GW00725950

See Corfu & the Ionians

See Corfu
& the Ionians

Paul Watkins

a complete guide
with maps
including
Paxos/Levkas
Cefalonia/Ithaca
Zakinthos/Kithira

FORMAT

For Tom

Acknowledgments

The author would like to thank the
following for their invaluable help in the
preparation of this book:

Mr Peter Analytis, who as Director of the
Greek National Tourist Organisation in
London offered practical co-operation and
advice, and Lia Mathioudakis of the Corfu
NTOG and other local tourist officers who
offered similar help in the islands.

Mr Vic Fatah, Mr Leo Morakis and the
late Michael Halikiopoulos whose father,
'Spyros Americanos', showed Corfu to
the Durrells in his taxi, and who in turn
showed the author a Corfiot Easter.

Mr Arthur Foss who kindly read the
manuscript.

Front cover photo: Antipaxos
Back cover: Easter procession, Corfu
town
Front endpapers: View from Kanoni,
Corfu
Back endpapers: Assos, Cefalonia
Frontispiece: Venetian buildings near
Nikiforos Theotoki Street, Corfu town

Photographs are by the author with the
following exceptions:
Archaeological Museum of Corfu 47, 71;
Museum of Pelikata 129; J. Burton 23;
J. Dermid 24

Map of Corfu by John Flower

In the same series

See Cyprus
by Paul Watkins

**See Madeira &
the Canaries**
by Annette Pink

See Malta & Gozo
by Inge Severin

See Sicily
by Paul Watkins

First published 1990
© Paul Watkins
Published by Format Books
23 Jeffreys Street London NW1

ISBN 0 903372 11 8

Photoset and printed by
Richard Clay Ltd,
Bungay, Suffolk, England

Contents

6 Introduction
The Ionian Islands · History maps
The Ionians and the *Odyssey*
Art and architecture · Countryside

25 Practical Information
Travel and transport · Inclusive holidays
Accommodation · Hotels and resorts
Recreation and entertainment · Food and drink
Restaurants · Greek restaurant menu
Festivals · Climate · Language · Currency
and banks · Museums and monuments
Reading and information

42 The Ionian Way of Life

44 Corfu
History · Discovering Corfu
Practical information · Corfu town:
Walking tour · Corfu and the *Odyssey*
Road map · Excursions · The Corfu Easter

96 Paxos

100 Levkas

110 Cefalonia

122 Ithaca

130 Zakinthos

140 Kithira

144 Writers and Rulers
Ionian travellers · The British in
the Ionians · Famous Ionians

159 Index

Introduction
THE IONIAN ISLANDS

'The Islands of Corfu, Zante, and Cephalonia,
are of more importance to us than all Italy.'
Despatch from Gen. Buonaparte, August 1797

NAPOLEON'S comment, at the outset of his great European conquests, underlined a certainty that has always existed for the
Ionians: they could never be the islands of a backwater. With the
submission of the Venetians, former custodians of the Adriatic,
Napoleon's way was now open to the mastery of the Mediterranean
and his greatest ambition: the foundation of a French empire in
the East. To that achievement, Corfu and the other Ionians were a
necessary key, serving the great strategic role that has been the
lodestar of their history.

The historical association of the Ionians has its physical parallel.
Although each island has its own character, the traveller who has
had the pleasure of visiting more than one of the 'Eptanisi' will
recognise the similar qualities which give them their special appeal.

Edward Lear observed it most famously—and most graphically—
in his *Views of the Seven Ionian Islands*, published in 1863. The litho-
graphs, based on his original pen and watercolour drawings, capture
the essential qualities of the pastoral landscape of the islands of

Greece's western seaboard; so different to the barren contours of their Aegean counterparts.

In Lear's time the islands had another affinity: they were British. The defeat of Napoleon—who had last held the islands from 1807–14—saw the assertion of another imperial power, on which the sun took longer to set. Though nominally a protectorate, the 'United States of the Ionian Islands' were effectively a colony ruled by a succession of plenipotentiaries from the Palace of St Michael and St George on Corfu. The colonial structure worked downwards through the British Resident responsible for the administration of the individual islands, in most cases a dedicated subordinate who was committed to a programme of public works— roads, bridges, aqueducts, harbours, schools—whose visible and practical legacy survives to this day.

Though it lasted 50 years, British rule of the Ionians can only be rated an interlude in the islands' history. In 1864, with the removal of Britannia from her barque, the Ionians regained their political identity with the Greek world, lost in the 12th-century erosion of the Byzantine empire. But another great power—usurped by competing European nations at the end of the 18th century— had an influence on the islands second only to the Greeks. Through four centuries their masters were the Venetians.

In taking possession of these precious links on the necklace of its trading routes, the Serene Republic was replaying the events of ancient history. Then, the Romans had sent a fleet to capture their first colony on Greek soil, the island of Corcyra (Corfu). Fifteen centuries later the bridge between east and west was crossed again by the Venetians, claiming their prize for their part in the Latin conquest of Constantinople. From their position, up to the end of the 12th century, as the western outpost of the Byzantine empire, the Ionians became under Venice the eastern outpost of free Christendom in the Mediterranean. By the end of the 17th century both mainland Greece and the Aegean were in Turkish hands and the Ionians were in the front line in the struggle against Islam.

Embattled against their seaborne foe, the island redoubts also had their internal conflicts—between the two great traditions of Byzantium and Rome, Orthodoxy and Catholicism, which helped to forge their unique character. The church architecture and decoration, the literature, painting and social history of the islands all bear witness to this blend of cultures, as essentially Adriatic as it is Mediterranean.

Opposite: Map of the Ionian Islands during the British Protectorate, with the islands' old Venetian names

The Ionian Islands, also known as the *Eptanisi* ('Seven Islands'), are mainly grouped off the west coast of Greece. Furthest north is **Corfu**, which lies in the Ionian Sea opposite the coastlines of Albania and Epirus. Immediately to its south lies the small satellite island of **Paxos**, and further south, close to the mainland and once attached to it is **Levkas**. South again, at the entrance to the Gulf of Corinth, are the neighbouring islands of **Cefalonia** and **Ithaca**, and to their south **Zakinthos**. Off the south-east coast of the Peloponnese in the direction of Crete lies the isolated **Kithira**.

The islands take their name from the sea in which the main group is located, the triangular Ionian Sea which lies between the boot of Italy and the west coast of Greece. Although not in the Ionian Sea, Kithira is nominally an Ionian island, as it has shared much of the history of the others.

Landscape The islands are mountainous, offshoots of ranges running from the western Balkans down to Crete. The highest peak (Enos, 1628m) belongs to Cefalonia, which is also the largest island. Coastal topography is extremely varied, ranging from steep bluffs and isolated coves on the mountain littorals to wide sandy beaches, backed by alluvial plains and often salt pans and lagoons, at the lower levels. The islands are green and temperate, with olives and vines growing in abundance. The mountain areas retain some of their original pine cover, although there has been much deforestation.

Geological phenomena are a special feature of the Ionians, the result mainly of the action of rain or sea water on limestone formations. Most impressive are the sea caves on the north-west coast of Zakinthos and on the west coast of Paxos, and the land caves near Sami on the east coast of Cefalonia. Another dramatic example of sea erosion is at Sidari on the north coast of Corfu, where deep coves and a spectacular tunnel have been carved out of the clay and limestone cliffs.

A natural phenomenon of the area whose effects have been less picturesque has left an indelible mark on the islands. The Ionians lie in the Mediterranean earthquake zone on the fault line whose shifts, in ancient times, destroyed the classical sites of Olympia and Delphi. In more recent times the victims were Levkas (1948) and the three-island group of Cefalonia, Ithaca and Zakinthos (1953). More than two-thirds of the buildings on these islands were destroyed during the earthquakes, including the greater part of the unique architectural heritage of the Venetians.

Population and economy The total population of the islands (200,000) is largely Orthodox Greek, though there are small communities of Roman Catholics descended mainly from Maltese settlers, most of them in Corfu. (The island is still the seat of a Catholic archbishop, one of only three in Greece.) The once flourishing Jewish population of Corfu, expelled by the Nazis, is now reduced to the handful who returned to their synagogue after the war.

In a group of islands which were decimated in the 15th–16th centuries by the Turks (many peasants, often the majority of the population, were captured and sold into slavery) it would be fanciful to trace an ancient Greek ancestry for the modern inhabitants, descended from the new population introduced by the Venetians (from mainland Greece, Albania, Italy and Venice). However, if every individual is reckoned to be a member of the race to which he or she *feels* they belong, there is no question of the Greekness of the Ionian islanders.

Despite earlier disasters and the continuing ravages of plague, population growth in the Ionians was greater than in the rest of Greece following the Venetian occupation. During a period of four centuries while the mainland was suffering the oppression of Turkish rule, the Ionians were protected by western European powers (principally the Venetians and British) who though themselves oppressive did much to encourage agricultural production and trade. The increase in population generated by this activity slowed after the departure of the British, however, and numbers were further diminished by emigration in the following decades to the lands of opportunity (America, Australia and—since the war—West Germany). Most affected were the smaller, poorer islands (Kithira, Ithaca) and those devastated by the post-war earthquakes (Levkas, Cefalonia and Zakinthos).

The only island to have maintained its numbers is Corfu, which accounts for half the population of the Ionians and has the largest town (Corfu, pop. 30,000). A recent growth has resulted from the development of tourism in the island, an improvement now also seen in the two islands which are most conspicuously following its example, Zakinthos and Cefalonia.

For many of the islanders, the traditional industries of agriculture and fishing are still the main source of livelihood. The most important crops—olive oil and currants—had their genesis in the activities of the Venetians and British, rivals in the commercial development of the islands.

In the early years of their occupation the Venetians offered Corfiot landowners special cash bonuses for the planting of olive trees, whose cultivation was impossible in Venice. The island now has about three million trees covering about half the cultivable land, and Corfu's olive oil is considered one of the finest in the Mediterranean. Paxos was similarly exploited and is now almost entirely covered by olive trees. Groves in the other islands bring the total to five million trees, making the olive the Ionians' most successful cash crop.

A similar enthusiasm was shown by the British for the currant, a coveted ingredient of the mincepies and plum puddings so dear to the nation. By the early 17th century the British were monopolising the islands' output, exporting directly from the three main producers—Zakinthos, Ithaca and Cefalonia—despite Venetian attempts to divert the trade to their own ports for the imposition of duty. Currants are still the major crop of Zakinthos and the Lixouri peninsula in Cefalonia.

The third most important traditional product of the Ionians is wine (see p. 33), produced in all the major islands. Although there is a growing export demand for Corfiot, Zakinthiot and Cefalonian labels, most of the wine is for domestic consumption.

Other exports from the islands include salt (Levkas and Zakinthos) and fish (Corfu). Fishing elsewhere is mainly for the benefit of the tourist industry, whose growth, though providing a tremendous boost to the islands' economies, is making a matching demand on their resources and bringing the inevitable changes. On the island waterfronts the old fishmen's cottages are now holiday villas.

History Maps

Any endeavour to plot the visual evidence of the Ionians' history is limited by the two great destructive forces, of man and nature, which have done much to erase it. The ancient sites which Davy depicted as 'undisturbed in noble tranquillity' during Roman times, were devastated by the Goths in the 6th century AD, further scattered by earthquakes and pillaged by fortress builders, leaving almost no record of early civilised settlement. Similar destruction of the architectural legacy of later rulers—notably the Venetians—was caused by the earthquakes of the more recent past. An outline history of the Ionians, divided into the most significant periods, is given with the related maps showing key sites.

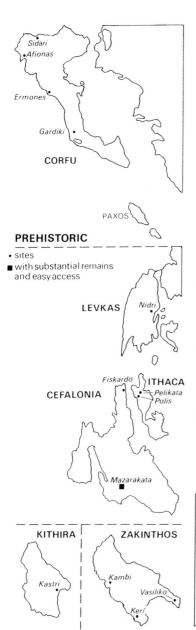

PREHISTORIC (50,000–850BC)

Corfu Sites in the south-west have revealed the earliest evidence of occupation of the Ionian Islands. The flint and stone tools at *Gardiki* and local sites belong to the Middle and Upper Paleolithic periods. Finds from later periods were plain and incised ware of the Neolithic (*Sidari* and *Afionas*) and pottery from the Early Bronze Age (*Ermones*). No evidence of Mycenaean settlement.

Levkas Middle Bronze Age site excavated at *Nidri* (proposed by Dorpfeld as Odysseus' city, to support his claim that Levkas was the mythical Ithaca).

Ithaca Middle-Late Bronze Age finds at *Pelikata* and *Polis* in the north indicate Mycenaean settlement and support arguments for Odysseian sites.

Cefalonia and **Zakinthos** Discoveries at various sites show a continuing occupation from at least Mesolithic times (Paleolithic finds at *Fiskardo*). Late Bronze Age rock-cut tombs at *Mazarakata* and other nearby sites in Cefalonia show a link between the Ionians and Mycenae at the time of the Trojan War. Mycenaean tombs at *Keri*, *Kambi* and *Vasiliki* in Zakinthos.

Kithira Minoan settlement at *Kastri* (1900–1450BC).

Key to Periods	
Paleolithic (Middle & Upper)	50,000–10,000BC
Mesolithic	10,000–6000BC
Neolithic	6000–3000BC
Early Bronze Age	3000–2000BC
Middle Bronze Age	2000–1500BC
Late Bronze Age (Mycenaean period)	1500–1150BC

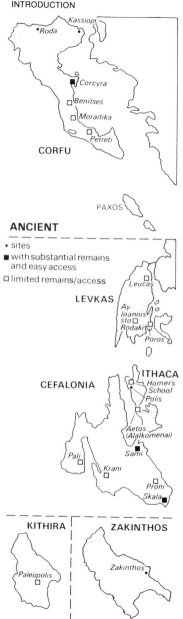

CORFU

PAXOS

ANCIENT

• sites

■ with substantial remains and easy access

□ limited remains/access

LEVKAS

CEFALONIA

ITHACA

KITHIRA

ZAKINTHOS

ANCIENT (850BC–330AD)

Corfu Previously occupied by Eretrians from Euboea, and a Corinthian colony from 734BC. Name of the capital, *Corcyra*, also given to the island. Corcyra wins independence from its parent state in history's first sea battle (*c.* 660BC). Continuing struggle with Corinth ended by alliance with Athens, and defeat of Corinthian fleet at Battle of Sivota (433BC) which provokes Peloponnesian War. Civil war in the island between pro-Peloponnesian aristocratic party and pro-Athenian democratic party ends in victory for the democrats. Independence maintained with intermittent occupations in the 4th–3rd c. BC from Macedonia, Epirus and Illyria. Romans expel Illyrians (229BC) and Corcyra becomes important Roman naval station. Settlements, villas at various sites on north and east coasts. Temples at *Roda, Kassiopi.*

Levkas, founded by Corinthians in 640BC, known as *Leucas* or *Nerikos*. Sparta's ally in the Peloponnesian War, Leucas later allied to Philip V of Macedon and conquered by the Romans (197BC).

Ithaca Settlement on Mt Aetos thought to be *Alalkomenai*, a Corinthian foundation of the 9th c. BC. Only other ancient building 'Homer's School', but pottery finds (3rd c. BC) show continuing use of Bronze Age shrine at *Polis.*

Cefalonia, probably colonised by Corinth at the same time as Corfu, has four city states by the 6th c. BC (*Sami, Proni, Krani, Pali*). Sides with Athens in Peloponnesian War, 431BC. Last stronghold of Sami captured by Romans, 189BC. This later becomes important Roman city: other Roman remains (mosaics) can be seen at *Skala.*

CORFU

Kassiopi
Angelokastro
Korifo (Old Fort)
+ SS Jason & Sosipater
Corcyra (Paleopolis)
Gardiki

PAXOS
Kastro (Gaios)

BYZANTINE/MEDIEVAL

remains of the period
■ substantial
□ limited
+ Byzantine church

LEVKAS
Castle of Santa Maura (Ay. Mavra)
+ Odiyitria

CEFALONIA
ITHACA
+ Vari
Paleokhora
Castle of □ St George (Ay Yeoryios)

KITHIRA
Paleokhora
□ Kithira (Khora)

ZAKINTHOS
Anafonitria □
Kastro Zakinthos □

Zakinthos Dependency of Achaia from 8th c. BC, sides with Athens in Peloponnesian War, then taken by Sparta, 431BC. Later occupation by Macedonia, and Romans (191BC).

Kithira Control passed from Kings of Argos to Sparta in 546BC; won by Athenians in 424BC (Peloponnesian War). *Paleopolis* site of ancient capital.

BYZANTINE/MEDIEVAL (330–1502)

Corfu As part of the Byzantine Empire, Corcyra strengthens its military ties with Constantinople to combat continuing barbarian attacks culminating in sack of the island by the Goths (6th c. AD). For protection the population resettles on promontory (site of present Old Fort, naming new town *Korifo* (from *korifai*, 'peaks'). Further raids by Saracens and occupations by Normans (1081, 1147) followed by Byzantine rule from 1187. After fall of Constantinople (1204) Corfu awarded to Venice but subsequently occupied by Michael I Angelos, Despot of Epirus, acknowledged builder of two Byzantine fortresses (*Gardiki, Angelokastro*). Later in 13th c. island falls into hands of the Angevins, who build fortress at *Kassiopi*. At the end of the Angevin dynasty Corfu accepts Venetian protection (1386).

Levkas (Santa Maura) Unlike Corfu and its three southern neighbours (see below) Levkas retains Byzantine rulers until its conquest by the Angevins (1295). Then like the others it is ruled by the Tocco family (1404–79) until its capture by the Turks. Castle of *Santa Maura* started by the Angevins.

Cefalonia By the 9th c. the island becomes capital of a *theme* of the

13

Byzantine Empire, based on Castle of *St George* (Ayios Yeoryios). Its history of occupation shared by **Zakinthos** and **Ithaca**. First the Normans (intermittent occupation between 1082 and 1194); second the Orsini, relatives of the Normans' Sicilian admiral Margaritone (1194–1209); third the Venetians (first occupation 1209–1218); fourth the princes of Achaia, subjects of the Latin Emperor in Constantinople (1218–67); fifth the Angevins (1267–1404); sixth the Tocco family (1404–79). Losing the islands to the Turks—by then in occupation of mainland Greece—the Tocchi maintain a struggle for their recapture. Their ultimate conquerors are the Venetians, established in all three islands by the early 16th c. Zakinthos' medieval capital the *Kastro*; Ithaca's pre-Venetian capital at *Paleokhora*.

Kithira (Cerigo) Depopulated by Arab raids, the island resettled from Crete in 961. Venetian Venieri family masters of the island from 1204, with one interval of rule by the Daimoyannes family of Monemvasia (1270–1309). Venetians take final control of the island in 1363. Medieval capital of *Paleokhora* (Ayios Dimitrios) abandoned after Turkish raid in favour of present capital *Kithira* (*Khora*).

MODERN (1503–1864)

Corfu Despite attempts on the island by the Turks, including the two great sieges of 1537 and 1716, *Corfu* remains a Venetian colony for 400 years (until 1797). The Byzantine fortress (Old Fort) is rebuilt and a New Fort (1588) constructed by the harbour. The coastal settlement of *Kassiopi* is

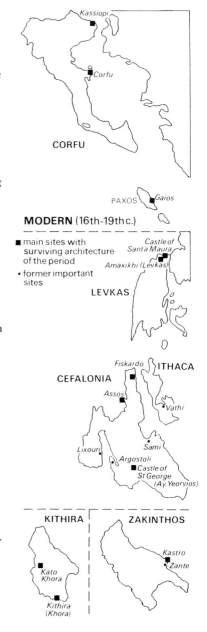

CORFU

PAXOS

MODERN (16th–19th c.)

■ main sites with surviving architecture of the period

• former important sites

Castle of Santa Maura

Amaxikhi (Levkas)

LEVKAS

Fiskardo   ITHACA

CEFALONIA

Assos

Vathi

Sami

Lixouri

Argostoli

Castle of St George (Ay. Yeoryios)

KITHIRA

Kato Khora

Kithira (Khora)

ZAKINTHOS

Kastro

Zante

developed by the Venetians. In 1797 Corfu and the other Ionians occupied by Napoleon prior to his campaign in Egypt. Following his defeat at the Battle of the Nile, two of the powers allied against the French—Russia and Turkey—occupy the Ionians and amalgamate them in an independent Septinsular Republic. In 1807 the islands reoccupied by the French, but then successively blockaded and captured by the British between 1809–14. The British Protectorate imposed on the islands lasts until 1864. In Corfu town a legacy of fine Venetian, French and British architecture.

Levkas (Santa Maura) Unlike other islands further from the mainland, Levkas occupied by Turks until 1684, when the Venetian leader Morosini captures the island at the start of his successful campaign against the Turks in the Peloponnese. In 1714 the island reoccupied by the Turks, but then recovered for Venice by Schulenberg (the triumphant defender of Corfu) in 1716. Thereafter it remains Venetian until 1797 when it shares the fate of the other Ionians. The vulnerable island, linked by a causeway to the mainland, continues to rely on the Castle of *Santa Maura*, reinforced by the Turks and Venetians, for its defence. The town of *Amaxikhi* (modern Levkas) develops on the shore of the island facing the castle.

Cefalonia, Ithaca and **Zakinthos** (Zante) share the modern history of Corfu. Their distance from the centre of power, however, and their general neglect stirs a greater sense of rebellion amongst the islanders against their foreign masters: Venetian, Russian, French and British. Recent earthquakes have destroyed most of the buildings of these periods in the major ports and towns: *Vathi* in Ithaca, *Sami*, *Argostoli* and *Lixouri* in Cefalonia, Zakinthos town (*Zante*). Venetian *Fiskardo* in Cefalonia was happily spared the last earthquake, in 1953, as were substantial parts of the Venetian fortresses of *Assos* and *Ayios Yeoryios.*

Kithira (Cerigo) Apart from a brief occupation by the Turks following the Venetian retreat from the Peloponnese (1714–16) the island remains Venetian until 1797 after which it shares the history of the other islands. Most important relics of the Venetian period are the Venetian rebuilding of the Venieri's fortress at *Kithira* (*Khora*) and the old village of *Kato Khora*. A few buildings also survive from the time of the British Protectorate.

UNION WITH GREECE (1864–)

The Ionians' political association ends with departure of the British and their incorporation as separate *nomes* or *eparchies* (administrative districts) of Greece. Foreign occupation occurs once more in 1941, when the Germans invade Greece and hand over control of the Ionians to the Italians. After Italian capitulation in 1943, the Germans take over the islands, but at the end of 1944 their forces withdraw from Greece.

The Ionians
and the
Odyssey

Ithaca Strait

THE LINKS between the Ionians are tethered not only in history
but in legend. Homer's account of the voyage of the Eternal
Wanderer, Odysseus, in search of his homeland Ithaca after ten
years' absence at the Siege of Troy, includes descriptions which
can be clearly related to the Ionians. Though a fabric of myth,
legend and travellers' tales, woven by one of the world's greatest
story-tellers, the *Odyssey* maintains an underlying reality in its por-
trayal of the people, places and events of the heroic age.

The Trojan War and its aftermath, the scenario of the Homeric
epic, have been placed in Greece's Late Bronze Age (*c.* 1200BC)
and since the first Victorian interest in the antiquity of legend, the
islands' identification with the Homeric sites has been keenly
debated. Romantically-minded scholars have converted Homer's
text into history and travelogue, and archaeologists—many of them
no less romantic—have supplied the supporting evidence. Whatever
the visitor cares to make of their findings, he will be unable to
resist, in the context of his surroundings, the fascination of the
tale.

According to Homer, Odysseus' domain consisted of his own island, Ithaca, and the neighbouring Same, Dulichium and Zakinthos. Same and Dulichium have been identified with Cefalonia, and together with the island of Zakinthos to the south were city states subordinate to Ithaca. In Homer's other great work, the *Iliad*, we learn that this confederacy contributed 52 ships, with their complement of fighting men, to Agamemnon's expedition against Troy. The co-operation which established the venture was betrayed, however, during the long absence of Odysseus—ten years at the Siege, ten years on the return voyage—by the action of the Suitors. These were the opportunistic princes who in the words of Odysseus' son Telemachus had taken full advantage of the situation by competing for the hand of the lost king's wife, Penelope:

Of all the island chieftains in Dulichium, in Same, in wooded Zakinthos, or in rocky Ithaca, there is not one that isn't courting my mother and wasting my property . . .

This state of affairs was brought to a dramatic end by the return of Odysseus and the dispatch of the Suitors: a bloody but fitting climax to the story. The setting of the drama, the island of Ithaca, is the most thoroughly described of the locations of the *Odyssey*, and as such the most identifiable. The other islands can also be identified by their descriptions or by their occurrence in the itinerary of the hero's wanderings.

Pushed southwards by the north winds of the Aegean at the outset of the voyage, Odysseus' ships drifted past the island of Kithira: ten years later, after some legendary diversions, the hero, bereft of his ships and comrades, was cast ashore on the island of Scheria, land of the Phaeacians. A study of the voyage and the topography of the landing site and of the Phaeacian capital has identified Scheria as Corfu: from here it was merely the distance from sunset to dawn to the final landfall in Ithaca.

Though Homer's references to Zakinthos and Cefalonia (Same) are brief, there is enough to relate them to the present-day islands. Of the large islands only Levkas (in Homer's time not an island but a peninsula) is omitted from the *Odyssey*, though the great German archaeologist Dörpfeld, who believed that the legendary Ithaca was in fact Levkas, would have us think otherwise.

The associations of the islands with the *Odyssey*, and a description of the suggested Homeric sites, is given under the entry for each island.

Churches Two buildings sum up the different styles of eastern and western church architecture in the islands: the modest 12th-century church of Sts Jason and Sosipater in Corfu and the elaborate 18th-century church of Makherado in Zakinthos. In the first building—the oldest surviving Byzantine church in the islands—a dome rises over a cross-in-square plan and barrel vaults; in the second a single-aisled basilica carries a pitched roof and flat ceiling.

Once the Venetians were established in the islands the basilican church became the norm, and by the end of the 17th century the addition of Baroque decor, both inside and outside, created a style peculiar to the islands and not seen elsewhere in Greece – the 'Ionian Baroque'.

Externally the decoration relieved what would otherwise have been a plain, flat façade: internally it had to synthesise with the features peculiar to Greek Orthodox churches, most notably the massive altar screen or iconostasis, spanning the east end, whose carving was more likely to be in the local tradition.

Ionian belltowers are one of two types, either a small Byzantine-style bellcote rising from the wall of the church or more often the distinctive Italianate campanile, usually standing separate from the church, capped by a dome or pyramid.

Art and architecture

Earthquakes and the ravages of invaders have left the Ionian Islands with a slender heritage of art and architecture: enough, however, to present that remarkable blend of east and west that is the 'Ionian style'.

Fortifications Most enduring of the islands' monuments are the great works of military architecture, which range from small coastal fortifications at the entrance to ports or strategic waterways (Levkas, Paxos) to the fortress-citadels (Corfu, Cefalonia, Zakinthos, Kithira). Though pine

Venetian carving on Town Hall, Corfu

trees now grow inside their crumbled walls these rambling castles have survived the ravages of time and earthquakes to commemorate their intrepid builders: Byzantine, Angevin, Turkish and Venetian. Excluded from this list are the British, who despite their restoration work can only be counted as despoilers after their removal of part of Corfu's historic fortifications to build a promenade.

Inevitably the most romantic of the Ionians' ruined castles owe their appeal more to their site than their structure. The hill-top mass of Angelokastro in Corfu, overlooking the beautiful bay of Paleokastritsa, is a haunting image engraved for us either in our own memories or by the hand of Mr Lear; similarly the fortress of Assos, at the foot of its snake-like peninsula in northern Cefalonia, puts its unforgettable seal on the cliff-top view.

Public buildings The civic architecture of the Ionians is mainly a legacy of the British Protectorate (1814–64), when a programme of public works was initiated by the Lord High Commissioner in Corfu and by the Residents of the other islands. The most imposing building of the period in Corfu town is the official residence of the Lord High Commissioner, the Palace of St Michael and St George, whose Doric colonnade and triumphal arches are in the best tradition of 'export Regency' seen in other British colonies of the early 19th century. (The stone for this building was, in fact, shipped in from Malta.) Many other buildings commissioned by the British in the neo-classical style may be seen on the walking tour of Corfu town (see p. 64).

Of the other islands, Levkas (British Residency and Courthouse), Kithira (schools, market place, viaduct) and Paxos (British Residency) have the best surviving examples, lost to the other earthquake-torn islands. Civic monuments of earlier occupations are confined mainly to Corfu. Most splendid are the Venetian town hall, originally a 17th-century loggia for merchants and later a theatre, and the French version of the public arcade, the Liston.

Houses Remnants of traditional domestic architecture are best seen in the islands which escaped the 1953 earthquake. In Corfu town the Venetian dwellings, originally single-storied but later enlarged within the confines of the walled city to the tall apartment buildings which now loom over the narrow streets, are a glimpse back into the 17th and 18th centuries, their façades refined by elegant cornices, window mouldings and painted shutters.

In the country, notably in the Pantokrator region, the record of Venetian settlements can be seen in farmhouses and other buildings of the old Corfiot villages, many now sadly abandoned. There is also an air of decay about the 19th-century mansions, once belonging to rich landowners, whose stuccoed, neo-classical exteriors fade gently behind a screen of cypresses.

In the major west coast islands apart from Corfu, all of which suffered serious earthquakes in this century, there are still domestic survivals in pockets which escaped the worst tremors. Although there are few churches which have not been reconstructed, smaller buildings from the 19th century and Venetian periods can still be seen in many of the villages and in Fiskardo (Cefalonia), Vathi (Ithaca) and Levkas town. The unique half-timbered construction of the Levkadian houses, designed to absorb shock, ensured their partial survival.

In addition to the Venetian (and Byzantine) heritage still much in evidence in Kithira's architecture, there is a strong element of Crete and the Cyclades in her domestic buildings, reflecting the island's Aegean orientation. Though the tiled roofs seen in the northern islands are commonplace here, there are also cement-covered flat roofs on plain, square whitewashed houses, drained by projecting waterspouts.

Artists In their art as in their architecture, the Ionian Islands reflect the influences of both eastern and western Europe, represented by the post-Byzantine painters of Crete and the Renaissance in Italy.

The Cretan connection was directed by events on the world stage, beginning with the conquest of Constantinople by the Turks in 1453. The diaspora of artists from the former Byzantine capital found its main refuge in Crete, which at that time was safely in the hands of Venice. For the next two centuries, the Cretan School developed a new approach to the painting of icons and murals which while maintaining the themes of Byzantine iconography began to express Renaissance ideas in a more realistic treatment of perspective and composition.

Inheritors of this artistic tradition, mostly Orthodox priests, subsequently travelled to Venice. They spent time *en route* in Corfu and Zakinthos, where they introduced the Cretan style. Most influential of these artists were the Cretans **Michael Damaskinos** (1535–91) and **Emmanuel Tzanes** (1610–90) whose works can be seen in the Byzantine Museum and various churches in Corfu town, and in the Zakinthos Museum.

The later conquest of Crete by the Turks (1669) created a further artistic exodus, this time to Venice and to the Ionians—the last Greek refuge. The artists who established themselves in the islands—mainly Corfu and Zakinthos—went on to study in Venice and other parts of Italy, which by this time had entered the age of the Baroque.

For the Greek artists it was heady stuff and led to their eventual rejection of the austere and rigid Byzantine style. The founder of this new school of religious painting (the Ionian School), was **Panayiotis Doxaras** (1662–1729) who had emigrated with his family to Zakinthos from the Turkish-occupied Peloponnese, and later travelled widely in Italy. His work, including the majority of his ceiling paintings in the church of St Spiridon in Corfu town, has largely disappeared, although there are fine examples in the church of Ayios Dimitrios in Levkas town. Little, too, survives of the work of his son **Nicholas Doxaras** who painted the ceiling of the destroyed church of Faneromeni in Zakinthos. The tradition which they established was carried on by two Zakinthiot priests: **Nicholas Koutouzis** (1741–1813), who studied in Venice under Tiepolo, and **Nicholas Kandounis** (1767–1834). The best examples of their work, which show the final acceptance of western ideas and techniques, may be seen in the church of Panayia ton Xenon (Koutouzis) and the convent of Platitera (Kandounis), both in Corfu town.

Countryside

Plants and flowers The vegetation of the Ionians is strikingly different to that of their sister islands in the Aegean for two reasons. The first is natural, the result of the higher winter rainfall which replenishes the earth and leaves a spring and summer bequest of wild flowers and shrubs. The second is man-made, the result of the commercial exploitation of the islands by their numerous colonisers.

In the Venetian period this was both a disaster and a blessing, for while the ancient forest cover of the islands was being plundered for shipbuilding, the Venetians were also grasping the opportunity to develop their other natural resources. As the countryside of Turkish-occupied Greece withered into neglect, the Venetians were managing their great estates and the islanders were planting acres of olive trees, encouraged by the special bounties offered by the Republic to promote their cultivation. Today these olive trees are still the dominant feature of the Ionian landscape—particularly on Corfu and Paxos where they have for centuries provided a major source of revenue. Some trees are thought to be more than 500 years old, but are still bearing fruit; a phenomenon observed by the British traveller Davy in the early 19th century.

In old age no tree is more venerable or picturesque, or more characteristic of the powers of vegetation and of the eternal youth of the living plant . . . It is not uncommon to see an aged olive,

Disused oil press, Paxos

hollowed out by decay, a mere shell,
the branches supported by props,
vegetating vigorously and bearing fruit.

Another familiar tree of the islands
is the cypress, whose dark vertical
spears, thrusting out from the silver
shields of the olive trees, give the
landscape the character of a
classical garden. Such an effect, one
might think, must be designed—
but the reverse is the case.
The absence of hedges, walls
and ditches, and the mingling
of the innumerable small plots of
the peasant farmers, preserves
the 'natural' look of the
countryside.

Although the pine forests have
diminished and are now confined
to the long ridge of Mt Enos on
Cefalonia and parts of Zakinthos,
there is plentiful tree cover at the
lower levels. The stalwart holm or
'holly' oak (*quercus ilex*) with its
prickly evergreen leaves, is mostly
seen in the wilder regions, along
with its more diminutive relative
the kermes oak—also an
evergreen—which vies for space on
the uncultivated slopes with the
myrtle, arbutus and lentisk (mastic
tree). On the plains and coastal
areas the deciduous trees—the
plane, silver poplar, eucalyptus and
deciduous oak—are more common.
In the towns the more ornamental
trees, including colourful tropical
species (jacaranda, pepper tree,
loquat) make a brilliant display in
gardens and avenues in their
flowering season: most splendid of
all is the spring-show on Corfu's
Esplanade, when the Judas trees
and horse chestnuts are in bloom,
their contrasting pink and white
providing a vivid backdrop to the
sombre Easter parades.

The climate of extremes that
typifies the islands of Greece's
western shores—hot dry summers,
cold wet winters—produces similar
dramatic changes in the appearance
of their landscape at different times
of the year: depicted most strikingly
by the variety of wild flowers for
which the Ionians—especially
Corfu and Zakinthos—are famous.

The violet *anemone blanda*,
peeping shyly from the tree roots,
is the first chink in the curtain of
spring: as it lifts, the vibrant
colours of crocus and hyacinth, iris
and tulip are revealed against the
green backcloth of mountain and
meadowland. The floral prelude of
February and March leads to the
climax of high spring: the months
of April and May when the
performance is at its most glorious,
the countryside decked with the
whites and golds of marigolds and
crown daisies, of speedwell and
camomile, and the contrasting
scarlet of poppies and the pinks and
purples of wild geraniums and
gladioli.

Summer's colours, though less
vivid, have a wider range: the *cistus*
or rock rose in its pink or white
varieties in the dry places together
with the lilacs and mauves of
thistles and scabious. The pale blue
campanula sprouts from rocks and
walls, the pink oleander thrives in
dry river beds. By the late summer
the flower-bearing plants have
withered, leaving the more
enduring growth of the evergreen
herbs and bushes to dominate the
hillsides and scrubland. The loss of
colour is compensated by the dusty
fragrance of lavender, rosemary,
sage and thyme.

The autumn rains which refresh
the parched earth, usually by mid
October, bring new life to the
countryside. The pink cyclamen
and pale purple *colchicum*—the
autumn crocus—are an unexpected
delight at this time of year.

Gecko

Road building and hotel development, and the spreading infrastructure of tourism, have had their inevitable impact on the natural environment of the Ionians. But the warily observant will always find a reward for keeping their eyes and ears open. Among the insects, the most audible are the cicadas, maintaining their seemingly endless castanet rhythm in the trees: the most visible (on late spring and early summer evenings) the fireflies, threading their luminous filigree in the velvety shadows of the shoreline.

Among the reptiles, the most conspicuous are the lizards, but the tiny gecko also pops up unexpectedly in all sorts of places and is something of a household pet, scurrying across walls and ceilings in pursuit of an insect prey. The most usual sightings of snakes are of dead ones, spread across the road like the discarded inner tubes of bicycles: most of the live ones are, however, equally harmless (the exceptions being two species of viper which you would have to be unlucky to encounter). A sudden genesis of frogs and terrapins occurs in the spring with the formation of pools from the mountain waters: the tortoises which share their awakening continue to lumber around the countryside in the summer and autumn months, browsing nonchalantly on the scrub-covered hillsides. The turtles which once came ashore on Zakinthos to lay their eggs are now, unfortunately, turning away, their nocturnal nesting disturbed by the intrusive backdrop of noise and light from the beach developments.

The wild mammals of the Ionians are much the same as those of the rest of Europe, although the

Wildlife Readers of Gerald Durrell's *My Family and Other Animals* will have an image of an island (Corfu) teeming with all manner of animal species, lovingly observed in their natural habitat (and occasionally retrieved from it) by the author. A compulsive animal lover, Durrell spent three idyllic boyhood years in the island in pursuit of its wildlife. The variety of creatures recorded in his account might well intrigue the modern visitor to Corfu or the other islands, who might count themselves lucky to have caught sight of the odd lizard on a garden wall, or heard the nocturnal hoot of a Scops owl. The enchanted island, was, after all, the Corfu of fifty years ago, an earthly paradise untouched by the tremors of mass tourism where the scorpions could enjoy their mating ritual disturbed by nothing more threatening than the curiosity of a twelve-year-old.

jackal, virtually unknown in western
Europe, is found in Corfu. Foxes,
weasels and hedgehogs are
occasionally seen but the most
active creatures—at least at night—
are the bats, which flutter and
swoop around the lights of the
beach walks and tavernas to gather
their insect harvest.

The marine mammal most
readily associated with the Ionian
Sea is the dolphin, glimpsed so
tantalisingly in the wake of a
steamer or fishing vessel or—
literally—'out of the blue', the
smooth silver arc of its body
momentarily breaking the surface of
the water. A greater and rarer thrill
would be the sight of a seal, lolling
in a rock-girt cove below the cliffs
that are a common feature of the
islands' western coasts: most
sightings have been made off Paxos,
near the Erimitis cliffs.

After insects, the bird life of the
Ionians is the most prolific.
Common species like magpies,
finches and wagtails abound:
familiar too is the hoopoe with its
distinctive fan-like crest. The
swallows and house martins are
busy spring visitors, building their
mud nests under the house eaves
and rearing their chicks—often up
to three broods—before their return
migration to Africa in the autumn.
Another spring migrant, the golden
oriole, with its ummistakable black
and yellow plumage, is a rarer
sight.

The more common birds of prey,
such as the kestrel and buzzard,
may be glimpsed hovering over the
fields or roadside verges in search
of rodents or smaller birds: for the
majestic sight of an eagle or vulture
the bird-spotter will have to
venture to the remoter fastnesses of
mountain and sea-cliff, most
rewardingly the wild heights of

Scops owl

Cefalonia and Ithaca. Sea birds and
waders frequent the islands'
lagoons, notably those on Levkas
(pelicans are common here),
Zakinthos and Corfu. Kingfishers
are also found in the coastal areas.
Gerald Durrell's hand-reared Scops
owl, Ulysses, was a representative
of the most common of the islands'
owl species: the barn owl, though
familiar elsewhere in Europe, is
only occasionally spotted, flitting
out of a ruined farmhouse or
derelict mill.

Apart from the disturbance of
habitat caused by tourist
development, the most apparent
threat to the wild birds of the
Ionians is an obsession of the
islanders themselves. Although
birds are not hunted as mercilessly
here as in other parts of the
Mediterranean, they are
nevertheless captured and popped
into cages, for display on the walls
of shops and houses along with
genuine cagebirds such as canaries
and ornamental finches.

Practical information   The Ionians

TRAVEL TO THE IONIANS

Air

In addition to the charter flights available from the inclusive tour operators (see p. 26) the three largest islands (Corfu, Cefalonia and Zakinthos) are served by Olympic Airways' domestic flights from Athens. The fourth largest island, Levkas, has connections to Athens from the nearby Preveza airport, and the fifth, Kithira, is also served by domestic flights from Athens. (For frequency of flights, see under individual islands.)

Sea

Corfu is reached by international car ferries from Italy on routes from Ancona, Bari and Brindisi to Patras. There are regular crossings to the island by car ferry from the Greek mainland (Igoumenitsa). *Paxos* is served by the 'Ionis' car ferry on the Brindisi–Patras route via Corfu, and by local car ferries from Corfu and Parga. *Levkas*, connected by bridge to the mainland, can also be reached by car ferry from Cefalonia in summer. *Cefalonia* and *Ithaca* are reached by regular car ferries from Astakos and Patras, also by the 'Ionis' ferry on the Brindisi–Patras route via Corfu. In addition, Cefalonia has a summer car ferry service from Killini in the W Peloponnese. *Zakinthos* has a regular car ferry service from the same port. *Kithira* is reached by car ferry from Piraeus, via Monemvasia, by a summer hydrofoil service also from Piraeus, by car ferry from Githio on the route to Crete, and by regular car ferry from Neapolis in the S Peloponnese. (For frequency of sailings, see under individual islands.)

Important note: Ferry sailings in the Ionian Sea are always subject to the vagaries of the weather, which from October is unpredictable. Sailings on some of the lesser-used routes are liable to cancellation without notice if the load is insufficient.

Land

Bus services (including the ferry crossings) operate from Athens to Corfu (via Igoumenitsa), Cefalonia (via Patras), Zakinthos (via Killini) and direct to Levkas. Ithaca has a ferry connection with the Athens bus to Cefalonia, and the bus to Parga has a ferry connection to Paxos. The bus to Neapolis in the S Peloponnese has a ferry connection to Kithira. The *railway* from Athens to Patras and Killini offers an alternative approach for ferries to Corfu, Cefalonia, Ithaca and Zakinthos. (For frequency of bus and rail services, see under individual islands.)

TRAVEL IN THE IONIANS

Roads

The first roads to be built in the Ionians during the British Protectorate are still in use today and all roads are generally well maintained, though drivers should always be on the lookout for the odd pot-hole and—in the mountain areas—the unexpected rockfall which might occur after a storm. Other roadblocks are caused by sheep, which tend to choose hairpin bends on which to demonstrate their right of way. They will eventually, of course, concede— but not so the stray dogs whose favourite activity is to leap out suddenly from the roadside and launch a determined, snarling attack on the nearest wheel.

Moped and scooter drivers are more vulnerable, from the hazards of both the roads and their machines. On some bends the cambers can be abrupt and slippery— a particular danger for overloaded bikes with pillion riders—and loose gravel can also cause skids. A more important precaution, however, is to check that the machine is not underpowered for the demands of local driving. The islands are all mountainous and some of the gradients should not be attempted by the lighter machines— most emphatically the climb up to northern Ithaca and the long haul from Sami to Argostoli in Cefalonia over the central mountain pass.

Unmade roads These are mainly forest roads, roads to remote coastal areas or mountain summits. They are not recommended for ordinary hire-cars, particularly after rainstorms when the loose surface can be dangerous. Rapid progress is however being made on road surfacing throughout the islands, and roads described on the tours as being 'unmade' may be surfaced by the time of publication.

Signposting This is generally good, and improving, with junctions marked with the place name in Greek first and then—further on—in the Roman alphabet. Village and town names usually show both versions.

Road maps

Although locally published road maps are obtainable in all the islands, the most accurate map of Corfu and the other Ionians (excluding Kithira) is the Clyde Leisure Map, published by Clyde Surveys. It includes a map of Corfu town, and shows the different grades of road—essential for motorists. Obtainable from Edward Stanford Ltd., 12/14 Long Acre, London WC2 or other good mapsellers.

Driving formalities

The only requirement for UK drivers is a current British driving licence. Drivers bringing their own vehicle will need in addition a Green Card, extending their insurance policy to foreign countries.

Self-drive cars

Most car-hire firms in the Ionians offer the following as part of their service

1. Full insurance, excluding
   a) Damage caused to the rented car by the driver. An exemption from this can be obtained by purchasing full collision (Collision Damage Waiver) at an additional daily rate. Such exemption does not apply, however, to damage caused to wheels, tires or the underside of the vehicle—a warning to keep off bad roads.
   b) Personal Accident Insurance. This must be purchased as an additional cover—but most drivers who are already covered by their own travel insurance do not require this.
2. Delivery to the airport or hotel to meet the visitor on arrival.
3. Oil and maintenance.

Most firms offer unlimited mileage for hire periods of one week or more. For shorter periods there is an additional charge for each km after the first 100km. When working out the final charge it is worth remembering that all rates are subject to 18% tax. Note: cars cannot be ferried without the authorisation of the car-hire firm. Minimum age limit is 23.

Availability With the exception of Paxos, all the islands have car-hire firms in the main towns and resorts. In the smaller islands, however, there are fewer cars available, and if the visitor is staying in a resort where there are no car-hire firms the arrangements for the hire, negotiated through a tourist agency, will incur an additional charge to cover the delivery of the car from another centre. (for example, from Levkas town to Vasiliki).
For car-hire locations, see under individual islands.

Scooter and bicycle hire

All the islands offer scooters or mopeds for hire in the main resorts. Before hiring them, their suitability for mountain driving should be considered. Bicycles, though generally available, are only practical in the immediate vicinity of the towns (an exception is Zakinthos, where the coastal plain around the main town offers pleasant bicycle excursions).

Petrol stations

These open at about 7.30am and close at 7pm. With the exception of a few selected stations they are closed on Sunday.

Other transport

For details of buses, taxis and inter-island ferries see under individual islands.

INCLUSIVE HOLIDAYS

UK tour operators offering hotel and self-catering holidays to a selection of the Ionian Islands (all include a choice of resorts in Corfu) are:

Falcon Holidays 33 Notting Hill Gate, London W11 3JQ

Grecian Holidays 31 Topsfield Parade, Crouch End, London N8 8PT

Greek Tourist Agency Morley House, 320 Regent St, London WIR 5AF

Olympic Holidays Westleigh House, 390 London Rd, Isleworth, Middlesex TW7 5AD

Starvillas 25 High St, Chesterton, Cambs CB4 1ND

Sunwheel Holidays Radnor House, 93 Regent St, London W1R 7TE

Thomson Holidays Greater London House, Hampstead Rd, London NW1 7SD

Redwing Holidays (inc. Enterprise, Martin Rooks, Sovereign & Sunmed) Groundstar House, London Road, Crawley, Sussex RH10 2TB

Sunmed offer the widest range of accommodation and choice of resorts in their 'Go Greek' brochure. Hotel and self-catering accommodation is offered in five of the islands (Corfu, Paxos, Levkas, Cefalonia, Zakinthos). Special features in their programme include 'Tailor-Made' holidays which offer resorts on two different islands (i.e. Zakinthos and Corfu) in the same package, and 'Split-Centre' holidays where two resorts served by the same airport are offered.

ACCOMMODATION

Hotels

The Ionian Islands offer a wide choice of hotels, listed below. They are divided into six categories: Luxury, A, B, C, D and E.

The first three categories all have a restaurant and rooms with *en suite* bathroom. C class hotels usually have private baths or showers but few have restaurants. D and E class hotels are also without restaurant or breakfast facilities, and have only communal showers, charged extra.

Booking In the high season (Jul–Sep) most hotels are fully booked, and it is virtually impossible to obtain a hotel room in this period without a reservation. Those arriving in the islands in the high season without a hotel booking should go to a travel agency in a main town or resort to find alternative accommodation. As a reassurance, there is always the long-stop of a private room (see below).

Prices All hotel prices are under the control of the National Tourist Organisation, and details can be studied in the hotel lists available in their offices in the islands. Room rates quoted include the service charge (15%) but not ATV (the government tax, levied at 6%) or the 4.5% community or city tax. Double rooms in the Luxury, A, B and C categories which are occupied by a single person are charged at 80% of the normal double room rate. There is usually a reduction in hotels for children, and an extra bed brought into the room will increase the rate by only 20%. In all but the luxury category an increase of 10% may be added if the stay is of two days or less. From Jul to mid Sep a high season surcharge of 20% may be added, but in the low season (Nov–Mar) prices in Greek hotels may be *reduced* by up to 30%. By law, a card showing the room rate and all extra charges must be posted in the room.

Pensions and tavernas

Pensions are the nearest alternative to hotels: like villas but operating as bed and breakfast accommodation. The breakfast will often be served in a local taverna or hotel. *Tavernas* also offer accommodation, where the guest can enjoy the additional pleasures of the table—and of local life.

Villas, studios and apartments

A wide range of self-catering accommodation is available for those who prefer the independence of this kind of holiday. *Villas* are generally blocks of purpose-built rooms with an *en suite* toilet and shower and sometimes—though not always—a balcony or terrace access. Kitchen facilities are usually available, but not in individual rooms. *Studios* are similar, but with an integrated kitchenette. *Apartments* are larger versions of studios, with two to four bedrooms, kitchen, bathroom and sometimes a sitting room.

The cheapest way of booking self-catering accommodation is through tour operators, many of whom offer it as an alternative to hotel accommodation in their package tours. (See *Inclusive Holidays*, p. 26.)

Private rooms

Rooms in private houses are available in all the islands. Some are licensed, with a classification and price card, others are unofficial, let to tourists by houseowners looking for an extra income in the summer months.

Travellers arriving by boat will usually find a gathering of locals on the quayside, looking for prospective customers: if you nod your head you will find yourself conducted to a family home in a side street, usually with a clean and comfortable room but sharing the facilities with the family. On the plus side this is a perfect introduction to the Greek way of life, and an opportunity to use those few words of Greek you have practised and which are always so well received.

If your arrival is less conspicuous and you find yourself in a strange place without accommodation, look out for the signs outside the houses offering the more official private rooms, which will say 'Rooms to Let' or the Greek equivalent *ENOIKIA-ZONTAI ΔOMATIA.*

Camping

Camping is permitted in the Ionian Islands (Corfu, Cefalonia, Levkas, Zakinthos) but only in officially organised campsites which have running water, electricity and toilet facilities and parking space for cars and caravans. They are generally open from May–Sep. For locations, see under individual islands.

Gaios, Paxos

HOTELS

P = Pension B = Hotel with bungalows

CORFU

Corfu town *Corfu Palace* **L**; *Cavalieri* **A**; *Anthis* (P), *Astron, King Alkinoos, Olympic, Phoenix* (P) **B**; *Arcadion, Atlantis, Bretagne, Calypso, Dalia* (Garitsa), *Hermes, Ionion, Phenix* **C**; *Acropole, Constantinoupolis, Europa, Metropolis* **D**; *Elpis, Karmen, Kriti, Kypros, Spilia* **E**

Ayios Yeoryios *Ayios Yeoryios* **D**

Ayios Yordis *Ayios Yordis* **A**; *Alonakia* (P) **B**; *Chrysses Folies* **C**; *Diethnes* **D**; *Pink Paradise* **E**

Ayios Ioannis *Marida* (P) **A**; *Vladimir* **C**

Ayios Stefanos *Nafsika, Saint Stefanos* **C**

Alikes *Kerkira Golf* **A**; *Alikes Beach, Salina, Sunset* **C**; *Triantafylia* **E**

Akharavi *Akharavi Beach, Ionian Princess* **B**; *Marie* **C** *Kormoranos Beach* **D**

Anemomilos *Arion, Marina* **B**

Arilas *Arila Beach, Marina* **C**

Aryirades *Golden Sands* **B**

Astrakeri *Angela Beach* **B**; *Astrakeri Beach* **C**

Barbati *Alexiou* **B**; *Barbati, Poseidon* **C**

Benitses *Regency* (Tsaki), *San Stefano* **A**; *Akhilleus* (Ghaena), *Belvedere, Evgenia, Potamaki* **B**; *Bavaria, Bella Vista, Corfu Maris, Kamares Benitson, Karina* (Tsaki), *Le Mirage, Loutrouvia* **C**; *Avra, Benitsa* **D**; *Eros, Riviera* **E**

Boukari *Boukari, Penelope* **C**

Dafnila *Eva Palace* (Kato Korakiana); *Grecotel Dafnila Bay* (B) **A**

Dassia *Corfu Chandris* (B), *Dassia Chandris, Elea Beach, Margarona Corfu* **A**; *Paloma Bianca* **B**; *Amalia, Dassia, Dassia Margarita, Galini, Las Karis, Primavera* (Kato Korakiana), *San Remo, Tina* **C**; *Scheria* **D**

Ermones *Ermones Beach* (B) **A**; *Athina Ermones Golf* **C**

Gastouri *El Greco* (P), *Montaniola* **B**; *Argo, Gefyra Kaizer* **C**

Glifada *Grand Hotel Glifada Beach* **A**; *Glifada Beach* **B**

Gouvia *Grecotel Corcyra Beach* (B) **A**; *Angela* (P), *Aspa* (P), *Molfetta Beach, Park* **B**; *Artemis, Constantinos, Elizabeth, Galaxias, Gouvia, Iliada, Maltezos, Pheacion, Sun Flower* **C**; *Hariklia, Louvre, Orfeas, Sirena* **D**

Ipsos *Ipsos Beach* **B**; *Doria, Ionian Sea, Jason, Mega, Platanos* **C**; *Costas Beach* **D**

Kalami *Villa Matella* (P) **A**

Kanoni *Corfu Hilton* (B) **L**; *Ariti, Corfu Divani Palace* **A**; *Royal, Salvos* **C**

Kassiopi *Oasis* **D**

Kavos *Roussos* (P), *Saint Marina* **B**; *Alexandra Beach, Kavos, Morfeas* **C**; *Cavo Palace Alexandra, Panela Beach* **D**; *Spyrou* **E**

Komeno *Astir Palace* (B) **L**; *Radovas* (B) **A**

Kontokali *Kontokali Palace* **L**; *Pyrros, Telessila* **C**; *Panorama* **D**; *Aleka* **E**

Liapades *Elly Beach* (B) **A**; *Liapades Beach* **C**; *Liapades Beach II* **D**

Messongi *Gemini* **B**; *Maria House, Melissa Beach, Rossis, Roulis* **C**

Moraïtika *Miramare Beach* (B) **L**; *Delfinia* **A**; *Albatros, Alkyonis, Capodistrias* (B), *Delfinakia, Messongi Beach, Solonaki* (P) **B**; *Margarita, Prassino Nissi, Sea Bird, Three Stars* **C**; *Fondana* **D**; *Moraïtika* **E**

Nissaki *Nissaki Beach* **A**

Paleokastritsa *Akrotiri Beach* **A**; *Oceanis, Paleokastritsa, Pavillon 'Xenia'* **B**; *Apollon, Odysseus* **C**; *Hermes, Zefiros* **D**; *Fivos, Paleo Inn* **E**

Perama *Alexandros* **A**; *Aeolos Beach* (B), *Akti, Oasis* **B**; *Aegli, Continental, Fryni, Pontikonissi* **C**; *Perama* **E**

Platonas *Platonas* **E**

Potamos *Elvira* (P) **B**; *Zorbas* **D**; *Spyros* **E**

Piryi *Piryi, The Port* **C**; *Ionia, Theo* **D**

Roda *Roda Beach* **B**; *Afroditi, Mandilas, Milton, Silver Beach, Village Roda Inn* **C**; *Ninos* **E**

Sidari *Afroditi Beach, Astoria, Mimoza, Sidari Beach, Three Brothers* **C**; *Sidari* **D**

Sinarades *Yaliskari Palace* **A**

PAXOS

Gaios *Paxos Beach* (B) **B**; *Ayios Yeoryios* **D**; *Ilios, Lefkothea* **E**

LEVKAS

Levkas town *Apollon, Lefkas, Niricos, Xenia* **B**; *Santa Mavra* **C**; *Averof, Patrae, Vyzantion* **E**

Ligia *Konaki* **E**

Nidri *Nidrio Atki* (P) **B**; *Gorgona* **E**

Nikiana *Alexandros, Galini* **B**

Vasiliki *Apollon* **B**; *Lefkatas* **C**; *Paradissos* **E**

CEFALONIA

Argostoli *Xenia* **B**; *Aegli, Aenos, Ayios Yerasimos, Argostoli, Armonia, Castello, Cefalonia Star, Galaxias, Mouikis,*

Phocas, Regina, Tourist **C**; *Allegro, Dido, Hara, Paralia, Parthenon* **D**

Ayia Evfimia *Pylaros* **C**

Fiskardo *Panormos* (P) **B**

Kounopetra *Ionian Sea* **B**

Lassi *Mediterranee* **A**; *Irilena, Lassi, Lorenzo* **C**; *Roma* **E**

Lixouri *Ionian Sea* **B**; *Poseidon, Summery* **C**

Platis Yialos *White Rocks* (B) **A**

Poros *Hercules* (P) **B**; *Atros Poros, Kefalos* **C**; *Galini, Poros House, Riviera* **E**

Sami *Ionion* **C**; *Kyma, Melissani* **D**; *Krinos* **E**

Skala *Skala, Tara Beach* (B) **C**

Svoronata *Irinna* **B**

ITHACA

Vathi *Mentor, Odysseus* (P) **B**; *Aktaeon* **E**

Frikes *Nostos* **C**

ZAKINTHOS

Zakinthos town *Kryoneri* (P), *Lina, Strada Marina, Xenia, Yria* (P) **B**; *Adriana, Aegli, Angelika, Apollon, Astoria, Bitzaro, Diana, Libro d'Oro, Phoenix, Plaza, Reparo, Tereza, Zenith* **C**; *Avrokhares, Diethnes, Ionion, Kentrikon, Kharavgi, Omonia, Rezenta* **D**; *Aktaeon, Astir, Dessy, Nea Zakinthos, Olympia* **E**

Alikes *Asteria, Astoria, Galini* (P), *Ionian Star, Montreal* **C**; *Alike* **D**

Argasi *Akti Zakantha* **A**; *Chryssi Akti, Levante* (P), *Lokanta, Mimosa Beach* (B), *Yliessa* **B**; *Argasi Beach, Captain's, Family Inn* **C**; *Kharavgi* **B**

Bokhali *Akrotiri* (P), *Varres* **B**

Kalamaki *Kalamaki Beach* **B**; *Crystal Beach* **C**

Laganas *Esperia, Galaxy, Megas Alexandros, Zante Beach* (B) **B**; *Alkyonis, Asteria, Atlantis, Australia, Blue Coast, Evgenia, Hellenis, Ilios, Ionis, Margarita, Medikas, Olympia, Panorama, Selini, Sirene, Vezal, Victoria, Vyzantion, Zefiros* **C**; *Anatoli, Galazia Thalassa, Hermes, Thalassia Avra* **D**

Planos *Dias* **B**; *Anetis, Cosmopolite, Orea Heleni, Tsilivi* **C**

Tragaki *Caraval* **A**

Vassiliko *Aquarius* (B), *Vassilikon Beach* **C**; *Porto Roma* **D**

Volimes *La Grotta* **C**

KITHIRA

Kithira town *Keti* (P) **B**

Ayia Pelayia *Kythera* (P) **B**

Manitokhori *Ta Kithira* (P) **B**

RESORTS AND RECREATION

The greatest recreation for visitors to the Ionians is provided by the very different landscape and coastline of each island, providing varied opportunities for walking, pic-nicing, swimming and sunbathing. Some of the best beaches are the least accessible, but there are good beaches at all the resorts. The greatest choice of resorts is in Corfu, but there are also two or three sizeable developments in each of the islands of Zakinthos, Cefalonia and Levkas.

The smaller islands tend to confine their tourist facilities to the main harbour areas.

For details of beaches and related resorts, see the practical information at the opening of the island sections.

ENTERTAINMENT

The principal resorts in the larger islands offer a variety of entertainment in the summer season. Some of the major hotels have night clubs with dancing and cabaret open to non-residents, and there are plenty of discos in the resort areas.

A trend in some of the more commercial resorts (Benitses in Corfu an inevitable example) has been the introduction of 'piped' entertainment such as day-time video shows: but the average tourist who sees 'unwinding' as an essential part of the holiday prefers more active enjoyment. Recognising this, most tavernas have an open space in the middle of the floor reserved for folk-dancing groups (diners are usually invited to join in) or budding 'Zorbas' wishing to practise their *sirtaki* (a popular Greek dance performed by two— or twenty—people with linked arms). Music is usually live, performed on a combination of either accordion, guitar, fiddle or *bouzouki* (a mandolin type of instrument with eight strings).

For the less energetic, participation can be confined to egging on the floor show, usually provided by one of the more sporting waiters who can lift a table in his teeth or balance a tower of wine glasses on his head while performing a solo dance!

For details of restaurants and tavernas, see the practical information at the opening of the island sections.

SHOPPING AND SOUVENIRS

Opening hours for shops in the summer are usually 08.00–13.00 and 17.00–20.00. There are few attractive handicrafts in the islands, an exception being the carved olive wood ornaments of Corfu: otherwise the most popular souvenirs are sponges, leather goods and clothing.

FOOD AND DRINK

Food

Despite the influence of Italy and the West on other aspects of their culture, the food of the Ionian Islands is predominantly Greek, with a nod in the direction of pasta. The raw materials are the resources of the land itself—the meat, fish and vegetables of the season. Processed foods have no place in the cuisine and all that comes out of a can or bottle is olive oil and the occasional pickle or preserve used as an appetiser or sweet.

The essential ingredients of Greek cookery are olive oil, garlic, herbs and lemon. **Olive oil**, which is one of the Ionians' major products, is used exclusively in cooking (no aminal fats) and for salads. **Garlic** is used in the majority of meat dishes, and in a number of sauces such as *skordalia*, a garlic and potato paste eaten with meat, fish and vegetable dishes. **Herbs** are abundant in the islands and similarly used. Most common are thyme, oregano, mint, fennel, rosemary and sage, which are usually gathered wild in the country areas. **Lemon** juice, like olive oil, is the *sine qua non* of Greek cookery. Apart from its familiar use as a counterpoint to meat and fish dishes it is also the basis for *avgolemono*, an egg and lemon sauce which is added to soups (mainly those made with fish or chicken) and to casseroles (chicken and lamb).

Starters (*orektika*) Though popular in home cooking, soups are rarely seen on restaurant menus, other than those of the fish tavernas. The traditional starter, the *meze*, is more commonly found in its plural form, *mezedes*, a variety of individual dishes which can sometimes be ordered as an alternative main course. Most famous are the *dolmades* (stuffed vine leaves) made with specially prepared vine leaves wrapped around a filling of rice and mince and served with an egg and lemon sauce. Other popular *mezedes* are the dips such as *taramosalata* (made either from grey mullet or cod's roe) and *tzatziki* (yoghurt and cucumber) and the many seafood specialities (see *Greek Restaurant Menu*, p. 36).

Meat (*kreas*) is something of a luxury in the Ionians as elsewhere in Greece. The poorer people consume it only on feast days, relying on fish or home-grown vegetables and home-made cheeses for their protein. Although there has been a recent growth of dairy farming in the south of Corfu, the terrain is generally unsuitable for cattle and most beef is imported. The word *moskhari* (erroneously translated on

Easter banquet, Corfu

menus as 'veal', which is not available in Greece) is used to describe beef dishes.

Where cattle founder, sheep and goats flourish, feeding on the sparse but varied vegetation of the hillsides. Lamb (*arni*) is the Greek national dish, presented in its most celebrated form at Easter when the young spring lambs (*arnaki*) are roasted on spits over charcoal fires. The combination of the slow cooking—three hours or more—the basting of olive oil and lemon juice and the seasoning of mountain herbs (usually oregano or thyme) imparts a succulent, aromatic flavour to the meat.

Lamb in restaurants comes in many guises, the most familiar being the miniaturised version of the Easter speciality. The *souvla* (spit) becomes the *souvlaki* (little spit) on which the cubed meat is skewered with sliced onions and peppers. Better known to foreigners as *kebab*, this is found in its pork (*souvlaki hirino*) and 'veal' (*souvlaki moskharizio*) variations.

Though not the gourmet traveller's most sought-after dish, goat (*katsiki*) is as popular with the Greeks (when it is young) as lamb. Tourists will not find it on the menus of the better class restaurants but may unknowingly have eaten it elsewhere and enjoyed it.

Meat is used in a great number of made-up dishes. Particularly good are lamb casserole (*arni yiouvetsi*) served with macaroni or potatoes, beef stew with onions (*stifado*) and pot roasts. Minced meat specialities are the celebrated *moussaka*, made with aubergines, and *keftedes*, the meat balls often served in soups. Minced meat, invariably mixed with rice, is also used for stuffing vegetables (see below).

Fish (*psari*) and seafood are abundant in the islands. Apart from the white fish, most commonly used in soups and fish stews, there are such specialities as *barbouni* (red mullet) and *xifias* (swordfish) which are best shallow-fried in oil. The flesh of swordfish is firm enough to allow it to be cut in cubes and skewered for kebabs. The tiny *marides* (whitebait) are usually served as a starter. Also popular are *ktapodi* (octopus) delicious cooked in wine sauce or grilled, *kalamarakia* (baby squid) best dipped in egg and breadcrumbs and deep-fried, and *garides* (prawns) served either as a pilaff or salad with olive oil and lemon. Although the most expensive seafood in the islands, lobster is cheap by European standards. The Greek name for it, *astakos*, is also sometimes used to describe the larger crayfish, which are more likely to turn up on the plate.

Pasta Known by the Greeks in all of its varieties as *makaronia*, pasta was introduced to the country (via the Ionians) by the Venetians. It is most commonly served here as an accompaniment to meat (*pastitsada*, *yiouvetsi*) or baked with minced meat in a pie (*pastitsio*). Simple spaghetti dishes with a tomato or cheese sauce are also popular.

Vegetables (*lakhanika*) are widely available in the islands and much of the production is sent to Athens. Artichokes (*anginares*) are a prized delicacy of the late winter months, followed by peas (*araka*), beans (*fasolia*) and courgettes (*kolokithakia*) in the spring to early summer. Aubergines (*melitzanes*) and okra (*bamies*) belong to the high summer, along with tomatoes (*domates*), whose season extends until November or December. Greeks are great bean eaters and have an enduring passion for *fasolia soupa* (white bean soup) a traditional family recipe which is, unfortunately, rarely found on restaurant menus. More common are *yemista*, or stuffed vegetables, where the chef can give full rein to his creative powers. Favourite vegetables for stuffing are tomatoes, peppers and aubergines, using a mixture of mince, onions, rice and herbs cooked in oil. There is also an interesting assortment of vegetarian stuffings,

using special ingredients such as pine nuts, raisins and *feta* cheese.

Cooked vegetables are rarely offered as a separate dish to accompany a fish or meat meal, but an honourable exception is the delicious *spanakhi may lemoni* (spinach cooked with lemon) served either hot or cold. Another popular side dish is *fasolakia* (runner beans cooked in oil and tomato purée).

No Greek meal is complete without the accompaniment of its **salad**: the essence of the cuisine at its simplest. A clean, fresh, *salata* is the natural complement to the well-cooked and savoury meat and fish dishes, and appears in its most celebrated form as the *horiatiki* ('the peasant's salad') which can include lettuce, tomatoes, onions, peppers, cucumbers, olives and the crumbly white *feta*, or goat's cheese. This is virtually a meal in itself, and is especially popular with the traveller on a budget. Simpler salads are cucumber and tomato (*angouri kay domata*), or the shredded white cabbage known as *lakhano*. Unique to Greece is *horta*, the wild greens gathered in the autumn which are boiled and then served cold with lemon and olive oil.

Fruit and desserts Like vegetables, the **fruits** (*frouta*) of Greece offer their seasonal repertoire. In Zakinthos and Corfu the curtain-raiser is the wild strawberry (*fraoula*) which appears between April and June. In early summer the islands have plentiful apricots (*verikokka*), cherries (*kerasia*) and plums (*damaskina*); in high summer figs (*sika*), peaches (*rodakina*) and the early pears (*akladia*). Late summer brings the apples (*mila*) and table grapes (*stafilia*). Melons, though not grown in all the islands, are always available in season in the markets and from wayside vendors: the refreshing, pink-fleshed water-melon (*karpouzi*) in the early summer and the golden honeydew melon (*peponi*) in the autumn.

A toothsome by-product of the fruits of the islands are the **spoon sweets** (*glika koutaliou*). These are very much a part of the Greek welcome and are offered to guests on arrival with coffee or liqueur. The preserves are made from a variety of fruits steeped in sugar syrup, and are treated as a fine art by the enthusiasts who prepare—and consume—them. Most popular are those made with the small bitter oranges and lemons—the dark green, unripened fruit which are preserved either whole or as peel, tightly rolled. (On Corfu a special miniature orange, the koumkouat—a Japanese variety—is used for making crystallised fruit or liqueur.) Quinces (*kidonia*) made into a paste with

31

slivered almonds, are another favourite, and nectarines, figs and cherries are also commonly used in preserves.

The celebrated sweet tooth of the Greeks is further cajoled by their **pastries** and **sweet dishes** (*glika*). The basis of these is *fillo*, the paper-thin pastry used in making most pies and pastries. Famed beyond the shores of Greece (not to mention Turkey or the Balkans) is the mouth-watering *baklava*, a mixture of chopped walnuts and almonds and layered *fillo* dipped in honey. This is sold either in wedges or in small cubes for those attempting moderation. *Kataifi* has the same honey and nut ingredients as *baklava*, but the pastry itself is in rolled strands, like shredded wheat. Another variation is *galaktoboureko* or 'milk pie', in which the pastry is wrapped around a core of custard or vanilla cream. *Loukoumades* (honey puffs) are often made 'while you wait'—small honey-dipped dough balls whose golden-brown colour, fresh from the sizzling vat, is enough to melt the resistance of the most self-denying.

The final temptation, when all the other whims have been indulged, are the sweet-meats. In Greek restaurants abroad these will often be offered as a *bonne bouche* with the coffee, but in Greece they are sold in delicatessens or the cake and coffee shop, the *zakharoplasteio*. Favourites are *loukoum* (Turkish delight) which can include almonds, and *halva*, a traditional Easter cake made with sesame seeds. A Zakinthiot speciality is *mandolato*, an almond and honey nougat.

Bread is basic to the Greeks' existence. It is baked fresh every day, and the bakeries are a focal point of the island villages. The loaves are usually round and flat, dense and with a good crust which may be sprinkled with sesame seeds. The Greek equivalent to the bread roll—the ring-shaped loaves known as *koulouria*, do service as the workman's breakfast.

For the Greek, the natural companions to bread are olives and cheese, which makes a meal in itself, or at the very least, an ideal *meze*. Apart from the fact that Greek cuisine would not exist without it, the **olive** (*elia*) is such a part of life that no table set for a meal can exclude a bowl of one of the many pickled varieties—green, black, purple or brown. **Cheese** (*tiri*) holds a similar place in the food hierarchy and here the foreigner will think immediately of *feta* (already mentioned as an accompaniment to the Greek salad), the salty white cheese made from goat's or sheep's milk which has a soft, crumbly texture. An essential ingredient of cheese pies (see p. 35), it is also eaten on its own with oil and black pepper. Made from the whey of *feta* and resembling cottage cheese is *mizithra*, which is unsalted and used for cooking sweet or savoury pies. A similar cheese is *manouri*. The creamy and mild *kasseri* is the nearest in flavour to cheddar and eaten with bread, and *kefalotiri* is a hard cheese similar to Parmesan and used in much the same way, either for cooking or grating.

Yoghurt (*yiaourti*) is another staple of the Greek diet. It makes its most familiar appearance in *tzatziki* (cucumber and yoghurt salad) or with honey (*yiaourti kay meli*) for breakfast or dessert.

Drink

Coffee If Greece has a national drink it is *cafe elleniko*. This, ironically, was once known as *cafe turkiko*—but times, and definitions, have changed. Whatever its history, its absorption into the life—and metabolism—of the Greeks is total. Its social significance is best observed in the *cafenion*, where its devotees linger eternally over the thimbles of dark liquid, discussing the state of the world. A glass of water is usually on hand to stretch the lubricant a little further.

Strangers to the cult of the *cafedaki* ('little coffee') should be advised of its mysteries. They should know that it is not a drink to be hurried; not only for social reasons, but because the coffee grounds are not filtered out and tend to take a little while to sink to the bottom of the cup. The degree of sweetness should be established with the waiter: *sketo* for unsweetened, *metrio* for medium, *gliko* for extra sweet.

Italian-style coffee is found in some bars, but bears no relation to the original ('capuccino' should particularly be avoided). The more predictable standby is the ubiquitous *Nescafé*. All that is needed here is the additional instruction, if required, of *may gala* ('with milk') or *may zachari* ('with sugar'). A refreshing variant in hot weather is *cafe frappé*—the same shaken and served cold. Tea (*tsaï*) is of the bag-in-a-cup variety and is best taken with lemon.

Soft drinks are in cans or bottles: orangeade (*portokalada*) and lemonade (*limonada*) and other drinks such as Coca-Cola can usually be bought at the street kiosks.

In Corfu, British visitors will be delighted to discover *tsintsibirra* (ginger beer); an odd, if touching, legacy of our Greek 'empire'. The old Victorian recipe—originally dispensed in stone jars—is still used, and it is worth the search (only a few bars in the town sell it) to enjoy a taste of this refreshing drink.

Beer and spirits Beer (the most popular refreshment for the average Greek) is usually of the lager type imported from Germany and bottled in Greece. The Greeks are also keen on whisky and other imported spirits, but visitors should try— just for the experience—the popular native *ouzo*.

Made from the fermented residue of grapes after pressing, this aperitif is similar in taste to the French *Pernod*, with a pronounced aniseed flavour. It has a high alcohol content and is better diluted, the 'Greek way', which turns the clear liquid to a milky white. Greek brandy (*Cambas, Metaxas*) is cheap but drinkable, and the measures always generous.

Liqueurs Less appealing, to some palates, are the islands' liqueurs. Corfu's most famous is *koum-kouat*. Made from locally grown miniature oranges (a type native to Japan) it comes in a variety of flavours: peppermint, strawberry, cherry brandy etc. The abundance of digestive liqueurs on display in the island distilleries is bewildering, the racks of bottles with their accompanying descriptions ('Very Good for Stomach', 'Keeps Stomach Warm') like colourful dispensaries.

Water A special note on the Greeks' most highly regarded and readily consumed drink: water. The nation's water-quaffing habits are well known, and go a long way to explaining their generally sober demeanour (a lesson here for some tourists). To reassure the rest of us, the tap water served in the restaurants can be drunk without any qualms, but those requiring a supply of water in their hotels or apartments are advised to purchase the large bottles of Loutraki mineral water, which is particularly good chilled.

Wine Strange to relate, in the land of Dionysus, but the Greeks are not the world's greatest wine drinkers. The main reason given for this is the growing popularity of beer and spirits, the former cheaper, the latter increasingly more fashionable. But the truth of the matter is that Greek wine, although a major product of the country in ancient times, has only in recent years been produced in a sufficient variety of labels to attract both domestic and foreign consumers.

Up to 30 years ago the main wine consumed in Greece was restina (described below) but now the majority of Greek wine is unresinated, produced by a number of wineries using grapes from different areas of Greece and other countries. Under a law similar to the *appellation controlée* system of France, the origin of the quality wines is protected.

The variety of wines includes white (*aspro, levko*), red (*kokkino, mavro*) and rose (*kokkinelli*). Most wines are dry (*xero*) or 'demi-sec' (*imigliko*) but the sweet (*gliko*) varieties such as muscadel (*moskhato*) make pleasant dessert wines. Greek wines are remarkably cheap, particularly when purchased from wine stores, but sometimes it is worth paying more for a *Cava* label. These are generally wines which have been made from selected grapes and given longer maturing.

Greek wines, available in supermarkets and served in Greek and Greek-Cypriot restaurants around the world, are familiar to many foreigners who have never been to Greece. On the mainland the principal wine-producing regions with their labels are:

Macedonia (*Boutari* of Naoussa and *Porto Carras* of Sithonia)
The Attic peninsula (*Cambas, Cellar*)
The Northern Peloponnese (Achaia Clauss's *Demestica* of Patras and the wines of the Nemea region).

Of these wines, which are all available in the Ionians, the best quality in the medium price range is offered by the Macedonian wines: the red *Cava Boutari* and the white *Lac des Roches* (also Boutari) and the *Cava Carras*. A popular wine from the Aegean, found throughout Greece, is the sweet white dessert, *Samos*.

Most famous—perhaps notorious—of all Greek wines is *retsina*, whose flavour of 'turps' comes as a shock to the untried palate, but can, with practice, become addictive. The unique taste belongs to the resin which is added by the producers, to preserve both the wine and a tradition which goes back to the days when the wine was kept in goat skins sealed with pine resin.

Produced mainly in Attica, retsina is served either from the barrel in the region or from the bottle elsewhere. It is best drunk 'same year' and served ice-cold. Good labels (also exported) are *Cambas* and *Kourtaki*. Some of the popular varieties sold in the tavernas such as *Marko* or *Plaka* come in the familiar $\frac{1}{2}$-litre 'beer' bottles—an added reason, perhaps, for their popularity.

Ionian wines Although conditions for vine growing are good in all the Ionian Islands, only Cefalonia and Zakinthos produce wines of exportable quality. Elsewhere the emphasis is on local wines produced in the villages for domestic consumption. In **Corfu** some restaurants offer Corfiot wines (*Corifo, Karpos*) at a price well below that of the better known labels, which are worth a try: in other islands not famous for their vintages (Paxos, Ithaca, Kithira) one should be encouraged, rather than enthused, by the labels which read 'Table Pure Wine, Special for the Taverna'.

Quality mainland wines, mentioned above, are available in most restaurants, but so too are the wines of **Cefalonia**, which have an excellent reputation throughout Greece and abroad. Climatically, and in the similarity of its varieties and vintages, Cefalonia is an extension of the Peloponnese: the liqueur wines *Muscat* and *Mavrodaphne of Cefalonia*, made from the island's muscatel grapes, are like those produced in Achaia. Another home-grown grape, *Robola*, has given its name to an 'Appellation of Origin' wine, on the Kalliga and Robola Wine Producers' Co-operative labels. The robust white *Robola* is particularly popular.

The pride of the vineyards of **Zakinthos** is undoubtedly *Verdea*, a light amber-coloured wine produced by Comouto and others. Its distinctive sherry flavour, though undoubtedly aristocratic, is for some an acquired taste.

Like Cefalonia, **Levkas** has its own grape variety, the red Vertzami, from which the island's best known wine, *Santa Mavra*, is made. At a more popular level, the red and white *Taol* is available in restaurants in half and full bottles.

Restaurants

In the smaller islands the only eating places are the village tavernas, popular with both locals and tourists. In the larger islands the range is varied and includes— at the more expensive level—hotel restaurants, which serve only international cuisine, and the *de luxe* restaurants which though often serving traditional dishes are not subject to price control. Apart from these, the different types of restaurant are:

Estiatorio This is the 'proper' restaurant— with white linen tablecloths, white-jacketed waiters and a full menu, with starter, main course, dessert and coffee. For the main course, both made-up (ready-cooked) and grilled *tis oras* ('of the hour') dishes are offered.

Taverna Like the Italian *trattoria* or the French *bistro*, the Greek taverna was until recently considered the 'working class' restaurant, providing simple local dishes for an unsophisticated clientele. With the advent of tourism and the ubiquitous international Greek taverna, all this has changed. In the more popular tourist areas the tavernas can be extremely smart, with tight-trousered waiters, loud music and more flamboyant dishes. The real thing is decidedly more modest, a local eating place situated either in the countryside or in the side streets of the island towns.

HERE YOU CAN FIND
THE BEST
SPECIALITIES
OF CORFU
FRESH FISH AND MANY
VARIETIES OF FOOD

VEAL PASTITSADA
VEAL SOFRITO
VEAL ANTALOUS
MOUSAKAS ALA AVEROF
PEPER STEAK
FILET MINION MATHERA
FILET STROGANOF
FILET MEXIKEN
FILET BEARNAISE
PRAWNS SAGANAKI
SNITSEL
HOFMAN
SOUVLAKI
LAMB CHOPS PANE

HAVE A LOOK
AT THE KITCHEN
HERE WE SPEAK
ENGLISH
GERMAN
FRENCH
ITALIAN

The place is usually run by the owner and his family, who will do most of the work— cooking and waiting at table—ensuring (for this is probably their home as well) the satisfaction of their customers, who they look upon as their guests. Specialities of the taverna are *mezedes* and grills.

Psarotaverna (Fish taverna) Usually located at the seaside or by the harbour.

Psistaria Much simpler eating places, with a takeaway counter and a few tables and chairs, serving exclusively spit-roasted and charcoal-grilled meats.

Kendro The word means 'centre' and in the towns these are working men's café-snack bars. The name also describes the temporary snack bars, often set up on beaches during the tourist season, offering refreshments and simple cooked meals.

Coffee shops

Apart from selling coffee, the two main types of coffee shop in Greece have little in common. The *cafenion*, traditional refuge of the older Greek male and the nearest thing to a Greek 'pub' serves Greek (Turkish-style) coffee, ouzo, brandy and the occasional *meze*. The refreshments, however, are almost incidental to the proceedings, which can vary from gossip to political discussion, from gentle musing to a game of *tavli* (backgammon).

A different type of coffee shop is the Greek patisserie (*zakharoplasteio*) which in addition to selling cakes and pastries offers the chance to sit down and enjoy them with a cup of coffee (usually continental). Like its French model, the *zakharoplasteio* appeals to the more sophisticated customer, the middle-class Greek who comes here after dining out to round off the evening with a coffee and *baklava*. The idea has caught on with the tourists, particularly those susceptible to the special delights contained in the Greek *fillo* pastry.

Choosing your meal

When ordering a meal in a 'typical' Greek restaurant, you must expect to abandon a few conventions, like sitting down and asking for a menu. There are, after all, so many other more interesting ways of making a choice. At some of the seaside tavernas, for example, the fresh fish and meat dishes of the day (*tis oras*) may be displayed outside in refrigerated cabinets, so that you can freely inspect what the restaurant has to offer. Having taken the bait, there may be further temptation inside when instead of being offered the menu you are presented with a tray of delectable *mezedes* brought to your table. When it proves impossible to make a selection the waiter will leave them all on the table, with the promise that 'you pay only for what you eat'.

The most familiar approach is for the proprietor to invite you into the kitchen before you sit down (if he doesn't, you should invite yourself). For your delectation there will be a cut of meat or a piece of fish from the refrigerator, or any of the variety of ready-made dishes in the oven or on the hotplates. Inevitably you will go for the tastiest-looking dish—and might forget to enquire the price.

A note of warning should be sounded about ready-made dishes, which may have been prepared early in the day. Some could be lukewarm later on and it is a good idea to make sure they are served hot (*zesto*).

Another cautionary note: there is a tendency in some restaurants and tavernas to serve the starter and main course together, so you should be prepared with the exclamation 'okhi tora' ('not now') or 'meta' ('after') when all the dishes arrive simultaneously. Greeks, who do not like their food hot, assume foreigners have similar tastes. For this reason *moussaka*, one of the most popular Greek dishes, is best ordered at lunchtime rather than in the evening, when it can be a little tired. Oil (*ladi*) and garlic (*skordo*) are widely used in Greek cooking, and are difficult to avoid except in the freshly-cooked (*tis oras*) dishes. Meat 'off the hook' will be spit-roasted or charcoal-grilled, and fish either charcoal-grilled or fried in the minimum quantity of oil (see also ps. 30–31).

Ionian specialities A few dishes native to the islands are worth trying, such as *bourdetto* and *veal sofrito* (Corfu), *saltsa* (Zakinthos) and *kreatopita kefalonitiki* (Cefalonia). See *Greek Menu*, overleaf.

The menu (*to kataloyo*) **the bill** (*to logariasmo*) Most restaurants in tourist areas display menus with dishes shown in both Greek and English. For a typical menu, see overleaf. Prices in the non-luxury categories are state-controlled and listed in two columns, the one on the right showing the addition of local tax, cover charge and service. (Although prices are inclusive, it is customary to leave the waiter another 10%.) Fresh fish is charged by the kilo rather than the portion and it is customary to choose the fish and have it weighed before agreeing the price.

Eating habits

The Greek breakfast (*proyevma*) is informal and usually consists of little more than a coffee and a Greek-style bread roll (*koulouria*) or yoghurt and honey. Cheese pies (*tiropitta*) and spinach pies (*spanakhopitta*) are also popular, usually bought at bread shops or snack bars on the way to work. For the sweet-toothed, there is an equal demand for the hot, freshly-made *bougatsa* (cinnamon cream pie) and the *milopitta* (apple pie). The pastry shops that sell these rare delights are usually found in the side streets of the business or shopping areas, away from the ports or other tourist-centred areas where the choice usually lies between the predictable English or continental breakfast. In Corfu town, the best oven-fresh pastries are found in the vicinity of M. Theotoki Street.

With office hours in Greece now stretching from 8 or 8.30am to 2 or 3pm, lunch (*yevma*) is generally eaten late, though it is available earlier for tourists. Dinner (*deipno*) is consequently also a late event for the Greeks, usually between 8 and 12pm.

GREEK RESTAURANT MENU   * specialities of the Ionian Islands

Typical dishes showing Greek word, pronunciation and English description. Note: the suffix ακι or ακια means 'little' as in ντολμαδάκια (dolmadakia)—small dolmades, or 'young' as in κατσικάκι (katsikaki)—baby goat.

ΣΟΫΠΕΣ/ΣΑΛΤΣΕΣ	SOUPEZ/SALTSEZ	SOUPS/SAUCES
αὐγολέμονο	avgolemono	egg and lemon sauce or chicken soup with rice, lemon and egg
φασόλια σούπα	fasolia soupa	white bean soup
ψαρόσουπα	psarosoupa	fish soup
σκορδαλιά	skordalia	garlic and potato paste
σούπα κρέατος	soupa kreatos	meat soup
'ΟΡΕΚΤΙΚΆ	OREKTIKA	STARTERS
ντολμάδες	dolmades	stuffed vine leaves
ἐλιὲς (γεμιστές)	elies (yemistes)	olives (stuffed)
μελιτσανασαλάτα	melitzanasalata	aubergine puréed with onion, garlic and tomato
ταραμοσαλάτα	taramosalata	cod's roe dip
τσατζίκι	tzatziki	yoghurt with cucumber
ζαμπόν	zambon	ham
ΚΡΕΑΣ	KREAS	MEAT
ἀρνάκι	arnaki	baby lamb
ἀρνί	arni	lamb
μπιφτέκι	bifteki	beefsteak
μπριζόλα	brizola	chop
χοιρινό	hirino	pork
κατσίκι	katsiki	goat
κοκορέτσι	kokoretsi	kidney, liver and tripe roasted
μοσχάρι	moskhari	veal/beef
παϊδάκια	paidakia	cutlets
σάλτσα	* saltsa	beef cooked in wine (Zakinthos)
σοφρίτο	* sofrito	beef stew (Corfu)
σούβλα (σουβλάκι)	souvla (souvlaki)	(shish kebab) chopped meat cooked on spit over charcoal
στιφάδο	stifado	meat stew with onions and red wine
κιμάς	kimas	minced meat
κεφτέδες	keftedes	meat balls
λουκάνικα	loukanika	sausage
μουσακά	moussaka	baked mince and aubergine pie
παπουτσάκια	papoutsakia	('little shoes') aubergines or marrows stuffed with mince and rice
παστίτσιο	pastitsio	baked macaroni and mince pie
σουτζουκάκια	soutsoukakia	meat balls in tomato sauce
ΨΆΡΙΑ	PSARIA	FISH/SEA FOOD
ἀστακός	astakos	lobster
μπακαλιάρος	bakaliaros	cod

μπαρμπούνι	barbouni	red mullet
μπουρδέττο	* bourdetto	white fish stew (Corfu)
γαρίδες	garides	prawns
καλαμαράκια	kalamarakia	baby squid (deep fried)
καραβίδα	karavida	crayfish
κταπόδι	ktapodi	octopus
λυθρίνι	lithrini	grey mullet
μαρίδες	marides	whitebait
σαβόρο	* savoro	fried fish salad prepared with oil, vinegar, garlic, rosemary, raisins (Levkas)
σουπιά	soupia	cuttlefish
συναγρίδα	sinagrida	sea bass
τσιπούρα	tsipoura	dentex
ξιφίας	xifias	swordfish

ΛΑΧΑΝΙΚΑ	**LAKHANIKA**	**VEGETABLES**
ἀγγινάρες	anginares	artichokes
ἀγγούρι	angouri	cucumber
ἀρακά	araka	green peas
μπάμιες	bamies	okra, lady's fingers
ντομάτες	domates	tomatoes
φασόλια	fasolia	white beans (pulses)
φασολάκια	fasolakia	string beans
κολοκύθακια	kolokithakia	courgettes
κολοκύθια	kolokithia	marrows
κρεμμύδια	kremidia	onions
λάχανο	lakhano	cabbage
μελιτζάνες	melitzanes	aubergines
πατάτες	patates	potatoes
πιπεριές	piperies	peppers
ρύζι	risi	rice
σκόρδο	skordo	garlic
σπανάχι	spanakhi	spinach
γεμιστά	yemista	stuffed vegetables

ΣΑΛΑΤΕΣ	**SALATES**	**SALADS**
ἀγγουροτοματα-σαλάτα	angourodomata-salata	cucumber and tomato
χοριάτικη	horiatiki	mixed salad with *feta*
χόρτα	horta	greens
λάχανο	lakhano	cabbage
μαρούλι	marouli	lettuce

ΓΛΥΚΑ	**GLYKA**	**SWEETS/SWEET PASTRIES**
μπακλαβά	baklava	flaky pastry filled with nuts and dipped in honey
μπουγάτσα	bougatsa	cinnamon cream pastry
γαλακτομπούρεκο	galaktoboureko	flaky pastry with custard filling
χαλβά	halva	cake made with semolina and almonds
καταΐφι	kataifi	'shredded wheat' pastry with nuts
κούμκουάτ	* koum-kouat	miniature oranges (Corfu)
λουκουμάδες	loukoumades	dough balls with honey
λουκούμι	loukoumi	Turkish delight
μαντολάτο	* mandolato	almond nougat (Zakinthos)
μηλόπιττα	milopitta	apple pastry

ΦΡΟΫΤΑ/ΞΗΡΟΙ ΚΑΡΠΟΙ	FROUTA/KSIRI KARPI	FRUIT/NUTS
ἀχλάδι	akhladi	pear
ἀμύγδαλο	amigdalo	almond
δαμάσκηνο	damaskino	plum
ἐλιά	elia	olive
φουντούκι	foundouki	hazelnut
φράουλα	fraoula	strawberry
καρύδι	karidi	walnut
καρπούζι	karpouzi	watermelon
κάστανο	kastano	chestnut
κεράσι	kerasi	cherry
κυδώνι	kidoni	quince
λεμόνι	lemoni	lemon
μῆλο	milo	apple
μηλοροδάκινο	milorodakino	nectarine
πεπόνι	peponi	honeydew melon
πορτοκάλι	portokali	orange
ροδάκινο	rodakino	peach
ρόδι	rodi	pomegranate
σταφίδα	stafida	seedless grape/raisin
σταφύλι	stafili	grape
σύκο	siko	fig
βερύκοκο	verikoko	apricot

ΠΙΤΤΑ	PITTA	SAVOURY PIES
κρεατόπιττα	kreatopitta	meat pie
σπαναχόπιττα	spanakhopitta	spinach pie
τυρόπιττα	tiropitta	cheese pie

ΤΥΡΙ	TIRI	CHEESE
φέτα	feta	salty white crumbly cheese made from sheep's or goat's milk
γραβιέρα	*graviera	Swiss-type gruyere (Corfu and Zakinthos)
κασέρι	kaseri	creamy yellow cheese like cheddar
κεφαλοτύρι	kefalotiri	hard salty cheese
μανούρι, μυζήθρα	manouri, mizithra	types of cottage cheese

Various			Methods of cooking		
ἀλάτι	alati	salt	καπαμά	kapama	cooked with potatoes and onions in tomato sauce and wine
αὐγά	avga	eggs			
γάλα	gala	milk			
κοτόπουλο	kotopoulo	chicken			
λάδι	ladi	oil			
μέλι	meli	honey	ψητό	psito	roasted
νερό	nero	water	σχάρας	skaras	grilled
παγωτό	pagoto	ice-cream	τηγανιτό	tiganito	fried
πιπέρι	piperi	pepper	τοῦ φούρνου	tou fornou	baked
ψωμί, ἄρτος	psomi, artos	bread	βραστό	vrasto	boiled
βούτυρο	voutiro	butter	γιουβέτσι	yiouvetsi	served with pasta
γιαούρτι	yiaourti	yoghurt			
ζάχαρι	zakhari	sugar			

* specialities of the Ionian Islands

Sea cave, Paxos

PUBLIC HOLIDAYS

Jan 1   New Year's Day
Jan 6   Epiphany
Mar 25   Greek Independence Day
Mar/Apr   Shrove Monday, Good Friday
May 1   May Day
May 21   Anniversary of the Union of the
           Ionian Islands with Greece
Aug 15   Assumption of the Virgin
Sep 14   Holy Cross Day
Oct 28   *Ohi* Day (Greece said 'no' to the
           Italian invasion ultimatum, 1940)
Dec 25   Christmas Day

FEAST DAYS AND FESTIVALS

Each island has its special feast days, and the most colourful are those in honour of the patron saints of the major islands: St Spiridon in Corfu, St Gerasimus in Cefalonia and St Dionysius in Zakinthos. The Easter celebrations in Corfu town (see p. 90) are particularly spectacular.

CLIMATE

Located near the mountain ranges of western Greece and Albania, Corfu and its five southerly neighbours have a higher rainfall than most of the rest of Greece, to which they owe the pleasant greenness of their landscape. This fact should not, however, deter holidaymakers, as most of the additional rain falls in the winter months. Summer temperatures are on the average the same as in the Aegean, with a peak in July and August. The best time to visit the Ionians is in the spring or early autumn, bearing in mind that the weather can sometimes break before mid October. Kithira, off the south-east coast of the Peloponnese, is much drier than the other Ionians.

Chart of average temperature and rainfall for Corfu-Zakinthos area

Month	Air temp	Sea temp	Av. days of rain	Av. daily hrs of sun
	C F	C F		
Jan	10/50	15/59	13	5
Feb	10/50	15/59	12	6
Mar	12/54	15/59	10	7
Apr	15/59	16/61	8	7
May	19/66	18/64	5	9
Jun	24/75	21/70	4	10
Jul	27/81	24/75	1	11
Aug	26/79	25/77	1	12
Sep	23/73	24/75	4	9
Oct	19/66	21/70	11	6
Nov	15/59	19/66	13	4
Dec	12/54	18/64	16	3

LANGUAGE

Greek alphabet	Romanised equivalent	Modern pronunciation
A/a	A/a	father
B/β	V/v	v (see *Note 1*, below)
Γ/γ	G/g	guttural g, but a 'y' sound when used before vowel (see *Note 2*, below) and an 'ng' sound when used as a double letter (*Note 3*)
Δ/δ	D/d	dh as sound in 'then' (see also *Note 4*)
E/ϵ	E/e	egg
Z/ζ	Z/z	z
I/ι	I/i	ee
Θ/θ	Th/th	*thin*
H/η	I/i	ee
K/κ	K/k	k
Λ/λ	L/l	l
M/μ	M/m	m
N/ν	N/n	n
Ξ/ξ	X/x	ks
O/o	O/o	hot
Π/π	P/p	p
P/ρ	R/r	r
$\Sigma/\sigma,s$	S/s	s
T/τ	T/t	t
Y/υ	Y/y	ee
Φ/ϕ	F/f	f
X/χ	Kh/kh	Ba*ch* (*Note 5*)
Ψ/ψ	PS/ps	a*pse*
Ω/ω	O/o	hot

1 The 'b' sound in Greek is rendered by the combination $\mu\pi$, as in the word $\mu\pi\acute{\alpha}\nu\iota o$ ('bath') pronounced 'banyo'.

2 An example of this is $\mathring{A}\gamma\iota o\varsigma$ (the Greek word for 'saint') found in many place names. This is pronounced, and shown in its Romanised Greek version in this book, as 'Ayios'.

3 Example: $\mathring{A}\gamma\gamma\lambda o\varsigma$ ('Englishman') pronounced 'Anglos'.

4 The 'd' sound in Greek is rendered by the combination $\nu\tau$, as in the word $\nu\tau o\lambda\mu\acute{\alpha}\delta\epsilon\varsigma$ pronounced 'dolmades'.

5 To avoid confusion with the alternative pronunciation of 'ch' as in 'church', this letter is rendered as 'kh' in this book as in the word $\chi\omega\rho\acute{\iota}o$ ('village') shown as 'khori(o)'. (The final 'o' is usually dropped from this word when used in place names, such as *Neokhori, Paleokhori*.)

Dipthongs

Greek	Pronunciation
AE/$\alpha\epsilon$, AI/$\alpha\iota$	egg
EI/$\epsilon\iota$, OI/$o\iota$	*is*
OY/$o\upsilon$	oo
AY/$\alpha\upsilon$, EY/$\epsilon\upsilon$	af, ev

Stress

When pronouncing a Greek word or name it is essential to put the stress on the correct syllable, otherwise a Greek will probably not understand you. Accents denoting stress are shown in the examples of Greek words in the Greek Restaurant Menu (p. 36). To help the traveller achieve the correct pronunciation when asking directions, etc., accents have been added to the place-names in the index, but for simplification of the text have been omitted from the rest of the book.

Use of Greek

English-speaking travellers in the Ionians will appreciate the ready use of their language in the towns and resorts—not only in hotels, bars, restaurants and shops but by the 'man in the street'. Excursions to the remoter, rural areas may bring communication problems, but it is not unusual to meet villagers in the islands least exposed to tourism (Ithaca, Cefalonia, Kithira) who speak perfect English. This is usually, however, with an American or Australian accent, and 'Christos' (now 'Chris') will probably have spent more of his life abroad than in Greece—as a chef in the Bronx, perhaps, or a taxi-driver in Melbourne. Back in his native island for a summer vacation, he is only too willing to show off his acquired language—and prosperity.

In spite of the prevalence of English it is a good idea to master a basic vocabulary of Greek words and phrases. These are useful when shopping in street markets, asking directions, etc., and some expressions are appreciated simply as a natural courtesy. The ideal phrase book should include numbers, weights, days of the week, time, and other essentials. The following brief list will get you started:

Yes   *nay*
No   *okhi*
Please/don't mention it   *parakalo*
Thankyou   *efkharisto*
Excuse me   *signomi*
Hello   **yiasou*
Good morning   *kalimera*
Good afternoon/evening   *kalispera*
Goodnight   *kalinikhta*
Goodbye   *adio*

*This is also used when offering a toast—the Greek equivalent to 'cheers' (the first and second person plural forms, used in larger company, are *yiamas* and *yiasas*)

CURRENCY AND BANKS

The currency in the Ionian Islands is the Greek drachma. The coins are 1, 2, 5, 10, 20 and 50 drachma, the notes 100, 500, 1000 and 5000 drachma. Banks are only located in Corfu town (hours Mon–Fri 8.30–2.00) but traveller's cheques, etc. can be changed at post offices in the main resorts (these are sometimes yellow-painted trailers located at central points) open Mon–Sat 08.00–19.00. Post offices generally offer better rates than banks and charge less commission. Money can also be changed in hotels and 'change' offices, but at a poor rate of exchange.

MUSEUMS AND MONUMENTS

The devastation of earthquakes, the plunder of barbarian invasions and the quarrying of ancient sites by the fortress builders has deprived the Ionians of much of their architectural heritage. All the islands, however, preserve remains of fortifications of the medieval and modern periods and all but Paxos have archaeological museums (Corfu, Zakinthos and Cefalonia also have art and historical collections). For the opening times of museums and monuments in these three islands see the practical information at the beginning of their sections.

TOURIST INFORMATION

The addresses of tourist information offices in the larger islands (Corfu, Cefalonia, Zakinthos) are shown in the practical information at the beginning of the island sections. Tourist information in the other islands can be obtained from good travel agencies or the local police.

House in the Campiello quarter, Corfu town

BOOKS ON THE IONIANS

General
Foss, Arthur *The Ionian Islands* (Faber, 1969)
Pratt, Michael *Britain's Greek Empire* (Rex Collings 1978)

Corfu
Chatto, James & Martin, W. L. *A Kitchen in Corfu* (Weidenfeld & Nicolson, 1987)
Dicks, Brian *Corfu* (David & Charles, 1977)
Durrell, Gerald *My Family and Other Animals* (Penguin, 1987)
Durrell, Lawrence *Prospero's Cell* (Faber, 1975)
Rochford, Noel *Landscapes of Corfu* (Sunflower Books, 1987) Detailed routes for walkers and motorists
Stamatopoulos, N *Old Corfu, History and Culture* (Corfu 1978)

The Ionians in Legend
Bradford, Ernle *Ulysses Found* (Hodder & Stoughton, 1963)
Homer *The Odyssey* (trans. E. V. Rieu, Penguin Classics, 1988) This celebrated translation is acknowledged as the source for the quotations in this book
Severin, Tim *The Ulysses Voyage: Sea Search for the Odyssey* (Hutchinson, 1987)

Selection of pre–20th century works, from which quotations used in this book are acknowledged:

Ansted, D. T. *The Ionian Islands in the Year 1863* (1863)
Davy, J. *Notes and Observations on the Ionian Islands Vols 1 & 2*
Holland, H. *Travels in the Ionian Isles, Albania, Thessaly, Macedonia, etc.* (1815)
Jervis-White-Jervis, H. *The Ionian Islands During the Present Century* (1863)
Kirkwall, Viscount *Four Years in the Ionian Islands Vols 1&2*
Leake, W. M. *Travels in Northern Greece Vol 3* (1835)
Lear, E. *Journals of a Landscape Painter in Greece and Albania* (1851); *Views in the Seven Ionian Islands* (1863)
Lithgow, W. *The Rare Adventures and Painefull Peregrinations* (1632)
Miller, W. *The Latins in the Levant* (1908)
Napier, C. *The Colonies: Treating of their Values Generally—of the Ionian Islands in Particular* (1833)
Strabo *Geography*, Book 10 (Loeb Edition)
Wheeler, Private *The Letters of Private Wheeler 1809–1828* (Michael Joseph edition, ed. Capt B. H. Liddell Hart, 1951)

Church of St Spiridon, Corfu town

Summer visitors from a northern clime will particularly enjoy the Ionian sensations: the warmth and the street life. The two go together, of course, but here the love of the outdoors has a special character. As elsewhere in Greece and the Mediterranean, the streets and squares of the towns and villages become, after dark, an extension of their inhabitants' houses, an *al fresco* living space in which the business of life can continue over an *ouzo*, *meze* or glass of wine, sitting at the pavement table of a cafe-bar or *taverna*. The social effect is everything: to see, to be seen, to communicate.

Like all Mediterranean people the Corfiots and their fellow Ionians enjoy their siesta, and in the summer months shut their shops and offices in the early afternoon and retire to their homes for lunch and a rest. This not only helps them recover from the long morning but prepares them for their 'second shift' when they reopen their businesses for a few more hours. The most pleasurable part of the day follows, when they finally finish work and go out with their families or friends to enjoy themselves.

Before settling into their chairs in the cafe-bars the more active—and socially conscious—members of the community will take part in the evening *volta*. This uniquely Mediterranean recreation,

42

known elsewhere as the *promenade*, *passegiata* or *paseo*, is strictly for the locals, but visitors can enjoy it from the sidelines. Down the central street, or around the central square, the greater part of the town or village population joins in a convivial perambulation: mothers and fathers with children in pushchairs, exchanging greetings with friends, more self-absorbed and sedate elders, and young girls, walking arm-in-arm with mothers or friends, pretending not to notice the lingering glances of the young men. This is the social concourse by which the nation renews itself—and provides the spectator with an evening's theatre.

The stage requirements are simple—a traffic-free open space near the centre of town, well-illuminated. In Corfu town the area in front of the Liston provides a perfect promenade, the arcades a viewing gallery for the diners and winers. In Zakinthos the Plateia Solomou (Solomos Square), the town's largest open space, is a natural congregating point—and a playground for the tireless army of small children who never seem to have a bedtime. Similar activity occupies the main square of Argostoli in Cefalonia, the main street of Levkas and the quaysides of the smaller islands.

The events of the Greek Orthodox calendar, and the religious festivals of the individual islands, provide a formal scenario for the gathering of their people. At the town or village level the most important event is the *panayiri*, a feast which marks the saint's day of the local church. The occasion is of particular importance when it is the island's patron saint who is being honoured, or if the church guards an icon with miraculous powers. After a special service the remains of the saint or the holy icon will be paraded in a colourful procession around the town or village, and the ensuing celebrations will include an outdoor feast with a sheep roasted on a spit, wine-drinking and dancing. The stranger is always welcome to join in these events—the best possible way of enjoying Greek hospitality.

The most splendid religious ceremonial and pageantry is seen in the annual processions of the three islands with patron saints— Corfu, Zakinthos and Cefalonia. In Corfu there are four processions in honour of St Spiridon, whose miraculous powers saved the island from plague, siege and famine (see ps. 55 and 91). Without exception the most spectacular event of all is on Easter Saturday in Corfu, with the celebrations in the town marked by the parading of the saint's relics, the *epitafios*, around the streets and Esplanade, accompanied by the solemn but stirring music of the town bands.

Corfu

(Kerkira)

Pop: 99,500

Area: 588 sq km

Capital/port: Corfu (Kerkira) pop. 37,000

Airport: 2km S of Corfu town

Highest point: Mt Pantokrator (906m)

Nearest island: Paxos (18.5km SE)

Distance from mainland: 3.5km from Albania

Festivals: Easter in Corfu town; processions in honour of St Spiridon around the town on Palm Sunday, Easter Saturday, Aug 11 and 1st Sun in Nov.

Information: National Tourist Organisation in the Palace of St Michael & St George, Corfu town

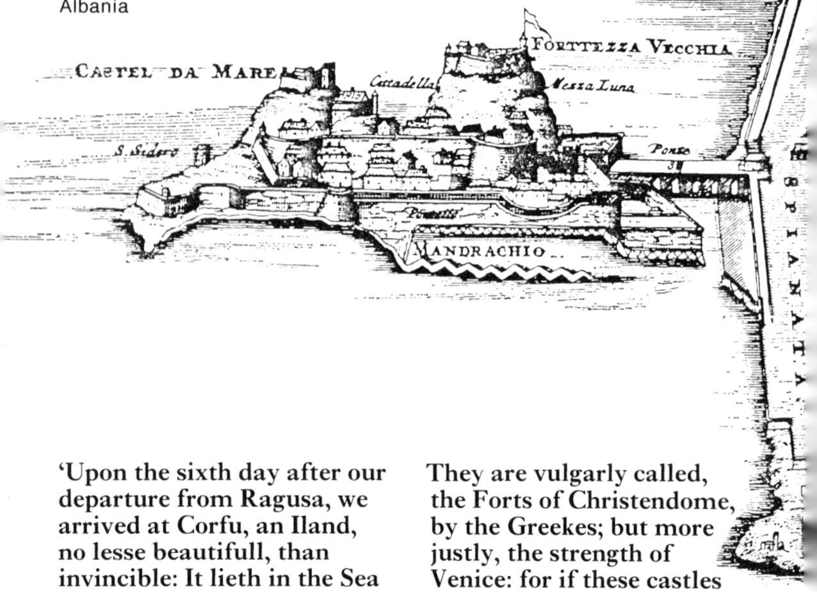

'Upon the sixth day after our departure from Ragusa, we arrived at Corfu, an Iland, no lesse beautifull, than invincible: It lieth in the Sea Ionian, the inhabitants are Greeks, and the Governours Venetians.

'The City Corfu, from which the Ile hath the name, is situate at the foote of a Mountaine, whereupon are builded two strong fortresses . . These castles are inaccessable, and unconquerable, if that the Keepers be loyall . . .

They are vulgarly called, the Forts of Christendome, by the Greekes; but more justly, the strength of Venice: for if these castles were taken by the Turkes or the Spanyard who would as gladly have them, the trade of the Venetian merchants would be of none account; yea the very meane to overthrow Venice it selfe.'

William Lithgow, *The Rare Adventures and Painefull Peregrinations*, 1632

Corfu town in the 16th century

Cioorn Werken

Patibu

S.Poco

FORTTEZZA NUOVA

Spilea Forteza

Corfu in history

The northernmost of the Ionian Islands and the westernmost part of Greece, Corfu lies at the entrance to the Adriatic Sea, commanding the Strait of Otranto between Italy and Albania. Its position has exposed it to the influence of western Europe, both in ancient times when the Romans submerged the Greek inhabitants, and during its modern history with occupations by the Venetians, French and British. The cultural legacy of these western rulers, together with the island's temperate climate and fertility, give it—and the other Ionians—a character unlike the rest of Greece.

Early settlement Two sites which have revealed prehistoric occupation of the island are Gardiki in the south-west (Paleolithic, *c*. 40,000BC) and Sidari on the north coast (Neolithic, *c*. 6000BC). Bronze Age settlement at various sites on the west coast shows no evidence of Mycenaean influence and nothing of Homer's *Scheria*, although there may have been contact with the Phoenicians, active in the Mediterranean at this time.

The first identified settlement was in the 8th c. BC by Greeks from Eretria in Euboea, later supplanted by a group from Corinth (734BC). The site of the original Greek city (*Corcyra*) lay to the south of the modern town, on the neck of land between Garitsa Bay and the Halikiopoulos Lagoon, identified now as Paleopolis.

The city state (8th–3rd c. BC) A key port on Corinth's western trade routes (southern Italy, Sicily), *Corcyra* was soon on equal terms with the mother city and they quickly became rivals. A naval battle between Corinth and Corcyra (*c*. 660BC)—the first recorded in Greek history—ended in victory for the Corcyreans, who went on to found their own colonies, most notably Epidamnos on the coast of Illyria (modern Durazzo in Albania).

Corcyra's success as a maritime state was similar to that of another island on the opposite side of Greece—Aegina. Like Aegina she had her own fleet of triremes and minted her own coinage: her athletes could also claim many honours at the Olympic Games. But whereas Aegina was subject to the dominance of Athens on the other side of the Saronic Gulf, the threat to Corcyra was always from the more accessible Corinth.

In 435BC another clash between Corcyra and Corinth came about in a dispute over control of Epidamnos. A Corinthian fleet was dispatched to the island, but like its predecessor it was destroyed by the Corcyreans. Corinth vowed vengeance, and Corcyra, fearful of a combined attack by Corinth and her Peloponnesian allies, formed its own alliance with Athens. An ensuing indecisive battle (Sivota Is., 433BC) in which Athens joined forces with Corcyra, was one of the direct causes of the Peloponnesian War.

In the course of the war there was a destructive struggle in Corcyra between two factions: that of the democrats, supported by Athens, and the oligarchs, supported by the Peloponnesians. The civil war, vividly described by Thucydides, ended in victory for the democrats (425BC) but only after a series of terrible massacres.

Corcyra's alliance with Athens suffered many vicissitudes in the next century (in 415BC the island's harbour was the assembly point for the Athenian fleet on its disastrous expedition to Sicily), and found its final commitment in 338BC on the field of Chaeronea. Here the Corcyreans joined the Athenians and other Greek allies in their stand against the invading army of Philip II of Macedon, and shared in their eventual defeat.

From that time the island was under threat and became the prize of competing generals, kings and tyrants, among them Kassander of Macedon, Agathokles of Syracuse, Pyrrhus of Epirus and Demetrius Poliorketes of Macedon. The Illyrians, traditional enemies of Macedonia, were also a threat. These people, who came from an area north of Greece occupied by present-day Albania, sent an invasion force from the mainland in 229BC which imposed a garrison on the island. The occupation of Corcyra by the 'barbarian' Illyrians, pirates of the Adriatic, antagonised the

Romans, who dispatched their own fleet of 200 ships from Brindisi. The Roman intervention, first thrust in the eastward extension of their empire, was welcomed by the Corcyreans. The Illyrians were expelled from the island and Corcyra became the first part of Greece to submit to the Romans.

Roman period (229BC–330AD) The island became an important naval base for the Romans for their campaigns in northern Greece and Illyria, which reached their climax in the defeat of the Macedonians at Pydna (168BC). The demand for timber for the Roman galleys took its toll of the island's forests; but throughout the period of Roman rule the Corcyreans suffered few other depredations at the hands of their masters and maintained a degree of independence.

During the Roman civil wars, however, the islanders were obliged to declare their sympathies and joined forces with Pompey against Julius Caesar. They later sided with Mark Antony against Caesar's heir, Octavian—a crucial mistake which brought the retribution of the man who as Augustus would be the first Roman emperor. On the eve of the great naval battle of Actium against Mark Antony (31 BC) Octavian's

Sculpture from Temple of Artemis, Corcyra

general Agrippa sent troops to the island to subjugate it and level the city.

Relationships with future emperors were more amicable and the island was granted many privileges in return for its loyalty. The most famous imperial visitor was Nero, who paid homage to the shrine of Zeus at Kassiope (66AD). Another significant event of the Roman period was the Christian mission of Sts Jason and Sosipater (before 200AD) which resulted in the building of the island's first Christian church (at Paleopolis). In 325AD the Corcyrean bishop Apollodorus attended the Council of Nicaea in Asia Minor convened by Constantine the Great. Among the other churchmen of the empire at the Council was the Cypriot bishop Spiridon, who would achieve immortality, after the many adventures of his earthly remains, as patron saint of Corfu (see p. 55).

Byzantine period (330–1081) After its transfer to the eastern section of the Roman empire ruled by Byzantium (Constantinople) Corcyra became prey to a series of barbarian invasions and was overrun many times, most devastatingly by the Ostrogoths (562) who destroyed the ancient capital. The Corcyreans, however, were able to reinforce their position in the empire by supplying military assistance, including warships, to various emperors for their campaigns against these foreign invaders. When Constantinople itself came under pressure from the Saracens in 717 the Corcyreans helped to raise the siege.

In the 8th c. Corcyra became part of a Byzantine *theme* based on Cefalonia and in the 9th c. the seat of an Archbishop under the jurisdiction of the Patriarch of Constantinople. By the 10th c. the population had moved from the ancient capital to the small promontory now occupied by the Old Fort, which offered a strong defensive location for a citadel. This new capital took its name, Korifo from the twin peaks (*korifai*, 'summits') which are its most prominent feature. (The name was also given to the whole island, the derivation of 'Corfu'.)

Normans to Angevins (1081–1386) Its position on the sea route from Venice and the boot of Italy to the Holy Land established Corfu as a port-of-call for the Crusaders. There were the inevitable attempts—some briefly successful—to capture the island for the interests of one power or another. Most persistent in the 12th c. were the Normans, who had established the rule of the de Hauteville family in southern Italy after the defeat of the imperial army. A force commanded by a member of the family, Robert Guiscard (the 'Wizard') captured Corfu in 1081. In the following century the island changed hands many times in a three-sided contest between the Normans, the Byzantine empire, and the Venetians.

After the subjugation of Byzantium by the Latins in 1204 Venice was awarded Corfu in payment for services in supplying and transporting the Crusader armies: her full occupation of the island was, however, thwarted by its annexation by a surviving enclave of the Byzantine empire, the Despotate of Epirus, under Michael I Angelos (1214).

For a brief period the island recovered the features of life it had enjoyed under the Byzantine emperors: low taxation and the precedence of the Greek Orthodox Church. A further change, however, occurred when the fourth and last Despot, Michael II (1236–66) gave Corfu to Manfred, the Hohenstaufen ruler of Sicily, as part of his daughter's dowry when she married Manfred (1257). The island was thereby drawn into the web of Italian politics, most significantly the contest between the Pope and the Holy Roman Empire. Manfred, as bastard son of the Emperor Frederick II, was the natural successor to the Empire and opposed to the Pope's temporal power: the Pope retaliated by backing Charles of Anjou, son of King Louis VIII of France, who subsequently defeated Manfred in battle. With Manfred's death the French prince was granted all his possessions—including Corfu—by his Pope.

Angevin rule (1267–1386) brought heavy taxation and religious persecution to Corfu. The Greek Orthodox archbishopric established in the 8th c. was abolished and a Roman Catholic archbishop installed, and the larger churches were given over to the Latin rite. With the decline of the Angevins and the continuing harrassment of pirate raids, the island was ready in 1386 to accept the protection of the Venetians.

Venetian rule (1386–1797)

The First Siege The long period of Venetian rule brought stability to the island and freedom from the thrall of the Turks, who by the mid-15th c. were in control of the mainland. Recognising the value of the Ionians to the Venetians as links on their shipping routes to the Levant, the Turks determined to seize them. Although most of the smaller islands were to submit to periods of Turkish occupation Corfu remained the major prize.

The island's defences, built up by the Venetians, were twice put to the test by the Turks in major sieges. The first attempt on the island, in 1537, was staged by Sultan

Corfu town in the Venetian period

Suleiman the Magnificent, who found an excuse for invasion when one of his supply ships was sunk by Venetian galleys. From his base on the opposite shore of Epirus, the Sultan launched a force under the command of his admiral Barbarossa. The notorious Barbary corsair, whose future naval victories would help bring the Ottoman empire to the height of its power in the Mediterranean, landed with an army of 25,000 men and artillery at Gouvia Bay and invested the town of Corfu. The town was soon overrun and ultimately only the citadel (the Old Fort) and the castle of Angelokastro on the west coast of the island were left in the hands of their Greek and Italian defenders. The citadel was particularly vulnerable, exposed to bombardment by the Turkish guns positioned on the high ground on either side of the fortress peninsula and on the islet of Vido. After three weeks, disease and starvation had brought the 4000-strong Christian garrison close to surrender, but the ranks of their besiegers were similarly ravaged and they were unable to maintain the siege. Their withdrawal was followed by a 'scorched earth' reprisal, which resulted in the wholesale destruction of the island's farms and villages and the seizure of

The Second Siege The armed neutrality which Venice had maintained since Lepanto, during the continuing conflict between the Ottoman and Hapsburg Empires, came to an end when the Turks conquered Crete (1669)—a major Venetian possession whose loss was a disaster to the Republic. Corfu, which had assisted in Crete's defence, now became the Republic's most important dependency, and the launching point for Venice's great campaign, under Francesco Morosini, to recover her lost territories in Greece.

Although the Venetian campaign was successful, carrying Morosini's forces to the slopes of the Athenian Acropolis and capturing the Peloponnese, it was difficult for the Republic to maintain its occupation. By 1714 the Turks were back, reoccupying the Peloponnese and seizing other Venetian outposts on the mainland and in the Aegean. The Sultan's army, determined to capture the major Venetian stronghold of Corfu, then marched on Epirus and launched an attack on the island in 1716.

Gouvia Bay was once more the landing place, for a host of 30,000 foot soldiers and 3000 cavalry. Although larger than the earlier invasion force the Turkish army faced stronger defences than in 1537, including the New Fort, and a line of fortifications stretching from Mandouki to Garitsa Bay. Commanding the defences was a Saxon Marshal, Count von der Schulenberg, whose 8000-strong force comprised a mixture of Germans, Italians, Slavs and Greeks.

For six weeks the motley garrison held out against sustained Turkish attacks, witnessing the successive capture of the suburbs of Mandouki, San Rocco and Garitsa, and the heights of Avrami and San Salvator, on which the Turks mounted their guns to bombard the city. An assault by the Turks on the north-west bastion of the New Fort, though successful, proved a turning-point in the siege when the defenders, led by Schulenberg, staged a counter-attack that was supported by a mass of civilians, pouring out from the fortress to repel the attackers.

Turkish losses were severe and the Sultan's troops fell back to their lines. The defenders' forces, too, were seriously depleted, and feared that any renewed attack would overwhelm them. But chance—or what many saw as the answer to their prayers to St Spiridon—brought a terrible storm which destroyed the Turkish encampment and carried their baggage out to sea. The demoralised Turkish army raised the siege and set sail, leaving 5000 dead as the memorial of their last attempt to capture the island they had prized for 300 years.

20,000 Corfiots for the slave-markets of Constantinople.

Reduced to a fraction of its ancient population, the island was only able to recover after the Venetians had repopulated it with refugees from their other colonies in Greece which they had lost to the Turks (Navplion in 1539, Monemvasia in 1540). By 1571 the island was sufficiently strengthened to act as a naval base for the armada of the Holy League, prior to its engagement with the Turkish fleet at Lepanto. The combined fleet, under the command of Don Juan of Austria, son of the Emperor Charles V, included 63 Venetian galleys. The Allied victory (which took place off the Echinades Is. between Ithaca and the mainland) dealt a crippling blow to Ottoman naval power in the Mediterranean. Corfu, however, was still vulnerable, separated only by a narrow channel from the Turkish-occupied mainland. Further Turkish raids brought demands by the Corfiots for a strengthening of the capital's defences. The *borgo*, or quarter which lay outside the citadel and which was always overrun in an attack, was walled in by the Venetians (this outer wall has since been dismantled) and the New Fort built between 1576 and 1588 to protect the city on its landward side.

Corfu under the Venetians In return for the Venetians' protection the Corfiots had to accept their autocratic system of government, which by the early 16th c. had been formalised by the appointment of a *Provveditore del Levante*, who had supreme authority over the Ionian Islands and commanded the Venetian naval force based on Corfu. Supporting this Venetian official was a Corfiot elite, consisting mainly of the descendants of the foreign landowners who had settled in the island under the Angevins. In 1572 the names of these privileged noblemen were entered in a register known as the Golden Book (*Libro d'Oro*).

The exclusion of the nobility from taking part in trade encouraged the advance of a merchant, or burgher class, who as they grew more affluent were tempted to bid for places in the ranks of the nobility. (A law of 1647 permitting the sale of titles to boost revenue for the Venetian Republic would eventually undermine the island's aristocracy.)

At the bottom of Corfu's economy were the peasant population who spent their lives working on land which did not belong to them, paying taxes on their produce but having no say in the island's government. In a bad year, when a poor harvest would make it impossible for the peasants to pay their tithe to the landowners, they would be imprisoned for debt. This feudal oppression led to the inevitable eruption and in 1640 the peasants stormed the town and released their comrades from the prison in the Old Fort. The rebellion, ruthlessly put down by troops from Venice, flared up again repeatedly in ensuing years as conditions for the islanders continued to deteriorate. The plagues of 1629 and 1673, which consumed whole villages, were a further penance from which the islanders looked to their saint for deliverance.

In religious affairs the Venetians endeavoured to contain the Orthodox faith, fearful that an increase of its influence would reinforce the Corfiots' sense of national identity. The Greek archbishop was kept in abeyance and the Latin supremacy maintained: the head of the Greek Orthodox Church in the island was referred to as the *Protopapas* ('First Priest') a title introduced by the Angevins. The island's culture was also strongly infected by the Latin spirit, notably in the influence of the Renaissance on architecture and painting (see p. 18). A special innovation of the Venetians was their introduction of opera to Corfu; the music school that was subsequently established becoming the progenitor of the colourful town bands that are very much a part of the contemporary Corfiot scene.

Venetian lion on the New Fort

French and Russian occupation and the Septinsular Republic (1797–1814) The decline of the Ottoman empire and the exhaustion of the Venetian Republic created opportunities for the rival European powers. The eyes of France, Russia and Britain were all focussed on the remaining Venetian possessions, particularly the Ionians whose strategic position in the Mediterranean theatre in which they were now competing offered vital opportunities. Each of the powers was to occupy the islands in turn, with Corfu as the main naval base and seat of government.

In 1797, after the capture of Venice by Napoleon, a French fleet sailed to Corfu to wrest control of the island from its Venetian garrison. The spirit of the French Revolution found its response in the Corfiots, who had suffered at the hands of their own *ancien regime*. Under the new order they were granted equal rights and celebrated their freedom by burning the Golden Book and destroying all the symbols of the nobility and of their Venetian overlords.

The ideals of liberty and equality, how-

The Liston, Corfu town

ever, were rapidly dispelled by the imposi-
tions of the French administration which
ran the islands as a *département* of
France, levying new taxes and confiscat-
ing property. An added provocation to the
Corfiots was the behaviour of the French
troops, who were unpaid and relied on
pillage for compensation. (The image of
'liberators' looting the churches of the 'liberated' would remain faithful to the
Grande Armée in the years to come.)

The French occupation was brief. In 1798
Russia and Turkey, threatened by Buonaparte's invasion of Egypt, sent as a count-
ermeasure a combined fleet to seize
the Ionian Islands, a mission which was
successfully accomplished as far as
Corfu.

Determined to resist, the French on Corfu
had first to quell a mutiny by the Corfiots.
Many of the inhabitants who had taken up
arms were in occupation of the suburb of
Mandouki, which the French were com-
pelled to reduce by bombardment.

Shortly afterwards the allied troops landed
simultaneously to the north of the town
(Potamos Bay) and the south (Garitsa),
capturing the heights of Olivetti (above
Mandouki) and St Pantaleimon (site of the
modern Mon Repos). From these strategic
points they were able to direct their fire
on the town, but it was not until they had
captured Vido Island, which commanded
the harbour, that they were able to force
the French to surrender.

Under a treaty drawn up by Russia and
Turkey (1800) the Ionian Islands were
made a semi-independent 'Septinsular Republic' (effectively a Russian protectorate)
and the allied troops withdrawn. The seat
of government, the Ionian Senate, was in
Corfu. The Greek Orthodox Church was
reinstated as the official faith, and with it
the Metropolitan See of Corfu. This gesture by their Russian Orthodox brethren
was welcomed by the Corfiots, but less so
their reinstatement of the old aristocracy
and the appointment of its members to the
Senate. The return to power of a privileged
minority was unacceptable to the Corfiots,
who appealed for British protection. Faced
by further unrest, Russian troops returned
and a very restricted constitution granted.
Although unsatisfactory, this enabled the

51

Greeks of the Septinsular Republic to enjoy a limited self-government: something unknown to their mainland brothers since the Turkish conquest.

Further confrontation with the allied powers over the constitution was averted by events in Europe, which saw a triumphant Napoleon, at the peak of his military successes, negotiating a Treaty of Peace and Alliance with a submissive Russia (Treaty of Tilsit, 1807). Under the terms of this treaty Corfu was ceded to France and the Septinsular Republic dissolved.

Once again the Ionian Islands became a French province, under the direction of a Governor-General whose powers included the appointment of the members of the Senate. Despite this autocracy, the second occupation by France was more benevolent than its predecessor, thanks to the guiding hand of a sympathetic Governor General, Donzelot, whose name is still honoured in Corfu. Under his inspiration the Ionic Academy and the first School of Fine Arts was established, agricultural methods were improved and parts of the town were remodelled on French lines.

By 1809, the Royal Navy had become the dominant force in the Mediterranean. This enabled British troops, which included two British-led battalions of Greek Light Infantry, to capture the Ionian Islands progressively, from Zakinthos (1809) to Paxos (1814). Corfu was meanwhile blockaded by a British fleet until Napoleon's fall.

British Protectorate (1814–64) Under the Treaty of Paris (1814) the islands became a British Protectorate with Corfu as the capital. Nominally independent, they were subject to an undemocratic constitution drawn up by the first Lord High Commissioner, Sir Thomas Maitland (1815–24), which gave the islanders only limited control over their own affairs. Members of the Ionian Parliament, which consisted of a Senate and an Assembly, were in part nominated by Maitland and in part elected on a limited franchise, leaving the power firmly in the hands of the Lord High Commissioner. The government of the other islands was delegated to British Residents.

One of the leading opponents of the British constitution was Ioannis Kapodistrias (1776–1831), a Corfiot who later became the first President of an independent Greece. During the War of Independence which raged on the mainland the British presence kept the island safe from attack from the Turks or their mercenaries such as Ibrahim Pasha, whose Egyptian army swept through the Peloponnese in 1824: on the other hand the Corfiots were unable to join their Greek compatriots in the struggle

against the Turks. After the liberation of Greece (1832) the British denied the Ionians their anticipated union with the mother country. The liberalisation of the constitution (1848) and a visit to the islands by the philhellene William Gladstone with the proposal of further reforms (1858) were seen as palliatives, and in the same year the Ionian Parliament made a formal demand for union with Greece.

When a deal was finally struck between Greece and Britain, whereby a monarch acceptable to Britain and her European allies was chosen for the Greek throne (the Danish prince William, who became George I of the Hellenes), the wishes of the Ionian Islanders were granted and the islands ceded to Greece on May 1, 1864.

Though undemocratic, the 50 years of British rule brought many advances to Corfu and the other islands. Fine buildings and roads and—on Corfu—the first system of water supply to the capital via the aqueduct at Benitses, were among the technical achievements; equally important was the abolition of the feudal system of land tenure and the eventual recognition in 1852 of Greek as the official language of the islands. Other achievements in the cultural life of the Ionians were the work of philanthropic individuals, such as Lord Guilford, who founded the new Ionian Academy—the first Greek university—in Corfu in 1824. Guilford, who personally financed the university, had already proved his devoted philhellenism by converting to the Orthodox faith.

The Union with Greece (1864) Mindful of the previous exploitation of Corfu's strategic position by rival powers, Britain had insisted as part of her agreement with Greece that the island be militarily neutralised, and to this end destroyed many of its fortifications before her departure.

The idea that an island in such a critical location could remain insulated from world affairs was, however, fanciful. During World War I Corfu played host to the exiled Serbian government and was used as a base by the allied forces, notably for the Macedonian campaigns.

Later in the 20th c. Corfu was twice the victim of Mussolini's aggression (a bombardment by the Italian fleet in 1923, and occupation by the Duce's forces in 1941) and once by the Germans, who wrested the island from the Italians in 1943. In the action a quarter of the town was destroyed.

The most dramatic post-war event was the 'Corfu Incident' when two British destroyers, patrolling the strait between Corfu and Albania, ran into a minefield and sank, with the loss of 44 lives.

Discovering Corfu

View north from Analipsis (see also p. 149)

The island is shaped like a sickle, 64km long and up to 32km wide. The highest mountains are in the north-east 'handle', rising to the summit of *Mt Pantokrator* (906m). To the west, *Mt Arakli* (405m) overlooks Paleokastritsa, and to the south at the centre of the 'blade' a chain of hills reaches its highest point at *Ayii Deka* (576m). The island flattens out between the two groups (*Plain of Ropa*) and at the dry southern tip.

The contours of the coastline show a dramatic variation: rocky and precipitous on the west and east sides of the 'handle' and yet shelving gently on the north: the edges of the 'blade' also more accessible with some natural harbours on the east coast. Best known of these are the twin harbours of Corfu town, on either side of its protective headland, which pre-ordained the site of Corfu's capital.

Corfu's climate is its greatest blessing. The rainfall, high for Greece, is concentrated mainly in the autumn, but the annual spread ensures a reasonable degree of humidity to alleviate the heat of high summer. A by-product is the island's rich vegetation, whose varied green tapestry is dominated by the interwoven cypress and olive. The density of olive trees on the island (there are 3–4 million, some more than 500 years old) is the result of a Venetian policy to encourage cultivation. Olives were a rare commodity for the water-locked republic and cash bonuses were offered for every 100 trees planted by the islanders.

Despite the demands of an energetic tourist development, catering for 300,000 yearly visitors, the majority of Corfu's population still works the land. The most fertile part of the island is found in the central (Ropa Valley) and southern plains. The former, irrigated by the Ropa river, is a popular area for market gardening and until recently for cattle and dairy farming. The decline in those industries resulted from the redirection of the economy towards tourism, although Greece's entry to the Common Market (1981) has brought the benefit of subsidies to encourage a return to livestock. Dairy farming and vegetable growing is also the major activity of the well-watered Lefkimi region in the south of the island.

The tradition of building villages on high points inland as a safe-guard against pirates deprived the coastline of settlements. The inland villages would instead build themselves a landing-stage (*skala*) for the purposes of fishing and trade. The fishing villages such as Benitses that were later established have now been taken over by tourism, but fishing is still an active industry, with the boats going out between midnight and dawn with their acetylene lamps and nets.

The demands of the restaurants and hotels in recent years have depleted the stocks in Corfu's waters, and now much of the fish served to tourists is imported. Grey mullet, sea-bass and bream are the most sought-after fish, with crayfish, octopus and squid also popular delicacies.

Although over 17% of the island's agricultural area is devoted to vines, the dry summer months are not favourable to growth and the quality of Corfu's red and white wines is variable, confining them to domestic consumption. Citrus cultivation also requires special conditions and is most successful in the Benitses and Lefkimi areas. Corfu's other fruit, however, is plentiful (see p. 31).

The impact of tourism on Corfu is now historical. In the vanguard of tourist development in the 1950s and '60s, it belongs to a different generation to the Aegean holiday islands, though of equal popularity today. In the early years the pioneer resort of Paleokastritsa was regarded somewhat disparagingly by the discerning traveller: now its commercialisation seems discreet in comparison with other developments. For these, it is unnecessary to look beyond Corfu's own recent excesses: the new resorts of Benitses and Kavos. Such places, with their strip growth of hotels, bars and gift shops, have changed the look of Corfu.

The island's life, too, is changing, with many Corfiots engaged in some aspect of the tourist industry. But happily the character of these people, and with it the real character of the island, is unaltered. The paradox is revealed in the glow of a thousand candles in the town square on Easter Saturday night; the cups of coffee never drained, the conversations never ended, in the wayside *cafenion*; the fruit plucked from its tree by a friendly villager for the pleasure of a passer-by.

Epitafios of St Spiridon, Corfu town

St Spiridon and the island festivals St Spiridon, patron saint of Corfu, has a devoted following. A bishop of Cyprus who attended the Council of Nicaea in 325, Spiridon's remains were taken to Constantinople to preserve them from marauding Saracens. For further safekeeping they were conveyed to Corfu before the capture of the city by the Turks (1453) and now rest in the Church of St Spiridon. The saint is credited with various miracles, including the dispersal of plague and famine and—in 1716—a dramatic appearance in a thunderstorm which put the besieging Turkish army to flight. These miraculous interventions are celebrated in four annual processions –

Palm Sunday, Easter Saturday, August 11 and the first Sunday in November – in which the saint's mummified remains are paraded through the streets of the town in a gilt casket. On these occasions the relics are accompanied in solemn procession by the Metropolitan of Corfu and escorted by state and city dignitaries, detachments of the armed forces, schoolchildren and the town's bands in their exotic uniforms.

The Corfiot Easter, one of the most splendid in Greece, includes a special event peculiar to the island: the 'breaking of pots' on Easter Saturday morning in the town. The significance of the ritual, in which large quantities of unwanted crockery are cast into the streets from upstairs windows, has been lost over the centuries (the stoning of Judas? the rending of the Tomb?) but symbolism apart, it is popular theatre which has not, so far, resulted in any broken heads.

Church architecture and art Only one church of the Byzantine period and style—the domed, cross-in-square Sts Jason and Sosipater—survives on Corfu. The Greek architectural tradition ended with the arrival of the island's Catholic rulers in the 13th century. Most of Corfu's historic churches were built by the Venetians in the 16th and 17th centuries and are typically single-aisled basilicas with flat ceilings under pitched roofs. Baroque exterior features—window and door mouldings, cornices and pilasters applied to stuccoed or stone façades are echoed by elaborate interior decoration: intricately carved gilded screens, painted ceilings, ornate candelabra.

A distinguishing feature of these Italianate Ionian churches is the campanile, either attached or free-standing, with a tiered balcony topped by a dome or pyramid. These belltowers often appear in the form also seen in Byzantine churches, as an upward extension of a wall or courtyard gate, pierced by arched openings in which the bells are suspended. The topmost tiers may have some Baroque ornament (volutes).

As a result of earthquake damage, wall paintings are very rare in Corfu and the best examples of the painters' skills can be seen in icons. Under the Venetians (14th–16th centuries) an Italianate style and technique created a more lifelike treatment, departing from the mannered formality of traditional Byzantine painting. Later on western ideas further asserted themselves in the work of the Cretan School (16th–17th centuries) whose best-known exponent is Michael Damaskinos (see also p. 20).

Catholic and Jewish populations Under the Angevins, the first Catholic power to enjoy a prolonged occupation of Corfu (1267–1386), Roman Catholicism was given precedence over the Greek Orthodox Church with the appointment of a Catholic Italian archbishop, and the relegation of the chief Orthodox priest to the title *Megas Protopapas*. The Venetians, however, endeavoured to maintain an equilibrium between the two churches, particularly after the influx of Greek refugees from Crete. Joint attendance of ceremonies was encouraged between the churches, and many Orthodox worshippers celebrated Mass with the Catholics.

Italian culture, projected by the language (used in official documents and in the law courts) and through Catholic ecclesiastical art and ritual, was absorbed by many of the educated Ionians, and was expressed most strongly in the twilight of the Venetian period by the religious paintings of the Ionian School, seen mainly in Corfu and Zakinthos. After the departure of the Venetians Catholicism waned, but Corfu is still the seat of a Catholic archbishop and there are 2500 members of the church still living in the island.

Tolerated by the Angevins, a Jewish community was established in Corfu by the late 13th century. They were not, however, popular with the Greeks who were jealous of them and would not permit them to own land or hold public office. In the late 15th century, the population was enlarged by an influx of refugees (Sephardis) from the Spanish and Portuguese Inquisitions, and later from Italy. Despite the hostility of the local population the Jews secured their position under the Venetians by their astute handling of the island's commerce. When a decree was enacted in 1572 banishing all Jews from Venetian territory, the Corfiot Jews were exempted.

Settled originally in the Campiello district, the Jews later formed another ghetto near the old port to the west of Voulgareos. (This quarter, known as *Hebraika*, still has a synagogue.) By the late 19th century it was estimated that the Jews formed a third of the town's population, but during the German occupation (1944) they were all deported to concentration camps in Europe. After the war a few of the survivors returned to the island to reoccupy their old quarter.

The name of the island Corfu's many names reflect the diversity of her history. Of the earliest, the best known is **Scheria**, immortalised by Homer as the land of the Phaeacians. These mythical people took their name from Phaiax, offspring of the union of Poseidon and the nymph Kerkira. The latter name was bestowed on the island by the Corinthian colonists of the 8th century BC: when referring to the ancient island the Doric version of the name—**Corcyra**—is generally used, and the people referred to as Corcyrans.

An alternative origin for the name **Kerkira** (geographical rather than mythical) may be the Greek word *kerkos* meaning 'tail' or 'handle', which is descriptive of its shape in the same way as another early name for the island, *Drepanon* ('sickle'). The modern name of the island, by which it is known outside Greece, also had a geographical origin. **Corfu** is an Italianised version of the Byzantine *Korifo*, which itself derives from the twin peaks (*korifai*) of the citadel.

TRAVEL TO CORFU

By air

Direct charter flights from London and Manchester

Direct weekly flights from London (summer only) by Olympic Airways

Daily flights from Athens to Corfu by Olympic Airways

By sea

International Car Ferries

A number of shipping lines run services from Italy to Greece which include Corfu on their routes and offer a Patras–Athens coach connection. These include:

Brindisi–Corfu–Igoumenitsa–Patras
Once or twice daily in summer, less frequently rest of year (average 8½hrs from Brindisi to Corfu)

Adriatica di Navigazione, Zattere 1411, 30123 Venice, Italy

Adriatic Ferries, 15–17 Hatzikiriakou Ave, 18537 Piraeus, Greece

Agapitos Lines, 99 Kolokotroni St, 18535 Piraeus, Greece

Fragline, 5a Rethymnou St, 10682 Athens, Greece

Hellenic Mediterranean Lines, Electric Railway Station Building, 18510 Piraeus, Greece

Brindisi–Corfu–Paxos–Ithaca–Cefalonia–Patras ('Ionis')
Alternate days Jun–mid Sep (9¾hrs from Brindisi to Corfu) weekly service in winter

Hellenic Coastal Lines, 12 Akti Possidonos, Piraeus, Greece

Bari–Corfu–Igoumenitsa–Patras
Once or twice daily in summer, less frequently rest of year (11hrs from Bari to Corfu)

Ventouris Ferries, Efplias 7, 18537 Piraeus, Greece

Ancona–Corfu–Igoumenitsa–Patras
Once daily in summer, less frequently Apr, May, Oct (23hrs from Ancona to Corfu)

From Patras
See *International Car Ferries*, above (12hrs from Patras to Corfu)

From Igoumenitsa
Frequent daily service (2hrs)

From Paxos
Two or three times daily (3hrs)

By land

By car from Athens to Igoumenitsa via Amfilokhia, Aktion, Preveza (476km) then car ferry to Corfu. By bus from Athens twice daily to Corfu via Igoumenitsa car ferry (10hrs). By train from Athens to Patras (frequent service, 4hrs) then car ferry to Corfu

TRAVEL IN CORFU

Buses Services are cheap and operate from Corfu town to all parts of the island. In Corfu town, buses to villages/resorts in other parts of the island and to mainland Greece (Athens, Thessaloniki) have their terminus in the main bus station in New Fortress Square, near the Old Port. Buses to villages in the area of Corfu town have their terminus in Plat. G. Theotiki (Sarocco Square) in the southern part of the town. There is also a regular service from Mandouki (by the New Port) to Kanoni via the Esplanade.

Taxis These are available in all the major resorts and in Corfu town from George II Square (Old Port), Plat. G. Theotoki (Sarocco Square), and the following streets: Kapodistriou, Mantzarou, Voulgareos.

Horse-drawn carriages (Corfu town only) These brightly-painted victorias, which can be hired for a scenic ride from the Old Port to the Esplanade via the sea wall (Odos Arseniou) are a colourful part of the scene in the old town.

Car hire is available from the airport, Corfu town and major resorts. The leading agencies are:

Hertz (at airport and New Port); Avis (at airport, New Port, Hilton Hotel and 31 Alexandras Ave); InterRent (at airport, New Port).

Scooter and bicycle hire is available in the major resorts and in Corfu town from George II Square (Old Port), the New Port and Alexandras Ave.

Petrol With the exception of one petrol station near Corfu town, these are closed on Sundays.

ACCOMMODATION

Hotels (see p. 28), villas, apartments and private rooms available throughout the island. Camping at Dassia, Ipsos, Karoussades, Kavadades, Kontokali, Messongi, Paleokastritsa, Piryi, Roda, Vatos (see p. 27).

RESTAURANTS

Corfu town and the major resorts all have a varied choice of restaurants and tavernas. Recommended are:

Corfu town

Averof Old Port
In a side street off George II Square, this long-established restaurant (Category A) offers good quality at reasonable prices. Mainly Greek, but with a few international dishes.

Barbarpipilas Alkiviadou Dari, Anemomilos
Informal restaurant near the sea in Corfu's southern suburb. 'Typical' cuisine, not expensive.

Orestes X. Stratigou 78, New Port
This attractive restaurant in Corfu's western suburb, Mandouki, is well-known for its authentic Greek cuisine, notably its fresh fish and seafood.

Rex Kapodistriou 6
In the street behind the Liston in the fashionable part of the old town. Unpretentious, popular with the locals and with a good selection of Corfiot dishes.

Outside Corfu town

Yiannis Perama (6km S)
Roof terrace restaurant by roadside overlooking sea. Varied fish menu, good atmosphere.

Taverna Tripas Kinopiastes (7km S)
Located in a small village on the northern slopes of Ayii Deka, this is Corfu's most talked-about restaurant. An inconspicuous frontage opens into an extraordinary 'grocer's shop' entrance with baskets of exotic fruit and vegetables and shelves of vintage wine in cobwebbed bottles on display. The *meze* presented at the table in the covered garden dining area is hard to resist—with such unexpected delicacies as caviar and salmon (although the salmon is imported, the caviar comes from the local grey mullet). *Souvla* and other meat dishes are among the best in the island. A good house wine, bottled for the restaurant, comes with the food. Diners worried about cost should ask for a menu/price list before indulging. Live music and folk dancing are added attractions.

BEACHES

A microcosm of the beaches of the Mediterranean may be found on Corfu's coastline, the range extending from the beautiful and desolate sandy bay of Ayios Yeoryios in the NW to the crowded shingle beaches of Dassia and Gouvia on the E coast. Although the beaches on the N and W coasts are more scenically attractive, they tend to be breezier than those on the more sheltered E coast, which also have the advantage of warmer sea temperatures (up to 25°C in early Sep).

Popular beaches/resorts

Key: **R** indicates location of resort including hotels, self-catering, **SC** mainly self-catering.

E coast, S of Corfu town

Mon Repos Beach (to the S of Corfu town in the suburb of Anemomilos) Within walking distance of the town (about 2km from the centre) this sand and shingle beach with diving jetty and shaded garden is the nearest for people staying in Corfu. Snack bar and changing rooms, small admission charge.

Kanoni (4km S of Corfu) Man-made beach below Hilton Hotel, open to non-residents. **R**

Perama (7km S of Corfu) Sand and shingle beaches close to main road, reached by steps. **R**

Benitses (11km S of Corfu) Long narrow strip of man-made sand and shingle beach backed by busy road with shops, bars, tavernas. **R**

Moraïtika (18.5km S of Corfu) Sand and shingle beach reached by tracks from main road. **R**

Messongi (20km S of Corfu) Narrow sand and shingle beach off main road backed by hotels, etc. **R**

Alikes (43km SE of Corfu) 2km sand and shingle beach. **R**

Kavos (47km SE of Corfu) Long sandy beach stretching 5km N of rapidly developing tourist area, with good watersports. **R**

E coast, N of Corfu town

Kontokali, Gouvia (6.5 & 7.5km N of Corfu) Pebble beaches of separate resorts on Bay of Gouvia reached by side road. Shallow sea. **R**

Dassia (13km N of Corfu) Sand and shingle beach backed by pine trees. N end used by Club Méditerranée (located on headland). Beach tavernas and bars, good watersports. **R**

Ipsos, Piryi (15 & 16.5km N of Corfu)
Narrow sand and shingle beach backed
by busy main road and tourist
developments. Shallow sea, safe for
children, with good watersports. **R**

Barbati (18km N of Corfu) Long pebble
beach at mountain foot with boat
connection to Ipsos. **SC**

Nissaki (23km N of Corfu) Tiny pebble and
rock beach in attractive mountainside
setting at foot of steep descent from
main road. Adjacent taverna. Further
beach to S and three to N, reached from
main road (Club Méditerranée hotel,
Kaminaki, Nissaki Beach Hotel). **SC**

Kalami, Kouloura (30 & 31km N of Corfu)
At mountain foot below coastal road,
the pebble beach at Kalami is 200m, at
Kouloura (on the other side of the
headland) tiny. Delightful fishing
harbours in heart of Durrell country.
Tavernas. **SC**

Ayios Stefanos, Kerasia (36km N of Corfu)
Reached by rough descent from main
road, these attractive twin coves on the
NE coast with white pebble beaches
and small tavernas are popular with
boat parties.

N coast

Kassiopi (36km N of Corfu) Kassiopi's
main beach (pebble) lies away from the
village on the W side of the fortress
hill. There are also pebble coves
accessible by footpath to the E. **R**

Kalamaki (40km N of Corfu) Sandy,
isolated beach, popular with the locals
for pic-nics. Reached by boat only or
steep path from road.

Ayios Spiridon (43km N of Corfu) Small
sandy beach on rocky shoreline at NE
corner of the island, close to lagoon of
Antinioti. Popular with Corfiots on
Sundays. Small villa complex and
taverna. **SC**

Roda, Akharavi (37 & 39km NW of Corfu
by central route) Long sand and
shingle beach, little developed, on bare
stretch of N coastline linking two small
resorts. **R**

Astrakeri (43km NW of Corfu by central
route) Sand and shingle. Modest
development. **R**

Sidari (37km NW of Corfu) A series of
beaches between eroded headlands of
sandstone and marl which create an
extraordinary setting. The sea can be
tricky around the cliffs, but rock
platforms provide refuge. *Canal
d'Amour* a famous feature. Shallow sea
near beach, fine sand. **R**

W coast

Arilas, Ayios Stefanos (44 & 47km NW of
Corfu) Remote bays accessible from
Sidari. Arilas has sand and shingle,
Ayios Stefanos a wide sandy beach.
SC

Ayios Yeoryios Bay (31km NW of Corfu)
One of Corfu's most impressive
beaches, a wide, windswept curve of
golden sand stretching 3km. Good
beach tavernas and little development.
SC

Paleokastritsa (25km NW of Corfu) Series
of six coves/small beaches set in
beautiful wooded coastline accessible
from resort. Sand and shingle, cliffs
and sea caves. Central 'clover leaf' bay
ideal for children. **R**

Liapades Bay (22km NW of Corfu) S of
Paleokastritsa, this bay has a large
pebble beach and a series of delightful
sand and pebble coves accessible only
by boat. Rock-screened inlets offer
enjoyable swimming and diving and the
water is crystal clear. Superb setting
of cliffs and cypress trees. **R**

Ermones (15.5km W of Corfu) Pebble
beach with funicular to hotel. **SC**

Mirtiotissa (16km SW of Corfu) Difficult to
reach, but worth the effort. Tucked into
the rugged W coast, the twin beaches
are set against a tree-clad cliff
backdrop. Fine sand, scattered with
boulders, completes a scene of great
beauty. Perfect swimming and
snorkelling. S beach nude

Nissaki

Glifada (16km SW of Corfu) Beautiful wide sandy beach below sheer cliffs reached by steep road. Increasing development limited by space. **R**

Ayios Yordis (18.5km SW of Corfu) Though one of the lesser-known beaches, this sandy bay, with rocks and cliffs at the S end, is being rapidly developed. **R**

Ayios Yeoryios (31.5km S of Corfu, not to be confused with Ayios Yeoryios Bay in the NW). Long isolated golden sand beach stretching 7km on SW coast with few facilities. Sand dunes on N stretch to Lake Korission, enclosed by sandbar. To the S, cliffs with small coves. Perfect swimming with shallow sea safe for children. **R**

SPORTS

Swimming In addition to the freely available beaches detailed above (officially there are no private beaches in Greece) many hotels allow non-residents to use their swimming pools free of charge, relying on income from sun-bed rental, etc.

Watersports The best centres for watersports are on the E side of the island (the sea here is shallower, warmer and usually calmer than on the W). Major centres are Dassia, Ipsos and Kavos, and sports include sailing, windsurfing, water-skiing and parascending. Most large resort hotels provide watersports facilities.

Boats Boat hire is available at most resorts, the choice either self-drive motorboats or *caiques* with a boatman who knows the ins and outs of the coastline. The latter are ideal for exploring the coves of the NE coast (starting from Ipsos) or the NW coast (from Paleokastritsa).

Golf There is an 18-hole golf course (*Corfu Golf and Country Club*) near Ermones, 15km W of Corfu Town.

Tennis The *Corfu Tennis Club*, at 4 Romanou Street, Corfu town, has four hard courts.

Cricket A visit to Corfu provides the British holidaymaker in the Mediterranean with a unique opportunity to indulge in his national sport. Those keen to take on one of the Corfu teams can make arrangements through the tourist office.

NIGHTLIFE

The best resorts for nightlife are Benitses, Kavos, Ipsos and Dassia. Entertainment includes folk dancing (offered as an attraction in some of the tavernas) discos and night clubs with cabaret (the latter usually in the larger hotels). A special attraction is 'Danilia Village' (9km N of Corfu town), a reconstruction of a traditional Corfiot village which offers regular evenings of folk dancing and a floor show in the summer.

In Corfu town night life revolves around the numerous restaurants and bars. The most popular social venue on summer evenings is the Liston arcade on the W side of the Esplanade, where the nightly *volta* or promenade can be enjoyed while lingering over a coffee or brandy.

SHOPPING

Corfu town is the best place in the island for shopping, both for souvenirs and quality goods. Most sophisticated shops are in Voulgareos Street (jewellery, furs, leathers) and the best area for popular crafts (woodwork, leather, lace) is in the warren of streets to the S of the port. Good value are sponges and the local olive oil, which can be bought in plastic bottles or cans in large quantities.

TOURIST INFORMATION

Corfu's Tourist Information Office is located by the arch at the W end of the Palace of St Michael & St George. Hours 08.00–13.30, 17.30–19.30, Sat 09.00–12.00, closed Sun. During the summer season there is another office on the port by the customs and passport office.

Corfu town

Undoubtedly one of the loveliest towns in the Mediterranean region, the attractions of Corfu's capital are combined in its site on a headland overlooking the mainland and the coast of Albania, with views of mountains to the north, and the elements of its stirring history inscribed in the architecture of its buildings and fortifications.

Dominating the town is the twin-peaked promontory bearing the massive but now ruinous defences of the Old Fort, built by the Venetians on the site of the Byzantine citadel. The later New Fort, overlooking the main harbour on the west side of the town, was connected to the Old Fort by the massive sea wall, much of which survives as a terrace wall for the road which skirts the north shore. Further fortifications to the south completed the enclosure of the old town, which within these confines grew vertically, leaving a legacy of splendid 17th–19th century buildings often reaching a height of six or more storeys.

The streets flanked by these buildings have another special feature peculiar to the Ionian Islands: the cool arcaded sidewalks whose colonnades support the upper storeys and provide a safe walking area for shoppers. The finest example of an arcade (this one French-built) is the Liston, overlooking the Esplanade: the others are found in the main shopping area of the town, whose radial streets are G. Theotoki, N. Theotoki, Filarmonikis and Voulgareos.

A lesser-known quarter is Campiello, above the sea wall in the north-east corner of the town. This densely-built and crumbling labyrinth of houses contains some of the island's finest examples of domestic Venetian architecture. Typically, these houses are constructed of the locally made brick surfaced in painted stucco, sometimes with carved stonework around the doors and windows.

More ostentatious are the stone-built neo-classical buildings of the British period, the 'colonial style' seen at its most assertive in the Palace of St Michael and St George, former residence of the British Lord High Commissioner, which dominates the north end of the Esplanade.

Main places of interest in Corfu town and area

MUSEUMS

Opening hours daily 09.00–15.00, Sun/hol 09.30–14.30. Closed Tue.

Palace of St Michael & St George (p. 64)
Staterooms and Museum of Asian Art

Archeological Museum (p. 71)

Byzantine Museum (p. 71)

Solomos Museum (p. 73)
Daily 17.00–20.00. Closed Sat, Sun

MONUMENTS

Old Fort (p. 67)
07.30–sunset

New Fort (p. 70)
Not open to public

Tomb of Menekrates (p. 79)

Paleopolis (p. 78)
Site of ancient city 2km south of town with remains of basilica, Temple of Artemis and city wall

Fountain of Kardaki
3km south of town on south side of Mon Repos park

CHURCHES

St Spiridon (p. 70)

Sts Jason & Sosipater (p. 79)
1.5km south of town

Platitera Convent (p. 73)
600m west of town centre

OTHER PLACES OF INTEREST

Town Hall (p. 69)

British Cemetery (p. 73)

Market (map, p. 72)
Corfu's major vegetable market (there are also fish and meat stalls) is picturesquely located beneath the walls of the New Fort. Open every morning except Sun.

Walking tour of Corfu town (see map, p. 72) Starting point:* **Esplanade** (N side). The open space known as the *Spianada* or Esplanade was originally created to secure a field of fire between the fortified rocks of the citadel (Old Fort) and the settlement that grew up outside its walls in the Middle Ages (the present town of Corfu). When the Venetians subsequently fortified the whole town (16th c.) the space was preserved as a parade and recreation ground. The British used it for similar purposes during their occupation.

Enclosing the N side of the Esplanade is the sedate **Palace of St Michael and St George** (Royal Palace) built for Britain's Lord High Commissioner in 1818–23. The architect, Col (later Gen Sir George) Whitmore RE, adopted the neo-classical style, *de rigueur* for colonial building of the period, using Maltese limestone. The Doric portico, with 32 columns, is extended to triumphal arches on either side of the building (one inscribed 'Gate of Archangel Michael' the other 'Gate of St George') and continued in a curve to lateral pavilions. The cornice has reliefs of the emblems of the seven Ionian islands (see opposite), with that of Corfu in the centre: above it is part of a stone carving of a Corcyrean galley. The figure of Britannia also surmounted the building, but this was removed after the British relinquished their Protectorate in 1864. In front of the palace stands the bronze statue of *Sir Frederick Adam*, the second British Lord High Commissioner.

In the British period the palace also served as the treasury of the Order of St Michael and St George, created to honour services to the Crown in Malta and the Ionians. It was also a meeting place for the Ionian Senate. After the union of Corfu with Greece the building was used as a royal residence by George I, but later abandoned after his death (1913). The palace was restored in the '50s (at the instigation of Sir Charles Peake, British Ambassador to Greece) as a museum.

Staterooms and Museum of Asian Art On the upper floor of the palace are the staterooms of the Order of St Michael and St George (central door facing staircase). These now contain part of the *Museum of Asiatic Art* (see below). The ante-room, in the form of a rotunda, has a coffered dome and the original parquet floor with its radiating design. To the right is the *State Dining Room* with its long mahogany dining table and ceiling painting incorporating the badge of the Order, to the left the *Throne Room*. Here the Lord High Commissioner presided over meetings of the Ionian Senate: the room was also used as a ballroom (note musicians' gallery).

Palace of St Michael and St George

To the left of the staircase the E wing houses the collection of *Grigorios Manos*, a Greek diplomat (d. 1928) who specialised in Oriental antiquities. These include bronzes, ceramics, armour and weapons. To the right of the staircase, the W wing houses a further Asiatic collection, that of *N. Hadji Vassiliou*. The two farthest rooms in the wing contain Christian art from local churches, including a floor mosaic (6th c.) from Paleopolis church, wall paintings (11th–18th c.) from the Chapel of St Nicholas and icons of the 16th–17th c. by Corfiot masters.

Before commencing the tour of the Esplanade, it is a good idea to pass through the W arch of the palace for the view from the sea wall at the corner by the St Nicholas Gate. On the way, note the attractive stepped and arcaded frontage of the building housing the *Corfu Literary Society*,

* Visitors starting the tour from the Old Port, see p. 70.

founded in 1836. The library here, the most important in Corfu, includes a unique collection of manuscripts and maps relating to the Ionian Islands.

Further on is the splendid neo-classical building which formerly housed the *Nomarchia* (Prefecture). This is the work (1835) of the Corfiot architect Ioannis Khronis, who also designed the Ionian Bank and Parliament Building, A plaque records that a house on this site was the birthplace of the first President of Greece, Ioannis Kapodistrias, in 1776.

From the Venetian sea wall there is a splendid view across the Gulf of Corfu to Mt Pantokrator. The islet offshore is *Vido*, from which the Turks bombarded the town during the sieges of 1537 and 1716, and which the French fortified in 1801. From here a ramp runs down to the original *Sea-gate of St Nicholas*. Here is the town's

Emblems of the Islands

Each of the Ionian Islands is represented by an emblem, seen together on the parapet of the Palace of St Michael and St George.

From the left:

Levkas Bellerephon holding Pegasus
Ithaca Head of Ulysses
Cefalonia Cephalus the hunter with his dog
Corfu Demeter, goddess of fertility, holding a cornucopia in front of a ship
Zakinthos A seated mythical figure
Paxos A trident
Kithira Aphrodite, goddess of love, with a dolphin

beach, a bathing area with a jetty. The derelict church of *St Nicholas* has an adjoining restaurant.

The area of the Esplanade to the S of the palace was used as a cricket pitch by the British during their occupation: a novelty which has now become part of the Corfiot scene. The wicket is maintained as a concrete strip covered by coconut matting; the field, once bare earth, is now green. The game is taken seriously by the locals and there are occasional fixtures in the summer with visiting British teams.

Bounding the cricket field to the W are the two rows of houses, with attractive arcades, known as the '**Liston**'. These belong to the island's French period (building started in 1807) and were designed by de Lesseps, architect of the Rue de Rivoli (and father of the Suez Canal engineer). Like their counterpart in Paris they were used by the more exclusive promenaders who were from the accepted 'list' of families (hence the name). The street in front serves a similar role today, though this is for all-comers on the evening *volta*. The pavements themselves are used by the cafés which occupy the ground floors: the most popular meeting places in town.

The tour is continued from the NE corner of the Esplanade. By the chapel of the *Mandrakina* (rebuilt after World War 2 bombing) a belvedere offers an impressive view of the stone-angled bastion of the Old Fort and the small boat harbour on its N side (Mandraki).

Proceeding S, a small enclosed garden lies on the left, with a statue of *Lord Guilford* (1769–1828) the founder of the Ionian Academy. Further on, at the entrance to the bridge across the moat, is a more imposing statue of *Marshal Schulenberg*, erected by the Venetians in honour of the man who conducted the defence of the city during the Turkish siege of 1716.

Citadel and yacht basin

Cricket on the Esplanade

Old Fort (Citadel) The original fortified town of Corfu took its name from the twin peaks (*korifai*) dominating the peninsula on which it was built. The E peak was fortified by the Byzantines, and the W peak by the Venetians in their first occupation at the beginning of the 13th c. Later on in the 15th c. the Venetians consolidated the defences.

They first dug a moat, to turn the peninsula into an island, and then built a double enceinte, the inner wall round the two peaks and the outer round the island. The two bastions and the W wall guarding the moat were constructed later, between the Turkish sieges of 1537 and 1571. At the same time the fortifications were extended to protect the town outside the citadel. Within the area of the citadel were the palace of the Venetian governor, the *Provveditore Generale del Levante*, and other important buildings of the civil and military authorities. During the British period these Venetian buildings were demolished and replaced by barracks: the citadel then served a purely military role, first for the British and then for the Greek Army. In 1979 the Old Fort was handed over by the army to the Greek Archaeological Service, which is now engaged in restoration work.

Tour The moat is crossed by a fixed iron bridge which replaces the old drawbridge. Entrance is by a vaulted *gateway* surviving the Venetian fortifications. Turning right in the direction of the S ramparts, there is shortly the spectacle of a monumental and incongruous building: the garrison church of *St George* (1830) built by the British on the lines of a Doric temple. From here a road skirts the W peak: on the first bend after the church a flagged path ascends through a vaulted passage to rejoin the road. At a fork in the road there is a choice of direction. For the **W peak**, go right uphill to the terrace by the lighthouse. Here is the best overall *view* of the town and island of Corfu.

The old town looks much as it would have done in the Venetian period, the street layout virtually unaltered. To the W of the Esplanade the streets lie at right angles to the open space, to allow cannon on the Old Fort to fire straight down them to repel an attack. On the N side of the rock below the citidel is the Venetian harbour, the *Mandraki*, and beyond the islet of *Vido*, where the Russians placed their artillery during their successful assault on the French-occupied citadel in 1798–9.

The view embraces much of the island, from Mt Pantokrator in the N to the curve of the Bay of Lefkimi in the S, taking in the Kanoni peninsula, Halikiopoulos lagoon and range of Ayii Deka.

Corfu town from the Old Fort

Town Hall and square

For the **E Peak**, keep left at the fork. Beyond the barrack blocks, steps, a path (right) and a tunnel with steps lead up to a further viewpoint which includes the old fortress.

Descending from the fortress, a short cut may be made. Emerging from the vaulted passage, go right by the old Venetian well-head below the clock tower and descend the steps.

Leaving the Old Fort, cross over to the central avenue of the Esplanade. The area to the S has been laid out as a **public garden**, and at its upper end there is a modern monument commemorating the *Enosis* (union) of the Ionian Islands with Greece. Reliefs of the symbols of the seven islands may be seen, similar to those on the front of the palace.

The centrepiece of the garden is the Victorian *bandstand*, where one of the town bands usually performs on a Sunday. Here also the Metropolitan of Corfu announces the risen Christ at midnight on Easter Saturday; a moving occasion in which thousands of the townsfolk take part, gathered round the square with lighted candles.

S of the bandstand is the Ionic *Rotunda*, commemorating the first British Lord High Commissioner *Sir Thomas Maitland* (1815–24). A statue in a separate garden at the foot of the Esplanade provides a pointed juxtaposition: this commemorates Corfu's most famous son, *Ioannis Kapodistrias* (1776–1831), crusader for the island's union with Greece and the modern state's first President.

Starting up the street which bears his name, the pink-stuccoed shell of the *Ionian Academy* is on the left. Built by the Venetians as a barracks in the late 17th c., this became the Academy's headquarters in 1840 and later on also housed the Municipal Library. Unhappily the building was bombed in 1943 with the loss of 25,000 volumes. Two doors down is the elegant *Cavalieri Hotel*, a conversion of a 19th c. mansion. Beyond this at *No. 10* is the two-storey building, ornamented by a cartouche of a Corfiot ship, in which Lord Guilford, the Philhellene and founder of the Ionian Academy, was received into the Orthodox faith (1791).

Continuing up Kapodistriou, a left turn is made at Odos Moustoxidhi. The building

'Ioniki'

halfway up on the right with the ornate balcony, now a clinic, was originally the *Ricchi mansion* (early 18th c.), the town house of a rich Venetian family. From this balcony, with its unusual keystone heads, the nobles used to watch jousting competitions. At the end of the street is the historic **Ionian Parliament Building** (Khronis, 1855) with a Doric portico, and an inscription in Greek and English on either side of the entrance recording the cession of the Ionian Islands by Britain to Greece in 1863. The building was subsequently taken over by the British community and used as their

church. Gutted by bombs in the war, it was restored in 1962.

A street near the top of Moustoxidhi, Odos Ioniou Voulis, leads down to Odos D. Kolla and thence to the square in which stands the Baroque **Town Hall** (1663). In the Venetian period this building was known as the *Loggia dei Nobili* (Lodge of the Nobles) and its open arcade served as a meeting place for merchants. In 1720 it was converted into a theatre and later on was used as an opera house. In 1903 the upper storey was added when the building became the Town Hall. This is the most elaborately decorated building in the town, with medallions and keystone heads, and the Corfiot ship emblem over the entrance. The E wall bears a bust of the Venetian admiral and later Doge, Morosini (1628–94), placed here in 1691 to commemorate his campaign against the Turks in Greece (during which the Parthenon was partially destroyed). The four children in the marble group represent Morosini's virtues. On the E side of the square is the *Roman Catholic Cathedral*, originally 1632, rebuilt after its destruction in 1943.

From D. Kolla cross E. Voulgareos into M. Theotoki. Here pause a moment in a little square: Plateia Vrakhlioti. This is the kernel of the town's market area, the foodstuffs and fancy goods spilling out on the pavements under the arcades. Off one corner is Odos Vasileou, the fish market. Continue to the busy thoroughfare of N. Theotoki, another popular food shopping street. (Its W end, not included in this tour, is worth a diversion to see the attractive arcading down the left-hand side.)

To the right, N. Theotoki leads to the most attractive small square in Corfu, known popularly as 'Ioniki'. One side is taken up by the elegant *Ionian Bank* (Khronis, 1846) which incorporates a *Paper Money Museum*, others by two churches. That on the E, opposite the bank, is the *Faneromeni*, more commonly the *Panayia Ton Xenon* (Virgin of the Strangers). This name refers to the community to whom the church belonged: the exiles from the Turkish-occupied Epirus. Inside are paintings by other exiles, of the Cretan school, including Michael Tzenos. The church on the S, *Ayios Ioannis o Prodromos* (St John the Baptist) is 16th c., the parish church of Kapodistrias. The preacher in his time, Nikiforos Theotoki, was so popular that the pulpit had to be moved to a position opposite the door (or the right hand side of the nave), so that the people outside as well as inside the church could hear him. To the left of the iconostasis there is a 17th c. painting of the *Baptism with 12 Scenes from the Life of St John* by the Cretan Michael Tzenos.

The Old Port

From the NW corner of the square, there is access to the town's major church of **St Spiridon** (Ayios Spiridonos). In this church, built in the late 16th c., are kept the remains of Corfu's patron saint.

The casket containing the saint's mummified body lies in the chapel to the right of the altar. Suspended above it is an array of silver and gold lamps, offered to the saint for some act of mercy, and the ship models suggesting deliverance from the hazards of the sea. Elsewhere in the church there are a number of exquisite chandeliers and oil lamps. Most notable are the *silver oil lamps* donated by the Venetians following the successful defence of the town against the Turks in 1716, inscribed with dedications to the saint. One, hanging near the pulpit, was given by Andrea Pisani, the Venetian Governor and Admiral of the Fleet; the other, hanging by the gallery, by the Venetian Senate.

Also worth noting in the church is the marble *iconostasis*, representing a neoclassical church façade, and the ceiling, a 19th c. repainting of the work of Panayiotis Doxaras (1727) portraying the miracles of the saint.

After visiting the church, have a look at the fine Venetian belltower. This is best seen from Odos Ayios Spiridonos, reached from the N side of the church. The street is the most characteristic of the Venetian town, the balconied façades of its houses jutting out at irregular levels.

At the W end of Ayios Spiridonos, turn right into Filarmonikis and then left into Filellinon. This narrow flagstoned street, whose gift shops herald the nearby port, opens into an attractive small square framed by the tall buildings of the old quarter, *Campiello*. To the right, take Ayia Theodora, then immediately left Timoxenou. Right again, Odos Komninon mounts to the square in front of the church of the *Panayia Kremasti*. This church has

a fine marble altar screen, and some tombstones of the Venetian period. The main feature of the square is the carved *Venetian well-head*, donated in 1699 by Antonio Cocchini.

Returning to the square on Filellinon, descend Theodora to the **Cathedral**. Built in 1577, this basilica contains many fine icons, including one of *St George Slaying the Dragon* by the 16th c. Cretan artist Michael Damaskinos (pillar to the right of door). To the right of the altar are kept the remains of St Theodora, brought to the island in the 15th c. together with those of St Spiridon.

From the cathedral, descend to the tree-lined Plateia Yeoryiou B' (George II Square). This is the *Old Port, from which the car ferry leaves for Igoumenitsa, and caiques for Paxos. (Passengers from Brindisi, Patras or Piraeus arrive at the W end of the harbour.) The attractively painted horse carriages are available for hire, for a trip round the sea wall and Esplanade.

On the S side of the square is the *Porta Spilia*, one of the four originally opened in the 16th c. Venetian walls. These walls have now largely disappeared, but their original depth can be ascertained by walking through the gate. In this area are concentrated many of the town's restaurants and gift shops.

To the W of the Old Port rise the grey creeper-clad bastions of the **New Fort** or Neon Frourion, built by the Venetians in 1577–88 and added to by the British. The fortress is now a naval headquarters and there is no access. One can, however, walk around the N and W sides and re-enter the town via a tunnel (see map). Venetian lions may be seen carved over the gates and elsewhere on the walls.

*This is an alternative starting point for the Walking Tour (see p. 64). From the port, ascend the sea wall by Odos Arseniou to the E of the square. This leads to the Palace of St Michael and St George and the Esplanade.

70

Other places of interest in Corfu town

Archaeological Museum Off Vas. Konstantinou, the boulevard to the S of the town, this museum was built primarily to house the statues from the Archaic Temple of Artemis at Paleopolis (see p. 80).

On the landing (**1**) are three interesting Archaic funerary monuments from the cemetery of the ancient city at Garitsa—all from the early 6th c. BC: a funerary *stele* of Arniadas with an inscription in Homeric hexameters; the Doric *capital* of a column from a tomb (note loaf shape of echinus, decorative frill, red colour of fluting and Archaic inscription on abacus); and a large clay funerary *pithos*. There are also two blocks from the sima (cornice) of the vanished temple at Mon Repos ('Heraion'?) with fragments and a reconstruction of a lion's head water-spout.

The courtyard room (**2**) has prehistoric finds from various sites; Corinthian and Laconian pottery (7th–6th c. BC) and fragments of a 5th c. BC Doric temple at Roda. The centrepiece is the Archaic *lion* found near the tomb of Menekrates: a magnificent work by a Corinthian sculptor.

The annex to the Gorgon Room (**3**) has finds from the Sanctuary of Artemis and other sites.

Gorgon Pediment (4) This finely restored Archaic work is from the Temple of Artemis at Paleopolis (*c.* 580BC). The work of a Corinthian sculptor, it is the oldest monumental stone pediment in Greece. It represents the Gorgon embracing her off-

Detail from the Gorgon pediment

spring Chrysaor and Pegasus with her wings, flanked by 'leopanthers' (fabulous beasts with lions' heads and panthers' bodies). At the right-hand angle of the pediment Zeus is striking down a Titan with a thunderbolt: to the left is an unidentified group with a slain Titan.

The purpose of the Gorgon figure (which had no association with the goddess Artemis) was protective. These grotesque mythological creatures, which had serpents for hair, terrifying grins, and eyes which could turn the onlooker to stone, were sculpted for temple fronts to ward off any intruder seeking to desecrate the building or its contents. They were later replaced by deities and more benign mythological figures.

Also displayed in this room are part of the frieze of the temple with triglyphs and metope; part of the terracotta sima from the first phase of the temple and part of the marble sima which replaced it, and other fragments of sculptural decoration.

The long gallery (**5**) is divided into three sections. The first contains terracotta roof fittings from temples in the grounds of Mon Repos (the Kardaki and 'Heraion') and other finds from the area. Especially attractive is the little bronze *komastes* or reveller, a decorative running figure from the edge of a cauldron (*c.* 570BC). On the partition is part of an Archaic *pediment* (*c.* 500BC) representing Dionysus and a youth on a banqueting couch. The second section has other finds from Paleopolis, including *terracotta figures of Artemis* from a shrine of Artemis at Kanoni. The third section has Hellenistic votive reliefs from the ancient city, also Roman copies of various works.

Byzantine Museum This fine collection of icons and other paintings, mainly of the Cretan and Ionian schools (17th–18th c.) is housed in the 16th c. church of *Antivouniotissa* located at the top of steps leading off Odos Arseniou (sea wall).

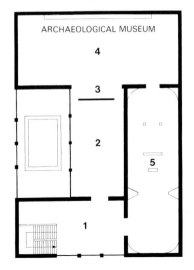

ARCHAEOLOGICAL MUSEUM

4

3

2

5

1

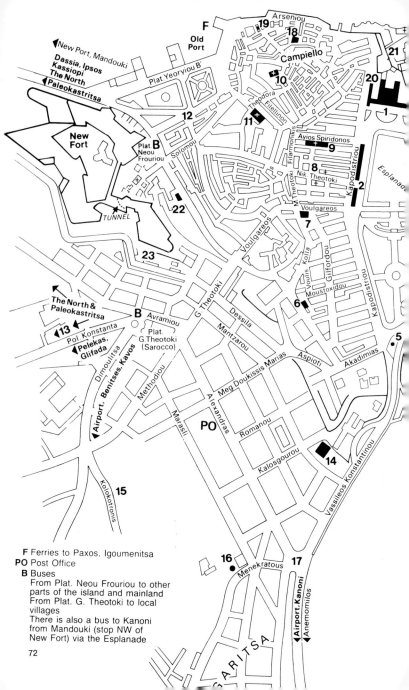

F Ferries to Paxos, Igoumenitsa
PO Post Office
B Buses
  From Plat. Neou Frouriou to other
  parts of the island and mainland
  From Plat. G. Theotoki to local
  villages
  There is also a bus to Kanoni
  from Mandouki (stop NW of
  New Fort) via the Esplanade

72

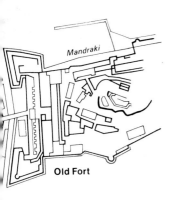

Mandraki

Old Fort

Corfu town

1 Palace of St Michael & St George
  Staterooms & Museum of Asian Art
2 Liston
3 Schulenberg statue
4 Maitland Rotunda
5 Kapodistrias statue
6 Ionian Parliament Building
7 Town Hall
8 'Ioniki' Square with Ionian Bank,
  churches of Faneromeni and Ayios
  Ioannis
9 Church of St Spiridon (Ayios
  Spiridonos)
10 Church of Panayia Kremasti
11 Cathedral
12 Porta Spilia
13 Platitera Convent
14 Archaeological Museum
15 British Cemetery
16 Tomb of Menekrates
17 Douglas Obelisk
18 Byzantine Museum (Church of
  Antivouniotissa)
19 Solomos Museum
20 Tourist Information Office
21 Sea-gate of St Nicholas
22 Synagogue
23 Market

  Paleopolis peninsula &
  Kanoni (see p. 78)

Solomos Museum At the W end of Odos Arseniou, the house of Greece's national poet has exhibits devoted to his memory.

Platitera Convent On the W outskirts of the town (Paleokastritsa road), this convent, founded in 1716, was rebuilt in 1801 after bombardment by the French three years earlier. The belltower of the church, similar to that of St Spiridon, was added in 1864 to commemorate the union of the Ionians with Greece. Entrance is through a passage beneath it into an attractive and secluded courtyard.

The church is of special interest for the work of 16th–early 19th c. artists, both Cretan and Ionian. In the upper tiers of the iconostasis are icons of the *Twelve Apostles* and the *Twelve Feasts of the Church* by Koutouzis in the 18th c. Italian style. Much earlier, and more interesting, are the paintings in the narthex. In the centre of the W wall is a finely detailed *Day of Judgement* by the Cretan George Klotzas (late 16th c.). To the left the damned and the blessed are depicted again in another beautiful scene, the *Upper Jerusalem* by an unknown 16th c. artist showing a Renaissance influence. On the opposite wall are two further excellent paintings: on the left a *Revelation of St John* by the Cretan Poulakis (17th c.) and on the right an icon by an unknown artist depicting *St Sabas and Archangels* (17th c.). Two large 18th-c. paintings by N. Kandounis (the *Washing of the Feet* and the *Last Supper*) are on the N and S walls. A painting by Tzanes, one of the leading exponents of the Cretan School (the *Panayia Lamboritissa*) is kept in the monastery library. The remains of *Ioannis Kapodistrias*, first President of Greece and a Corfiot, are entombed behind the main altar. While he was serving as a diplomat in Russia Kapodistrias sent the convent a special gift: the bejewelled frame on the icon to the right of the iconostasis.

British Cemetery To the S of Plat. G. Theotoki and branching left off the Airport/Benitses road, a minor road leads up to this secluded memorial of the British years in Corfu, located on the low hill (San Salvator) which was one of the fortified strong points defending the W of the city in Venetian times. Maintained by the War Graves Commission, this cemetery does not have the air of dereliction of those of the earthquake-damanged Zakinthos and Argostoli. The British who served the Protectorate are buried here, as are some of the unlucky 44 British sailors who were killed in the 1946 'Corfu Incident' (the mining of two British destroyers by the Albanians in the Corfu Channel).

Corfu and the *Odyssey*

If the sickle-shaped isle was just a fable, it would begin —and end—with Homer: the story of a pleasant land called Scheria, inhabited by a prosperous sea-faring people called the Phaeacians. The setting for the final chapter of the tale of an epic voyage, which countless generations have passed on, from its earliest recital, as the *Odyssey*. Attempts to link the legend with the stones of Corfu have so far failed, but the prospect remains to excite our imaginations.

'On the eighteenth day there hove into sight the shadowy mountains of the Phaeacians' country, which jutted out to meet him there. The land looked like a shield laid on a misty sea.'

Thus Homer describes Odysseus' first glimpse of Scheria, the land that lies near the end of the hero's voyage. After ten years, it must have looked tantalising, but within moments the ever vindictive Poseidon, furious at being cheated yet again of his revenge on the wily wanderer, stirred up winds and sea to capsize Odysseus' makeshift boat, casting him once more on the mercy of the waves. Happily the hero's plight was observed by the friendly goddess Ino, who gave him a protective veil, and the faithful Athena, who smoothed his way to the shore with a helpful breeze. Landfall, however, was not easily achieved:

'There were no coves, no harbours that would hold a ship; nothing but headlands jutting out, sheer rock and jagged cliffs.'

A grim encounter with a hostile shore that would surely have committed the hero to his doom, had he not swum clear of the breakers and progressed to the 'mouth of a fast-running stream' where he stumbled ashore and found shelter under a 'wild olive'.

Had Odysseus found Corfu? Most of the theorists who have come to this conclusion would have to admit that it is based largely on a single assumption: that the preceding link in the chain of Odysseus' journey, the mythical Ogygia (Calypso's Isle) was the Maltese island of Gozo. Journey time in a makeshift boat from Gozo to Corfu could well have been the 17 days described by Homer, and from a western approach the shield-like appearance of the island is unmistakable, with Mt Pantokrator forming the boss in the centre. The physical features of Corfu's west coast can then be studied for further similarities.

The hero's landing site is fully described by the poet: first the unfriendly rocks and cliffs which are a feature of the north-west coast, and then the more hospitable river estuary which Odysseus reaches after swimming down the coast. There is only one point on the west coast where a substantial stream runs into the sea, with an accessible landing place, and that is the bay of Ermones—still a tranquil spot where one can picture Nausikaa and her maidens washing their clothes in the pools, close by the olive tree where the exhausted Odysseus lay sleeping.

Although Ermones is plausible as the site of Odysseus' landfall, the location of the city of the Phaeacians, to which Nausikaa conducted Odysseus after the hero had revealed himself, is still in dispute. In 1867 the enthusiastic and ever-impatient Heinrich Schliemann, on a brief foray to the island, declared the features of Paleopolis (Corcyra) the ancient city to the south of Corfu town, to be consistent with Homer's description. Like King Alkinoos' capital, Schliemann observed that the ancient city, lying between the bay of Garitsa and the Halikiopoulos Lagoon, had an 'excellent harbour on each side and is approached by a narrow causeway'. In search of the washing place of Nausikaa, the great archaeologist found the estuary of the River Potamos, to the north of the modern town, fitted all the requirements.

Although there is no evidence of any occupation of the site of Paleopolis before 734BC (the Corinthian colonisation) Schliemann's theory is probably as good as any other. The strongest question mark against it, however, is the placing of the mythical city on the *east* side of the island, when to be accessible to Odysseus' landing site it needed to be on the west. Such was the argument of the historian Victor Berard, who in 1901 proposed Paleokastritsa as the most likely site. Accessible to Ermones, its features match Homer's description perfectly, its double bay enclosed by headlands forming the twin harbours. Unfortunately, as in the case of Paleopolis, no supporting archaeological evidence has been found here of occupation by—or even the existence of—the mythical Phaeacians.

Who were these people, who received Odysseus with such warmth and made it possible for him to return to his native island?

The safe conduct that they offered him, and the treasure which they bestowed on him suggest a wealthy people who were in command of the local seas: possibly an early colony of the Phoenicians. Whatever the identity of these Bronze Age people, their wealth is consistent with an island where

trees hang their greenery on high, the pear and the pomegranate, the apple with its glossy burden, the sweet fig and the luxuriant olive . . .

The description of the orchards of King Alkinoos depicts an earthly paradise which must have been a revelation to a Greek traveller from the barren mountains of the mainland or the arid Aegean. Such a description is fitting of Corfu, an island additionally endowed with splendid natural harbours and a position commanding the sea lanes between Italy and Greece and the Adriatic and Ionian seas.

The last stage of Odysseus' journey, from Scheria to Ithaca—the passage of a single night—places Corfu even more squarely on the map of the *Odyssey*. This compares favourably with the journey time for the modern ferry (about five hours), and can be seen as a tribute to the seamanship of the Phaeacians. It was in their ship, as part of the hospitality of King Alkinoos, that Odysseus returned to his native island. A myth attached to this voyage, which has made such an impact on the tour guides' imaginations, is the fate of the ship: turned into stone by a vengeful Poseidon as it re-entered the harbour of Scheria. Modern visitors to Kanoni, on the tip of the peninsula embracing one side of the lagoon, will be shown the islet of Pontikonisi at its entrance, which at twilight resembles a ship under sail coming into the harbour.

Corfu

Key

$\boxed{5}$ Routes for excursions with distances in Km

——— Other roads

Scale

0 1 2 3 4 5 kilometres

600
400
200
0 Height in metres

1 Tomb of Menekrates
2 Church of Sts Jason & Sosipater
3 Paleopolis church
4 Convent of Ayios Theodoros
5 Temple of Artemis
6 Kardaki Spring

Excursions from Corfu town

Paleopolis peninsula and Kanoni

The ancient city The pursuit of evidence relating Corfu to Homer's *Scheria*, land of the Phaeacians, has been inexhaustible, and much of the search for King Alkinoos' city has centred on the Paleopolis peninsula, site of the ancient capital of the Corinthians (*Corcyra*) established here in the 8th c. BC. No archaeological remains before this date have, however, been uncovered, and there are scant relics even of the Corinthian city, whose buildings were quarried for the medieval town to the N.

Corcyra was located on the peninsula to the S of the modern town on the E shore of the Halikiopoulos Lagoon (see plan). The N angle of the peninsula (now formed by Garitsa Bay) was more deeply indented in ancient times, to form the fancifully named *Alkinoos Harbour*. Much of the harbour, which silted up, is now covered by Anemomilos, the suburb to the S of Garitsa Bay.

On the W side of the peninsula, within the Halikiopoulos Lagoon, was a second ancient harbour, the *Hyllaic Harbour*. These two harbours served Corcyra's fleet, which in the 5th c. BC was one of the largest in Greece, rivalled only by those of Athens, Corinth and Aegina. In an age when all sea voyages were made by coasting, the advantages of Corcyra as a port-of-call for western bound fleets are obvious from a glance at the map: the island was chosen as a natural rendezvous for the Athenian fleets for the disastrous Sicilian expedition (415BC).

At that time the Halikiopoulos Lagoon, now site of the airport runway, would have been much deeper, and its sloping shores ideal for the drawing up and launching of the galleys. The line of the city wall ran between the two harbours, across the neck of the peninsula: part of one of the towers of its S gate has been preserved, incorporated in a ruined Byzantine chapel.

The *acropolis* of the ancient city is assumed to have been located on one of the hills in the area of Mon Repos and Analipsis: traces of a number of temples have been found on the slopes.

Church of Sts Jason and Sosipater

Tour The first antiquity of interest lies outside the ancient city, in what is now the suburb of Garitsa. This was the area of the ancient cemetery, and the major find here was the **Tomb of Menekrates**, uncovered by the British during road works in 1843. The tomb, which lies in the grounds of the police station, can be reached from the *Douglas Obelisk* on the S of the town (Odos Menekratous). Menekrates was a Corcyrean consul who represented the island state in Lokris on the mainland: drowned at sea he was commemorated by this tomb *c.* 600BC. The tomb is circular in form with a conical roof, its most interesting detail the Archaic Greek inscription which records the event.

From the Douglas Obelisk, Mitropolitou Athanassiou runs S to Alex. Dessilla (s/p 'Kanoni'). In a further 200m, beyond the *Belle Epoque* restaurant, take the signposted left turn (Iassonos Sossipatrou). Shortly on the right is the 11th c. church of **Sts Jason and Sosipater**, the only complete church of the Byzantine period to survive in the island. It is dedicated to the two saints who brought Christianity to Corfu. The caretaker who lives beside the church will open it for visitors.

The church is cruciform with an octagonal dome and Byzantine-style belfry, added later. The walls are of limestone blocks—mostly taken from ancient sites in the area—with interposed courses of tile. At the E end of the church, notably on the central apse, these tiles are arranged vertically in 'Cufic' decorative friezes between denticulated bands. The S wall, originally destroyed in the siege of 1537, is a modern restoration.

Much of the material inside the church is, like the exterior, from ancient sites: note particularly the two marble columns supporting the dome. Inside the church are some fine icons: on the narthex pillars, *Sts Jason and Sosipater* by Father Emmanuel Tzanes (mid 17th c.) and on the reverse side of the pillars, *St John Damascene and St Gregory* by the same artist. The paintings on the altar screen, of the *Pantokrator* and the *Virgin Mary with Jesus*, are also by Tzanes. Further icons by these artists are in the Byzantine Museum. One fresco survives: that of the 10th c. Bishop of Corfu *St Arsenius* in the narthex.

The tombs on either side of the altar screen are supposed to be those of the two saints, but in fact belong to two individuals who took refuge here in the 15th c.: a man and a woman. The woman has been identified as Catherine Paleologos, wife of the last Despot of the Morea, who escaped here after the Turkish conquest. Her robe is in the apse to the right of the altar.

Returning to the main road, continue S for 300m. Here is the entrance to **Mon Repos**, the royal villa which was originally built as a summer residence for the British Lord High Commissioner, Sir Frederick Adam, in 1824. Subsequently used by the Greek royal family (Prince Philip was born here) it is now closed and there is no admission to the public. Opposite the Paleopolis church, take the road s/p 'Analipsis'. This skirts the park of Mon Repos and climbs in 1km to the village, which lies on the acropolis of Corcyra. Save for a few vestiges the temples and sanctuaries which stood on these slopes have disappeared. One survival is the *Temple of Kardaki* (6th c. BC) probably dedicated to Apollo, which was discovered accidentally by British engineers in 1822 while digging to uncover a blockage in the nearby spring. Although this temple (Doric, 6 × 11 columns) is the best preserved in Corfu, there is little to see, for it lies partly hidden in the grounds of Mon Repos. A glimpse of it may be obtained on the way to the *Kardaki Spring*, whose course was blocked by its collapsed foundations.

To reach the spring take the rocky path to the left at the end of the road just before the grassed traffic island. A drink here is recommended, particularly as a quotation by the poet Mavilis next to the spring reminds the stranger that if he does so he is destined to return to Corfu.

The Venetian lion which serves as a waterspout shows the continuing use of the ancient spring, which was channelled via the temple. This lies above it, on the other side of the boundary wall of the villa.

Paleopolis Church Located opposite the gates of Mon Repos is the shell of the great basilica (also known as Ayia Kerkyra) which was the mother church of the early Christian city. Built in the 5th c. AD on the site of pagan buildings (a Doric temple and a Roman odeum) whose stones it incorporated, this five-aisled basilica was subsequently rebuilt several times following the Gothic invasions and other depradations, only to be finally destroyed by a bomb in 1940. The inscription of its foundation is on the architrave over the W door. This cannot be seen from the road, but access to the site may be obtained through the Archaeological Museum.

The road to the right before the church leads to further remains of the *lower city*. This road is one way, so the tour must be done on foot. Next to the site of the Paleopolis church, in the gardens of the Olive Cultivation Institute, are the remains of Roman *baths* (*c.* 200AD) which were destroyed in the 6th c. The site is overgrown and there is no public access. Following

the road to the left around the Institute, a winding lane leads in 1km to the *Convent of Ayios Theodoros*, built on the site of an early Christian basilica. The convent was subsequently taken over by the Latin rite, and the plaque above the entrance in Greek and Latin commemorates the restoration of the nuns by Sir Thomas Maitland (1816).

At the W end of the convent lie the remains of the altar of the great *Temple of Artemis* (Doric, 17 × 8 columns). This temple of the early 6th c. BC was discovered by French sappers in 1812, and subsequently excavated by the German archaeologist Dörpfeld, at the request of Kaiser Wilhelm II who had visited the site during one of his regular sojourns in the island. It was from these ruins that the Gorgon pediment, showpiece of the Archaeological Museum, was recovered.

Vlakherna and Pontikonisi islets from Kanoni

A footpath leads in 500m to the modern Greek cemetery: on a ridge just before stands a small section of the ancient *city wall* to a height of 10m, topped by a ruined Byzantine chapel. Traces of the wall may be followed to the lagoon.

Kanoni Continuing S from the Paleopolis Church, take the right fork (s/p 'Figareto') for the one-way circuit road to the point of the peninsula (2km). In the days of the Protectorate, this was a popular walk or drive for Corfu's British community, who knew it as the 'walk to the one-gun'. The gun was the battery (*kanoni*) which once stood on the point.

At the end of the road there is a tourist pavilion (parking) with a terrace overlooking the most celebrated view in Corfu, over the mouth of the Halikiopoulos lagoon towards Perama. Two small islands lie close to shore: in the foreground the tiny *Vlakherna*, with its whitewashed convent, further out *Pontikonisi*, or 'Mouse Island' with its little chapel masked by trees. Vlakherna is reached by a short causeway, and a boat may be taken from the smaller island to Pontikonisi. A romantic concept is that the latter island may be the ship of the Phaeacians, turned into stone by Poseidon after it had returned Odysseus to Ithaca.

Another longer causeway connects the peninsula to Perama: the jet aircraft fly in low over this to land on the runway which extends along the lagoon. Despite the noise of the aircraft, and the incongruous block of the Hilton Hotel, the serenity of the spot is not completely lost.

The return to Corfu town is made by taking the right exit after leaving the pavilion parking area.

Akhilleion

The approach for the Akhilleion is the same as that for the S of the island (p. 88), turning off the Benitses road after 10km for Gastouri. The Akhilleion is reached after a climb of 1.5km.

Built as a pleasure palace for the Empress Elizabeth of Austria in 1888–91, the Akhilleion is a fanciful recreation of a Phaeacian palace of legend, set oddly—but superbly—on its wooded throne of rural landscape overlooking the E coast and the town of Corfu.

Dedicated to Achilles, a Greek hero who fascinated the Empress, the palace is an elaborate confection of the neo-classical and neo-Pompeian styles, surrounded by luxuriant Italian gardens. After the Empress was assassinated in 1898 the palace was bought by the German Kaiser Wilhelm II who came here every summer from 1907 up to the Great War. The building is now the property of the Greek government and is open to the public as a museum. It is also used as a *Casino* in the summer season.

Inside, the ground floor rooms contain mementoes of the Empress and the Kaiser which include a portrait of Elizabeth by Winterhalter and a writing desk used by the Kaiser with a saddle-seat on which he composed his despatches. The terraced garden at the upper level of the palace has copies of Greek and Roman statues and two sculptures of Achilles: one—the dying hero—commissioned by Elizabeth and the other—a huge, upright and belligerent bronze—by the Kaiser, inscribed 'To the greatest of the Greeks from the greatest of the Germans'. The hero is also portrayed in a vast fresco, the *Triumph of Achilles* on the upper floor, visible from the outside.

Mt Pantokrator
(69km return)

Leave Corfu town by Paleokastritsa/North exit and follow route to Piryi (16.5km, see Excursion to the North, p. 85).

Climbing from Piryi, a left turn is made in 500m s/p 'Spartilas'. Carved out of the S flank of Pantokrator, this is the island's steepest road. It offers glorious views, however, and after 7km the prospect of one of Corfu's most attractively sited villages, *Spartilas*. Banked against the mountainside, the old houses and the pretty Baroque church are painted in gay pastel colours. 1km further on the road levels out and there is a right turn for Pantokrator (s/p 'Petalia') on an unmade road. This leads through increasingly barren uplands to *Strinilas* (4.5km). 700m from the village the road divides, left to *Petalia* and right to Pantokrator (5km). The road to the summit is extremely rough, but motorable.

Akhilleion

Mt Pantokrator (906m), the highest point on Corfu, is topped by the monuments of two ages: a television transmitter and the *Monastery of the Pantokrator*. The 17th-c. monastery church, standing on the site of an earlier 14th-c. building, was itself re-modelled in the 19th c. Also of the 19th c. are the exterior cells which circle the court-yard, used by the pilgrims who come here for the feast of the Transfiguration (Aug 6). The pinnacle view of Corfu embraces the whole island, with the Othonian Is to the NW. Further W, the coastline of Italy may be seen on a clear day. To the E, only 3.5km across the strait, lies the mysterious littoral of Albania, with the blue basin of Lake Butrinto enclosed by its coastal rim and backed by the country's mountainous interior. To the S, beyond the Lefkimi peninsula, is the shape of Paxos and sometimes—in the far distance—the other Ionians.

Paleokastritsa
(50km return)

Leave Corfu by Paleokastritsa/North exit (see map). At the junction for Kontokali (6km) continue on the main road. After 2km, on the left is a turning for the *Village Danilia*, worth a diversion as a curiosity among the island's new tourist developments. This is not an authentic village but a reconstruction, using parts of traditional buildings from elsewhere. The 'main street' has echoes of Disneyland. In addition to arts and crafts there are tavernas, bars and an open-air night spot. Open for the season (admission charge) this is a popular attraction.

In a further 1.5km at *Tsavros* keep left for Paleokastritsa. This is one of the pleasant-est drives in Corfu, on a road built by the Royal Engineers in the 1820s to a con-valescent station at Paleokastritsa. (This was given as the official reason for the road, but it was no coincidence that Paleo-kastritsa was the favourite beauty spot of the Lord High Commissioner of the day, Sir Frederick Adam.) After 9.5km, keeping left at junctions, there is the first of two recommended diversions.

> *Diversion 1:* **Liapades** The 3km detour to the village and beyond it the beach is worth while for the setting of the bay, enclosed by towering cypress-clad cliffs and rock debris which forms its own warren of inlets and pools. The main beach is of white pebbles and there are several other coves tucked into the indentations of the bay, accessible only by boat. Taxi-boats serve the bay and there is a hotel and beach taverna. The continuation of the journey to Paleokastritsa can be made

by turning left at the cross-roads N of the village. 1km from the junction with the main road the second diversion, to Lakones, should be taken.

Division 2: **Lakones** This is the belvedere of Paleokastritsa and before going to the resort it is a good idea to drive up here to enjoy the panoramic view of the coastline below. The village is reached after a 4km climb: the viewpoint is at *Bella Vista* 1km further on. From here you can see the three major promontories of Paleokastritsa which enclose its bays: to the E *Alipa*, shaped like a clover-leaf, and to the W the smaller bay of *Ayios Spiridon*. The twin harbours of Alkinoos' city, where Odysseus was taken after his Phaeacian landfall, could well be here, but the Homeric shades are dispelled by the scattering of modern hotels, whose sites might have been better chosen.

An even finer view of Paleokastritsa can be enjoyed further on. From Bella Vista, continue 2km to *Makrades* and thence 300m to *Krini*. From *Odos Angelokastro*, an unmade road leads in 1km to the foot of the peak on which lie the ruins of *Angelokastro*, a 12th-c. Byzantine fortress which saw service in defence of the island against the Turks, in the 16th c. and again in 1716. On none of these occasions was the castle taken, and it offered refuge to thousands of villagers who would otherwise have been slaughtered.

Of the castle, painted by Edward Lear from the bay to the E, there are only crumbled remains (a church, cave chapel and cistern survive). The 15min climb to the summit, however, offers a stunning view, not only of Paleo-kastritsa but across the island to Corfu

Angelokastro

town. (There was once signal communication between the two points.)

From Makrades a road (not part of this excursion) can be taken to the Troumpeta Pass (7.5km), an attractive drive along a ridge with views to either side.

Returning to the Paleokastritsa/Lakones junction, it is 3.5km along a wooded road (campsites) to **Paleokastritsa**. This is Corfu's most popular holiday area, for reasons which began with its site—a series of sandy coves and bays backed by wooded hills and cliffs—and continue with its development. The tourist offerings are the best in the island, but hopefully expansion will be contained before the character of the setting is lost.

The road ends at the promontory which closes the W bay. On its highest point is the white-painted *Monastery of Paleokastritsa*, conjecturally founded in the 13th c. The present buildings are 18th and 19th c., and comprise an interesting layout of courtyards, monks' cells, storerooms and oil presses. The church has some fine 17th and 18th c. icons.

Paleokastritsa and (above) monastery

Venetian arsenal at Gouvia

The North
Corfu–Kassiopi–Roda–Sidari–
Troumpeta–Corfu (95km)

This excursion goes by way of the popular E coast resorts on a tour of the mountainous NE, with three alternative return routes: one via the W flank of Mt Pantokrator, the others taking in parts of the N coast and returning via the Troumpeta pass.

From Corfu town take any of the Paleokastritsa/North exits (see map). These roads merge at the Potamos river and there is a coastal run to *Kontokali* (6km from Corfu). At this village the main road turns inland and a side road runs right along the Bay of Gouvia. For the 'Village Danilia' see p. 83.

The pincers of land at its entrance make this bay into a sheltered lagoon, excellent for water sports. The village is a resort area, with a hotel on the E headland: 1.5km further on is the second village resort of *Gouvia*. Just before the village there is a sign on the right to 'Gouvia Marina'. Entering the marina at this point and following the track 300m to the left there is the relic of another period of maritime endeavour: a *Venetian arsenal*. This roofless structure, with its graceful pillars and arches, was constructed after the Turkish siege of 1716, and used as a shipyard for the repair of the Republic's galleys. The main road is rejoined at Gouvia village and in 1.5km,

after *Tsavros*, branches right for Ipsos, leaving the Paleokastritsa road.

In 3.5km a crossroads is reached. On the right is the side road for *Dassia Bay*, which has a long, well-shaded beach with excellent water sports facilities. (The Club Méditerranée have colonised the headland to the N.) On the left of the crossroads is a side road to the *Castello Hotel*, a conversion of a pseudo-Venetian palace in the *quatirocento* style. Built in 1880 by an Italian count, this was the summer residence of the Greek king George II. The next beach, 2km further on, stretches from *Ipsos* to *Piryi*, an area of hotels, camp sites and private accommodation. After 1.5km the road starts its climb up the E flank of the Pantokrator massif. At the first hairpin bend a road leads left to Ayios Markos.

Diversion 1: **Ayios Markos** (2km) This village has two frescoed churches of special interest. One, on the hillside above the village (reached by steps from the road at the W end) is the 16th c. church of the *Pantokrator*, which has the most complete cycle of frescoes of the period on Corfu. The frescoes of the narthex are about 1c. later. It is possible to gain access to the narthex, but the main part of the church is locked and it is necessary to ask in the village for someone to open it. Similarly, a guide should be

85

obtained to locate the church of *Ayios Merkourios* in the valley below the village. This is the most historic rustic church in Corfu, retaining the island's oldest dated wall paintings (11th c.). The images display the highly-expressive, frontal treatment of the early Byzantine period. Other frescoes are of the 14th and 15th c. The church, which until recently was half-ruined and used as a stable, has been restored.

From the Ayios Markos junction the road continues uphill and past the turn (500m) for Spartilas and Mt Pantokrator (for excursion to the mountain, see p. 83). The road follows a beautiful route around the olive and cypress-clad spurs, passing occasional side roads down to beaches and fishing villages. After 2.5km *Barbati* has a beach with restaurants and villas: in a further 3.5km *Nissaki*, a village at the S end of a series of quiet coves and beaches terminated by *Nissaki Beach* 2km to the N (hotels). After the Nissaki turn it is 6.5km to the next side road, to the perfectly-sited fishing village of *Kouloura* and its companion village *Kalami* on the next bay. (The road down to them divides: left for Kouloura, right for Kalami.) Kouloura's fishing harbour (restaurant near the jetty) is one of the prettiest in the island: Kalami has a café-bar, beach and Durrell associations (the 'show-white villa' was here).

From the Kouloura turn it is 6.5km to **Kassiopi**, a large village with a N facing harbour tucked between two scrub-covered promontories. Although there are no hotels here the pleasant setting has been overdeveloped, a profusion of villas breaking up the pattern of the village houses. The place has aspects, however, that are worth exploring. The *Castle* on the N headland is 13th c., built by the Angevins to protect the N entrance of the channel between Corfu and the mainland. Its strategic importance is indicated by the Venetians' dismantling of its walls in 1386 for fear that it would fall into the hands of the Genoese. The main *gateway*, reached by the path opposite the church, survives with parts of the thickly overgrown walls and bastions. On the far side of this headland is a bay with a shingle beach, the best bathing place.

At the bend in the road before the harbour is the white-painted church of the *Panayia Kassiopitra* with its belfried gate and small cemetery. The church stands on a historically sacred site: originally that of the Temple of Jupiter of the Roman settlement (visited by Nero) and subsequently a Christian basilica. This church was built in 1590 following the destruction of its predecessor by the Turks, and preserves the

Sidari

icon of the Virgin dating from this period, whose healing powers have made this place a shrine. The silver-cased icon is to the right of the altar; to the left is another icon of the Virgin by the Cretan Theodore Poulakis (1622–92) who offered it in gratitude for his salvation from a shipwreck. This icon portrays in its corner the Virgin's most famous miracle, the healing of a youth wrongly blinded for theft. On the N and S walls of the church are remains of 17th c. *frescoes.*

Kassiopi is connected with Corfu town by a daily boat service.

6km from Kassiopi a minor road is crossed. To the right is the sand beach of *Ayios Spiridon* (2km); to the left a mountain road to Perithia.

> *Diversion 2*: **Perithia** (8km) This inland diversion, though over a rough road, is worthwhile for the encounter with an authentic 18th c. village. Although it has few inhabitants Perithia is not a derelict village, and the stone Venetian buildings are well preserved. But there are no streets, only grassy flagged walks, and a single *cafenion* open in the summer. The village, which covers two hillsides, has a ruined watchtower, a reminder of the age of piracy when it was safer to site villages inland.

From the Perithia turn a level road is followed along the N coastline of the island to *Akharavi* (4km). 200m W of the roundabout is a minor road to *Ayios Pandeleimon*: this is the first of three alternative routes back to Corfu town, with the opportunity of a side excursion to Mt Pantokrator (see p. 83).

2km from Akharavi is the *Roda* junction. Here are three choices. To the left a second alternative return route to Corfu town, via the Troumpeta pass. To the right is the attractive sand and shingle *Roda Beach*, the longest in the island. Ahead the main route continues to Sidari, a new

road with (at the *Karoussades* junction) a turning right for *Cape Astrakeri* (beach, restaurants).

After 5km, watch out for a sign to 'Hotel Sidari Beach'. The side road runs down to the E end of Sidari Bay: for the W end, continue for 1km on the main road to a left turn uphill which curves right for the descent to Sidari village (4km) via a T-junction (Sidari–Arkadades road) and a river bridge.

The new hotels and restaurants indicate the growing popularity of **Sidari**. Driving through the village, there is a view of the most unusual feature of the Corfiot coastline, the formations of soft eroded rock in Sidari Bay which have created a swimmers' paradise—a series of coves and headlands with tunnels and diving ledges. To reach them, a right turn should be made beyond the village, following the sign to 'Canal d'Amour'. The tavern (ample parking space) is named after Sidari's most celebrated natural feature, a long tunnel gouged out of one of the headlands (beyond the bay to the W). The popular legend is that if it is swum for its full length the swimmer—a maiden, of course—will win her heart's desire.

From Sidari the route heads S for the Troumpeta pass and Corfu town. This is an attractive road, following wooded valleys and slopes on a gentle ascent to the island's transverse range. After 12km at *Arkadades* a side excursion can be made to *Ayios Yeoryios*, a curving, golden beach in a well-sheltered bay. The route (6km) descends to the coast through a landscape of gaunt rocks, rising out of a forest of olive trees. Though remote, the bay has a few small hotels, villas and tavernas.

From Arkadades it is 3.5km to the *Troumpeta Pass* with a panoramic view at its summit over the interior of the island. After 7.5km the junction with the Paleokastritsa road is reached, and in a further 14km Corfu town.

Pelekas and Beaches of the West Coast
*Corfu–Pelekas–Glifada–Mirtiotissa–
Ermones–Ayios Yordis–Corfu (55km)*

In addition to the climactic view of the island from Pelekas, this excursion gives the car-borne traveller the opportunity to explore a choice of beaches on the central W coast that offer alternatives to Paleokastritsa. The four beaches are close together and two—Glifada and Ayios Yordis—are easily reached by tarmac roads. The other two—Myrtiotissa and Ermones—are approached by rough tracks.

From Corfu take the exit s/p 'Pelekas' (see map). Follow signs to *Pelekas* (13.5km), a hill village which offers reasonable accommodation for visitors not wishing to stay at Glifada resort. The village has another recommendation: one of the best views of the island from the vantage point popularised by the German emperor Wilhelm II and now known as *The Kaiser's Throne*.

The viewpoint is reached by taking the right fork beyond the church at the top of the village: from here a climb of 1km is rewarded by a panorama embracing Mt Pantokrator and the northern ranges, the port and town of Corfu and Mt Ayii Deka to the S. From the terrace of the restaurant the view is the other way, to the Ionian Sea and the striking coastal peak of Ayios Yeoryios.

From Pelekas the descent to *Glifada Beach* is 5km. The broad strand of golden sand has made this one of the most desirable beaches in the island: its character has inevitably changed with the construction of the large Glifada Beach Hotel at its S end. Water sports are among the best in the island, and the N end, described as the 'Main Beach' has its own smaller hotel and beach facilities. (Note: there is no access to the adjacent Mirtiotissa Beach from here.)

Mirtiotissa Beach, named after the little tree-girt monastery ('Our Lady of the Myrtles') at its N end, has a special character, its sand and shallows scattered with rocks and backed by a high bluff from which spring water trickles. Its seclusion and supply of fresh water have inevitably attracted unofficial campers, and the more militant nudists. From the N end of the beach the climb may be made to the peak of *Ayios Yeoryios* (392m).

To reach Mirtiotissa, ascend from Glifada. A left turn (s/p 'Ermones') is made at 2.5km. At the main road, bear left and after a further 1.5km note the track to the left by the farm building. This is the only approach to Mirtiotissa, a rough track of about 1.5km which ends in a rather

Mirtiotissa

The South
Corfu–Benitses–Kavos–Ayii Deka–Corfu (99km)

This is a full-day excursion to the S tip of the island, taking in the E coastline (Benitses, Messongi) the inland villages of Lefkimi and Kavos, Cape Asprokavos, the S coast (Ayios Yeoryios, Korission lake and Ayios Mattheos) and returning via the central mountain road (Ayii Deka).

From Corfu town take the Plat. G. Theotoki exit (s/p 'Airport, Lefkimi'). After 5km turn left for **Perama**, reached in a further 2km. Although the cliffs are steep here and the beaches negligible, its nearness to the town has promoted the rapid growth of this resort. Kanoni is only a walk away across the causeway, and from here a bus can be taken into town. A good eating place on the corniche is the fish restaurant *Ioannis* with its belvedere.

2.5km S of Perama is the ruined jetty, the 'Kaiser's Bridge', which served as a landing-place for the German emperor on his visits to the Akhilleion. Shortly afterwards is the turning for the Akhilleion (see p. 82) close to the entrance of the San Stefano Hotel (s/p 'Gastouri'). 1km further is **Benitses**, still a fishing village but hardly recognisable as such. The take-over by souvenir shops, café-bars, car-hire firms and other tourist paraphernalia is complete, overwhelming the village and narrow stretch of beach. To prove Benitses had another existence one should ask to see the *mosaica*, the remnant of the Roman era that survives in a back garden at the N end of the village near the promenade garden. These are the floor mosaics of a bath-house belonging to one of the many villas built by the Romans on this coast.

7.5km S of Benitses there are further Roman remains on the outskirts of *Moraïtika*, from where a road runs left to the first of the Messongi beach developments.

dangerous descent recommended only for four-wheel drive.

Returning to the road, in 2km the route crosses the Ropa river beyond *Vatos*. To the right is the *Corfu Golf and Country Club*; to the left, in 500m, a fork. The road uphill goes to the Ermones Beach Hotel bungalows, the track downhill to the shingle beach. Although it lacks some of the physical attractions of the other beaches on this coast, *Ermones* has its place in the island's most famous legend. The river here has been determined as the washing place of Nausikaa, the beach as that on which Odysseus was cast after his shipwreck (see p. 74).

For those not wishing to include the beach of Ayios Yordis in this tour, a direct return may be made to the capital after recrossing the Ropa. The left-fork after Vatos leads in 4km to the junction of the Corfu town (Kerkira)/Pelekas roads. From here the return can be made to the capital.

The tour is extended to Ayios Yordis by continuing to *Sinarades* (5km). From the centre of the village a side road ('Aerostatos St') leads in 1km to one of Corfu's most attractive coastal views at *Plitiri Point* (café). From here it embraces the bays and headlands N to Mirtiotissa and the peak of Ayios Yeoryios; S the beach of Ayios Yordis.

To reach *Ayios Yordis*, turn right after Sinarades and descend 3.5km to the beach. The setting is attractive, but development on this long sandy stretch (2km) has been piecemeal: a few hotels and a scattering of villas. The return journey to Corfu town (18km) is made over the lower ridge of the Ayii Deka range via *Kinopiastes*. After Kinopiastes the right turn to Gastouri climbs to the Akhilleion (see p. 82).

> *Diversion*: **Boukari** After 1km, a left turn can be made to *Messongi* village, at the centre of a development that has been dubbed 'Corfu's Costa Brava'. A rough road leads 6km along the shoreline to *Boukari*. A fishing jetty, fresh lobster, and well-shaded tavernas provide a peaceful alternative. From Boukari a return inland is made to *Kouspades*, from where a road leads left to another fishing village, *Petreti*, with the ruins of a *Roman piscina*. The route back to the main road, joined at *Aryirades*, is 4km.

Staying on the main road, without the above diversion, a left turn is made at *Messongi Bridge*, 2km from Moraïtika, for *Aryirades*, reached in a further 9.5km.

From Aryirades it is 9km to *Ano Lefkimi*, the first of a series of agricultural villages that are the economic centre of the S of the island (a left turn leads in 4km to *Alikes*, where a sandy beach runs up to *Cape Lefkimi*). The southward drive of tourism to Kavos has not affected the character or self-sufficiency of these villages: the women, anchors of the working community, still wear the traditional folded headscarves and aprons. In the last village, *Potami* (2km from Ano Lefkimi) there is an unexpected sight: caiques loaded with produce moored by an iron bridge on a substantial river which has its source in the coastal range to the S.

In a further 6km **Kavos** is reached. This village lies at the end of a 6km stretch of flat coastline with sandy beach, and in a few years has been converted into a fast-living resort to rival Benitses—sadly inappropriate in this remote part of the island. Here the coastal plain terminates and the land rises gradually to the thickly wooded Cape Asprokavos, the S tip of the island. A pleasant walk to the cape may be made in about 1hr, but the approach described below may be altered by tourist developments.

> Follow the tarmac road to the point where it ends beyond the furthest hotel and enters an olive wood. At the fork (300m) keep left. At the next fork (200m) before the holiday villa keep ahead up the rough stone track. In 2km the track which has run through dense olive groves and out on to a headland narrows to a shaded walk. After 500m the ruined *Monastery of Arkondillas* is reached. A stone archway, topped by a charming Baroque belfry, has a carved keystone with the date 170–. Inside, a building on the left

with a vaulted upper chamber is faced by a flight of steps that stand detached from the entrance, requiring a plank to bridge the gap: this was a defensive measure against any pirates who might land on the S cape. The church is still intact, but the rest of the buildings and walls ruinous. The monastery stands on the dramatic *Cape Asprokavos*, with superb cliff-top views.

From Kavos the return is made to Aryirades (17km). In 1km there is a left turn to *Ayios Yeoryios Beach* (2.5km) with its 'village' of tavernas and rooms to let. Back on the main road there is another turn after 2.5km (*Linia*) for the unmade road to the *Korission Lake*. This small lagoon lies to the N of the road, across a barrier of sand dunes. Largely dry in the summer, the lagoon is sown with fish traps.

6km N of Linia a third diversion to the left may be made before the Messongi Bridge junction.

> *Diversion*: **Ayios Mattheos** The village itself, tucked into the oak-covered mountain barrier on the W side of the island, is not the first objective: 2.5km from the junction is a minor turn to the Byzantine fort of *Gardiki*, the only building of its kind in the S of Corfu. This dates back to the 13th c., when the Despots of Epirus were in possession of the island. The castle is built on a low mound surrounded by hills, an unusual site that can only be explained by the proximity of springs. Its vulnerability brought its eventual abandonment, but although crumbling and overgrown the outer walls (octagonal with square postern towers) are still standing to their original height. 3km further on the village lies at the foot of the mountain which shares its name (*Ayios Mattheos*, 463m). A road (from which a path ascends to the summit) leads 2km from the village to its beach (taverna).

Returning to Messongi Bridge, take the inland route via the Messongi river valley to *Ayii Deka* (14km). This village lies below Corfu's second highest peak (576m) of the same name, meaning 'The Ten Saints'. From the village there is a ½hr climb to the summit, where there is an old monastery and the best view in the island of Corfu town, with the Kanoni peninsula and Halikiopoulos lagoon lying before it and the massif of Pantokrator in the distance.

After a swift descent from Ayii Deka to *Kinopiastes* (1.5km), famous for its taverna *Tripa*, the road reaches the junction for the return to Corfu town, a further 10km.

Potami

The Corfu Easter

EASTER, the major festival of the Orthodox calendar, is celebrated with particular splendour in Corfu town. The narrow streets and the open stage of the Esplanade provide a perfect setting for the numerous processions, whose mixture of pomp and brio, orchestrated by the church dignitaries and the town bands in their colourful robes and uniforms, is unequalled in Greece.

The colour and vitality of the celebrations are an image of the spring season in which they take place: up to a month later than the Easter in Western Europe. At this time the Esplanade is aglow with the pink and white blossom of the Judas trees and the horse chestnuts, the warm air tinged with the fragrance of renewed life. This is the setting for many of the parades and other spectacles of Holy Week, which reach their climax in the joyful revelation of the Resurrection on Easter Saturday night.

First is the procession of the *epitafios*, the holy table bearing the image of Christ. Every church in the town parades its *epitafios* on Good Friday, a symbolic bier beautifully decorated with flowers and borne on the shoulders of the mourners. In the labyrinth of Corfu's streets, with their closely-built Venetian houses, the route and timing of each procession must be carefully planned, and the contingents of official mourners—servicemen, boy scouts, high school boys and girls—divided equally amongst them. The musical resources of the town—no less than four bands—are also tightly stretched. The players of the bands, divided between half-a-dozen or more processions, are the heroes of the hour, providing a diligent, sombre accompaniment to each slow-moving cortège.

Throughout the afternoon and evening of Good Friday the processions wind their way round the tight, flag-hung streets, a continuous spectacle that can be as tiring for the spectator as the participant. By nightfall the keen *epitafios* follower will be in training for the major procession of the day. The *epitafios* of the cathedral commands a special reverence, and is led by the Metropolitan, clergy and a host of official mourners bearing candles. The bands are also in attendance but the music is subdued and in its pauses the sober column, moving at a measured pace around the old sea walls, is ushered only by the sighs of the Mediterranean. The tall Venetian houses built over the walls frame the silence with their dark façades and spread a warding arm along the way for the trembling threads of candlelight. The townsfolk also take part in this procession and maintain their solemn progress, returning to the cathedral to restore the venerated bier to its sanctuary.

The Epitafios of St Spiridon

The following morning (Easter Saturday) is reserved for the most splendid procession of all. This is the *epitafios* of the church of St Spiridon, the island's patron saint, and commemorates simultaneously the saint's miraculous alleviation of a 16th-century famine. In this procession, as in the three others commemorating the saint's miracles (see p. 55), the saint himself takes part, his shrunken body borne reverentially in a gilt casket. The processional route, around the Esplanade, is lined by most of the town's population, many of whom will proudly identify a member of their family in the procession. Their numbers are swelled by the tourists, who after a day's rehearsal with the other parades are eager for the final performance.

The Metropolitan of Corfu leads the epitafios of St Spiridon
Inset: Flowers for the holy table

The great moment for all the spectators is when the head of the procession comes in sight, its slow and deliberate pace conveyed on a tremor of music filling out to a vibrant crescendo. This is the Dead March from *Saul*, triumphantly rendered by the band of the St Spiridon Philharmonic Society. Before them advance the neat ranks of schoolchildren: the boys in dark suits and white gloves, the girls wobbling on high heels, diligently keeping step. Then the scouts, bare-thighed, staves reversed; the cubs skittering along like nervous lambs. Half of them (the boys) will be called Spiros after the saint they are honouring.

Following the band the priests, in their stovepipe hats and robes of many colours, escort the precious relic. The Metropolitan strides in their midst, a diminutive but glorious figure in his mitre and vestment of blue and gold. Behind him, flanked by the perspiring bearers of the great votive candles, is the golden sedan of St Spiridon, decked in flowers and carried by four priests. The blessed saint—head askew, eyes tightly closed—treats the whole thing with a stoic calm.

The breaking of the pots

After the procession, when the streets are cleared, the Corfiots find a release for their emotion in a strange ritual. One of the oddest bits of symbolism, peculiar to the folklore of Corfu, is the breaking of the pots on Easter Saturday morning, At eleven o'clock precisely a church bell rings and the streets to the west of the Liston, recently hushed in respectful tribute to St Spiridon, suddenly explode with the impact of a thousand missiles.

Wine jars, crockery and flower pots splinter at the feet of the startled onlookers, an earthenware shrapnel that in seconds decks the streets with a mosaic of brown and white fragments. The bombardment continues until the last pot has been launched from window ledge or balcony, and the streets have become a no-man's land of broken pottery.

With its protective arcades, Nikiforos Theotokis Street is probably the best place to witness the spectacle. The first brave spirits to venture forth from the arcades, glancing cautiously upwards, signal a ceasefire, and within moments the street is filled with people again, crunching the scattered sherds under their feet.

The significance of the ritual (which presumably goes beyond the smashing of unwanted crockery) has been lost over the centuries of its performance. According to one theory it represents the stoning

The breaking of the pots in Odos N. Theotoki

Town band in epitafios procession, Corfu town

of Judas, another the rending of the Tomb. More plausibly, it is a throwback to the Middle Ages, when members of the town's large Jewish community were expelled from the streets in this manner during Holy Week. Symbolism apart, it is popular theatre—not only with the Corfiots but with Holy Weekenders from the mainland and further afield.

Christos Anesti

After the pottery smashing on Easter Saturday the spirit of penance gives way to the more joyful aspects of the festival. The end of the Lenten fast is nigh and the preparations for Sunday's feasting begin. The paschal lambs, last seen tethered in gardens and doorways with red ribbons tied to their fleeces and red crosses marked on their faces, are no longer on view. Their next and final appearance will be the following morning, on a slowly revolving spit. Cheese pies, red-dyed Easter eggs and sesame cakes are all in preparation for the special day.

The signal for the great absolution comes at midnight, when the Metropolitan announces the happy tidings of Christ's resurrection from the bandstand on the Esplanade. Fifty thousand people, each clutching an unlit candle, are there to hear the news. All lights save those on the bandstand are extinguished, and the eyes of the hushed crowd are fixed on the mitred figure, swinging a censer as he proclaims Christ's triumph over Death.

'*Christos Anesti!*' ('Christ is Risen!')

The chimes of midnight are still sounding as the Metropolitan's cry rings out. Immediately the bands strike up an Easter hymn and the square is ablaze with candlelight. A conflagration of tiny flames spread beyond the square into the streets, blossoming at the windows of the houses. The boom of cannon from the fort is answered by the artillery of fireworks, and in the town the church bells add their peals of joy.

'*Alithos Anesti!*' ('Truly He is Risen!')

The cry is taken up by the people as they leave the square, guarding the precious light of their candles. They will see that light safely home, and into the Easter dawn. Once home, they will also attend to another duty—the breaking of their fast. This is performed by cracking and eating the special Easter eggs—dyed crimson to symbolise the blood of Christ—and joining in a midnight feast. This is, however, a mere appetiser for the main feasting which takes place the following day when the Easter lambs are roasted on the spit. This can be witnessed—and enjoyed—by the visitor in various parts of the town where there is an open space for a charcoal pit.

After the slow cooking the lamb is superbly tender and spiced with the resin of the pine embers. Two counterpoints are provided by the tangy Corfiot wine, balancing the flavour of the meat, and the fresh spring flowers on the tables, tingeing the charcoal smoke with their scent. The visitor should always remember to respond to any hospitality that may be offered with the traditional Easter greeting—'*Chronia Polla!*' ('Many years—long life!').

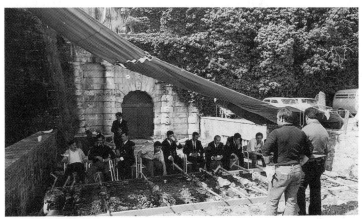

Roasting Easter lamb on spits by the New Fort

Paxos

(Paxi)

Pop: 1300
Area: 31 sq km
Main village/port: Gaios (pop: 450)
Highest point: 248m
Nearest island: Corfu (18.5km NW)
Distance from mainland: 13km W of Epirus
Festival: August 15 (Assumption of the Virgin

Travel to Paxos

From Corfu (3hrs)
Car ferry 'Ionis' (Brindisi–Corfu–Paxos–Ithaca–Cefalonia–Patras)
Alternate days Jun–mid Sep
Passenger boat 'Kamelia'
Daily
Day Trips 'Paxi'
Three times weekly

From Ithaca/Cefalonia (4hrs)
Car Ferry 'Ionis'
Alternate days Jun–mid Sep

From Parga (2hrs)
Daily Jun–Sep
Excursions are also available in high season from Kavos, Benitses and Igoumenitsa

Travel in Paxos One bus five times daily, Gaios–Longos–Lakka. Boat, taxi, scooter hire in Gaios, Longos and Lakka

Accommodation Hotels (see p. 28). Villas, apartments and private rooms available throughout the island

Restaurants Tavernas in Gaios, Longos and Lakka. Also at Mongonisi and Antipaxos beaches in summer

Boat trips Round-island boat trips available from Gaios and Lakka. Also 'express' services to Mongonisi and Antipaxos from Gaios.

Beaches At Gaios, Mongonisi, Lakka, E coast and Antipaxos (see also p. 99)

Water sports At Lakka, Mongonisi and at the *Paxos Beach Hotel* at Gaios

Despite its small size, Corfu's satellite island has many features which make it an attractive port of call. It is also growing in appeal as a retreat for those disenchanted with the conventional resort holiday.

Its principal charm is its landscape: unexpectedly hilly and green. The greenness comes mainly from the dense growth of olive trees, which cover much of the island. Like those on Corfu they are unpruned, mighty and ancient (some 500 years old or more) but unlike them they are systematically terraced, the stone walls almost merging with the rocky landscape. Another attraction, for sea-going explorers, are the grottoes beneath the steep cliffs on the west coast, perfect for snorkelling or scuba-diving.

History Though it shares the history of its mother island, Paxos has always been tested by its greater vulnerability, isolated off the southern tip of Corfu and with a harbour accessible to foe as well as friend. When the Venetians came, their priority was the defence of Gaios and for this purpose they built the fortress of St Nicholas (1423) on the island enclosing the harbour entrance. Unfortunately it was not enough to deter the raids of the assorted Algerian, Tunisian and Turkish pirates who regularly pillaged the island. The Turks were a particular menace and in 1537 (the year of the first great siege of Corfu) and 1571 totally devastated Paxos.

The later Venetian period saw the development of the island's agriculture – mainly the cultivation of the olive and the vine – and the growth of a Paxiot fleet which joined forces with both Corfiot and Venetian galleys in their forays against the Turks.

The change to French rule brought the island's worst civil crisis when, in 1810, the English blockade of Paxos (the last of the Ionians to be wrested from the French before Corfu itself) reduced the population to starvation. A rebel mob, assembling at Lakka, marched on Gaios and sacked the houses of the authorities, killing the military governor. The French punished the rebels with great severity, but it was, in effect, a stay of their own execution. In February 1814 the French garrison surrendered to a British landing party whose number included – significantly – the man who would later be one of the heroes of the Greek Independence struggle, Theodore Kolokotronis.

It was the campaign for the union of the Ionians with the newly liberated Greece which brought the island its most distinguished foreign visitor. In 1858, the specially appointed Lord High Commissioner Extraordinary WE Gladstone came to Paxos as part of his goodwill tour of the Ionians and his mission to present a new liberal constitution for the administration of the islands. Received with great courtesy by the Bishop of Paxos and other island dignitaries he made a great personal impression – and left with a large Greek flea in his ear.

The island The changing base of economic life in the Ionian islands is reflected in Paxos as elsewhere. Although its olive oil – extolled as the finest in Greece – is still the island's major product, the methods of production have changed. Modern factories have outmoded the traditional olive press, and transformed the country scene.

Tourist developments, until recently the by-product of Corfu's popularity, have been given the spur of the island's own reputation as a separate destination. Happily new accommodation is on a modest scale and confined to Gaios and Lakka, although country villas are being built in various locations.

Gaios

The island has three main villages, connected by tarmac road. The principal is the port of **Gaios**, located on a curving inlet protected by a wooded islet. The approach to the port is like entering an estuary, as the steamer negotiates the narrow channel between island and port. With its graceful, tile-roofed houses and small square opening off the waterfront Gaios has a 19th c. air about it, reminiscent of the days when Gladstone called. The British *Resident's House* is still standing, at the approach to the steamship dock: it is now used by the port authorities. Its four stories make it the tallest building on Paxos.

On the islet of *Ayios Nikolaos* which screens the harbour from the open sea stand the ruins of the Venetian *fortress* (1423) and an old *windmill* now obscured by a thick growth of pine and cypress. The smaller island of *Panayia* to the N (with a lighthouse and chapel) is the scene of the island's major festival on Assumption Day (August 15). On this occasion the Paxiots embark en masse on a pilgrimage to the chapel, returning for celebrations in the main square.

The waterfront can be followed in either direction from Gaios. 1km to the N, round the headland, is the *New Port*, now used by the car ferries and other large vessels. To the S, the coast road leads in 2.5km to Mongonisi (see below).

Gaios has a good choice of tavernas, centred on the square, and a few quiet shingle beaches within walking distance. The crystal clear water is ideal for bathing. Boats can be hired from Gaios to explore the interesting W coast of Paxos with its sea caves: trips can also be made around the island and to Antipaxos (see below).

A village bus travels from Gaios five or six times daily to **Lakka** on the N coast, a distance of 8km. Lakka is a small fishing port set in a horseshoe-shaped bay ideal for water sports. There are sand and shingle beaches and tavernas. The third village is the attractive **Longos** on the NE coast, to which the Gaios–Lakka bus makes a detour.

The interior Wrapped in its shroud of olive trees, the shape of Paxos is barely apparent to the traveller inland. The single road which runs the length of the island, from Gaios to Lakka with a diversion to Longos, offers only occasional glimpses of the coastline, most notably from the ridge W of the island's highest point (248m). To get a more intimate view of the interior it is a good idea to get off the bus

Eremitis Cliffs

near this point and walk downhill, either to Lakka or Gaios. (Taking the village of *Magazia* as the central point it is an hour on foot either way.) Beneath the canopy of the olive trees, the walker can discover glimpses of the island's rural past, the simple mechanics of a farming life that has gone forever.

By the roadside, the abandoned oil presses are sad relics of this past, their rusted screws vainly poised over the broken grinding stones. Elsewhere, derelict well-houses, abandoned farmhouses and sailless windmills may be seen. The latter are very much a feature of the Paxiot countryside, their ruined, stone-built towers standing out above the thickets of olive trees on the hillsides. All this is desolation, but a symbol of the continuing life of Paxos is in the villages, whose stone houses and whitewashed belfried churches present the well-kept image of communities thriving on the island's new resources.

Different aspects of the island can be enjoyed on short diversions from the main road, following the tracks leading to the smaller villages. From *Magazia* a popular short walk is to the small church of *Ayii Apostoli*, with a fine view from the churchyard of the Erimitis Cliffs.

The coastline The wedge-shaped island, with high cliffs on the W and a sloping E coast, offers surprising variety and spectacle. The W coast is famed for its **sea caves**, which though seen elsewhere in the Ionians are particularly spectacular here, carved by the relentless waves out of the cliffs of limestone. The best way of seeing the caves is by a round-island boat trip, possible in 1 hr by express boat (the normal trip takes about ½hr longer, allowing time to explore the caves).

The smaller boats are able to enter the caves, where the translucency of the water, enhanced in places by a luminous blue, may be seen to full effect. A different spectacle is provided by the rock formations, which have transformed the coast into a monumental sculpture gallery, centred upon the massive *Erimitis Cliffs*, the highest in the island.

To the S, the needle-shaped *Ortholithos*, the 'upright stone' guards the *Petriti Cave* which forms a deep, crag-vaulted chamber in the rock. After the obelisk, the triumphal arch: a weathered replica of an imperial monument, the *Arch of Tripiti*, extends from the crumbling masonry of limestone further south. At the tail-end of the coastline, *Mongonisi* islet has its own small cave whose lapis-lazuli mirrors glimmer magically in its otherwise unfathomable darkness.

What the **beaches** of Paxos lack in quantity they make up for in the quality of their setting. The least exceptional, however, are those of Gaios, small rock and shingle bathing places immediately to the S of the port. A better equipped beach, 1hr's walk further on (or by the Mongonisi Express taxi boat from Gaios) is at *Mongonisi*, an islet which with its smaller companion *Kalkhionisi* form the small toe-bones on the island's foot. From the road above Mongonisi looking towards the narrow channel separating it from the main island, there is a fine backdrop view of Antipaxos. Reached on foot by a rock causeway, Mongonisi has a sand beach and taverna. The bay formed by the gap between the two islands offers a safe harbour for windsurfing and sailing.

Beaches on the E coast of the island (mostly pebble) are accessible either by boat or rough paths from the interior, although the road northwards from the new port now makes the southernmost more accessible from Gaios. *Lakka* has a pleasantly shaded pebble beach on the W shore of its bay, and excellent watersports facilities. The beaches on *Antipaxos* (see below) are worth the boat trip to the smaller island.

Antipaxos This small island to the S of Paxos is a popular excursion (reached in 18min by express boat from Gaios). Only 3 sq km in area, it is covered in lush vegetation including vineyards. The 40 inhabitants live in scattered dwellings reached from the harbour (*Agrapidia*) on the east side. To the north of this harbour lie two beautiful beaches, one of white pebbles (*Voutoumi*) and one of sand (*Vrika*) both with tavernas. The wine of Antipaxos, the main product of the island, is primitive but drinkable.

Levkas
(Lefkada)

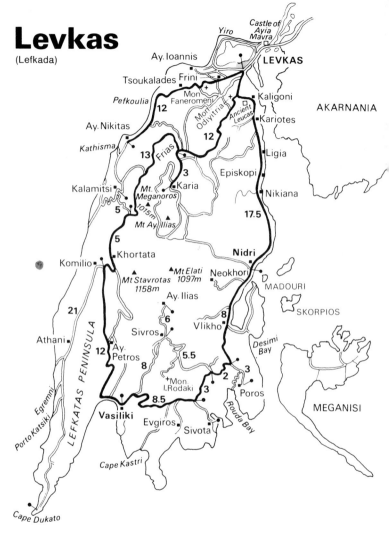

Pop: 22,000
Area: 293 sq km
Main town: Levkas (Lefkada) (pop: 6500)
Highest point: Stavrotas (1158m)
Nearest island: Ithaca (6km S)
Distance from mainland: 1km by causeway

Festival: Levkas Folklore Festival (end August)
Information: There is no Tourist Information Office on Levkas. Information about excursions, vehicle hire, etc. can be obtained from travel agents or from the Tourist Police

Levkas town and the Yiro

Travel to Levkas

By air
Charter flights from London and
Manchester to Preveza. The airport is
located near Aktion on the mainland,
16km by road to Levkas town (bus
connection).
Daily flights from Athens to Preveza by
Olympic Airways

By sea
Daily connections by car ferry from Ithaca
and Cefalonia to Nidri and Vasiliki

By road
From Athens: By car or bus (daily, 9hrs)
via Corinth, Rion-Antirion car ferry (every
20min), Missolonghi, Agrinion, Amfilokhia
(362km)
From Corfu (via Igoumenitsa): By car
via Morganiti, Preveza, Preveza-Aktion
ferry (every 10min) (116km); by bus
(daily) via Paramithia, Gliki, Kanalaki,
Preveza, Preveza-Aktion ferry, separate
bus to Levkas town (3hrs).

Travel in Levkas Buses are available to
most of the villages from Levkas town
(see map for location of bus station).
There are at least four buses a day to
the resorts of Nidri and Vasiliki. Taxis are
only available in Levkas town and in Nidri
and Vasiliki in summer. Car hire is
similarly available in these places,
though in the case of the resorts, if there
is an extra demand, the car may have to
be brought in from Levkas town. As a
result of the limited supply of vehicles,
car hire tends to be more expensive in
Levkas than the other larger islands.
Scooter and boat hire is also available.

Accommodation Hotels (see p. 28), villas,
apartments and private rooms are
available in the main resorts, and there
are also rooms on Meganisi island.
Camping at Kariotes Beach (4km S of
Levkas town), Episkopi Beach (8km S of
Levkas town), Desimi Bay (5km S of
Nidri), Poros (2 sites) and Vasiliki (see
also p. 27).

Restaurants Levkas town has a number
of restaurants and tavernas in the area
of the main street. There are also good
tavernas (most open only in summer) at
Ligia, Nidri, Poros, Sivota, Vasiliki, Ayios
Petros, Ayios Nikitas and Karia.

Boat trips Available from the main
resorts. Among the most popular trips
are to the small island of Meganisi (from
Nidri) and to Porto Katsiki on the Levkatas
peninsula (from Vasiliki).

Beaches In the area of Levkas town the
best beaches are on the *Yiro*, the sandy
isthmus which encloses the lagoon. The
stretch on the N side, backed by sand
dunes, has no cover and tends to be
windswept: the beach to the W, curving
round to the fishing village of Ayios
Ioannis, is more protected.
The sheltered E coast of Levkas, facing
the mainland, has the safest and most
accessible beaches, but these tend to be
of the narrow pebbled variety and the
water in the area of the Levkas channel
(*Ligia, Nikiana*, 6.5 and 11km S of Levkas
town) and the land-locked bay of Vlikho
(*Nidri*, 17.5km S of Levkas) less clear
than elsewhere.
Beaches on the S coast are confined to
those in the deeply indented bays: most
popular are the white pebble *Poros
Beach* in Rouda Bay (28.5km S of Levkas)
and the 3km shingle beach to the NW of
Vasiliki (39.5km SW of Levkas).
In striking contrast, the exposed and
mountainous W coast, which is barely
developed, has some fine sandy beaches,
though only easily accessible at *Pefkoulia*
and *Ayios Nikitas* (9 & 12km SW of
Levkas). Further S the beaches are only
reached by rough road: *Kathisma* from
Ayios Nikitas and *Kalamitsi* from the
village, via a steep descent from the main
road. The deserted beaches on the W
side of the Lefkatas peninsula (*Porto
Katsiki, Egremni*) are best reached by
boat from Vasiliki. They lie at the foot of
cliffs and can only be reached by tracks.

Castle of Ayia Mavra

Once forming a peninsula on the west coast of the mainland, Levkas is separated from Akarnania by a narrow strait and a canal. Despite its proximity to the mainland the island is relatively undeveloped and its attractive countryside and natural character are its greatest virtues. It has superb, but remote beaches on the west coast and two attractively sited village resorts: Nidri and Vasiliki.

History The ancient settlement of *Leucas* (*Nerikos*) to the south of the modern town of Levkas, was founded (640BC) by the Corinthians, who cut a canal through the isthmus to shorten the sea routes to their other colonies to the north. The newly created island flourished, and in the 5th c. supported a population of 20,000. It joined the struggle of the Greeks against the Persians, sending ships to Salamis and troops to Plataea. Later in the century, however, the loyalty of Levkas to its mother city brought attacks from the enemies of Corinth: Corcyra (436BC)

and Athens (427BC, during the Peloponnesian War).

Allied to Philip V of Macedon (220–197BC), Levkas was captured by the Romans and the canal, which had silted up, was reopened by them after Augustus' vistory over Mark Antony at the nearby Battle of Actium (31BC). In the late Roman period Levkas became the seat of a bishop, who attended the Council of Nicaea in 325AD.

In the Middle Ages the island was influenced by its accessibility from the mainland. While the more southerly islands of Ithaca, Cefalonia and Zakinthos were under the seafaring Normans, Venetians and Latin Crusaders, Levkas remained part of the Byzantine Empire, and subsequently the Despotate of Epirus. Control by the Angevins and by the Tocco family brought it in line with its southern neighbours in the 14th–15th c. During the Latin period the building of the castle of Ayia Mavra on the mainland side of the canal caused the population to abandon the old city for its protection, thus establishing a new capital.

After its conquest by the Ottoman Turks (1479) Levkas became the only Ionian island to submit for any lengthy period to Turkish rule. It remained Turkish until 1684, when its capture by the Venetians marked the first success of Morosini against the Ottoman army. During the Venetian occupation the island was known as Santa Maura.

Its nearness to the mainland made Levkas more vulnerable to attack than the other Ionians. There was a continuing threat of Turkish reoccupation from across the narrow Levkas Strait (achieved briefly in 1714–16), and during the Septinsular Republic (1807) the island was besieged by Ali Pasha, tyrant of Ioannina. On this occasion Levkas was saved by the sturdy defence of the troops of the young Kapodistrias: three years later the French, at the end of their second occupation, were not so successful. Besieged in the fortress of Ayia Mavra at the head of the causeway, Napoleon's troops managed to resist the allied infantry attacks (including that of the Greek Light Infantry under the command of Major Richard Church) but succumbed eventually to the British artillery.

During the British Protectorate Levkas shared the unrest of the other islands, and in 1819 a serious riot—against the imposition of taxation by the government for the dredging of the canal—resulted in the execution of local agitators.

After the departure of the Venetians, Levkas shared the history of Corfu and the other Ionians. In 1948 the island suffered severe earthquake damage, though escaping the 1953 disaster.

The island The name of Levkas derives from the *Levkas Petra* (White Rock) mentioned in the *Odyssey*, a striking feature of the spear-shaped promontory at the southern tip of the island. Like its southern neighbours Cefalonia and Ithaka, Levkas is a mountainous island with its twin peaks of *Meganoros* and *Ayios Ilias* (both 1015m) in the north and *Stavrotas* (1158m) and *Elati* (1097m) in the south. High plateaux and coastal plains are however much more of a feature, and the driver will find the roads here easier than in the other islands.

Apart from the area of Levkas town, and the east and north-west of the island, access to the coast is limited, with openings to the sea through the rugged cliff barrier only at Poros, Sivota and Vasiliki. *Meganisi* islet, off the east coast, offers a pleasant excursion from Nidri.

Dörpfeld's Ithaca The archaeologist Wilhelm Dörpfeld (1853–1940), convinced by his own reading of Homer's geographical descriptions that Levkas, and not Ithaki (the modern Ithaca) was the Homeric Ithaca, and that the name of the island had been transferred to its modern location by a migration from Levkas, devoted much of his life to a search for archaeological evidence to support his theory. His excavations in the plain of Nidri revealed a prehistoric settlement which he claimed was the city of Odysseus: the nearby Bay of Vlikho became its harbour. Other Homeric sites were identified, but later scholars have dismissed Dörpfeld's findings as hypothetical.

Homer's own description of the land of Odysseus as 'unfit for horses' was offered as one contradiction, considering the suitability of the plain of Nidri for horses; the principal objection, however, was Dörpfeld's siting of the main harbour on the east coast of Levkas, with no outlet to the north (in Odysseus' time, they claimed, there was no canal through the isthmus). In such a confined location, and facing inland, the site would have had serious strategic limitations. The arguments for the heights of Ithaca's north range as the site of Odysseus' capital are made stronger by comparison.

Approach to Levkas The sandbank which once formed an isthmus connecting the island to the mainland now carries the road across the strait to the town of Levkas. At the point where the canal cuts through the isthmus the *Castle of Ayia Mavra* stands guard. This castle, which once gave its name (Italian *Santa Maura*) to the island, was built by the Orsini in 1300 and later enlarged by the island's succession of overlords, mainly the Turks and Venetians. It was taken from the French in 1811 by Major (later General Sir Richard) Church, who was to become one of the great allied military leaders in the Greek War of Independence.

Across the newly constructed bridge a causeway leads directly to the town, with the remains of the old Turkish causeway (which once carried an aqueduct to the castle) submerged in the lagoon to the right. The right-angled sandbank enclosing the lagoon to the W provides an alternative circular route to the town (5km), passing the attractive *Yiro Beach*.

Typical Levkadian houses

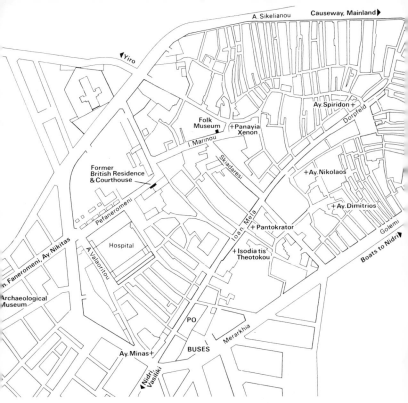

Levkas town

The air of impermanence that pervades the towns of the southern Ionians with their tragic history of earthquakes is strongly felt in Levkas, which suffered its most recent disaster in 1948 when much of the town was destroyed. Enough survives of its original character, however, to make it more interesting to the visitor than its sister towns of Argostoli, Vathi and Zakinthos.

In the Middle Ages the island's centre of population was concentrated around the castle of Ayia Mavra, but moved back to the island, to the S end of the causeway, following the destruction of the aqueduct by an earthquake in the 18th c. The architecture is Epirot rather than Ionian, the houses timber-framed with a filling of stone or brick with a cladding of boards or corrugated iron on the upper storey. This style of building provides a structural flexibility which reduces the effect of earth tremors.

A similar adaptation can be seen in the unique belltowers of the town's churches which are built of openwork iron like miniature Eiffel towers.

These churches, originally built in the late 17th–18th c. Venetian period, are among the most attractive in the Ionians, and preserve much of their Baroque decoration (see map for location). Most interesting are the church of the *Pantokrator*, founded by the Venetian commander Morosini after his capture of the island in 1684, which has a richly decorated stone façade and contains the tomb of the writer *Aristoteles Valaoritis* (1824–79), and *Ayios Minas* with its fine iconostasis and ceiling paintings by *Nicholas Doxaras* (d. 1761). To the S of the main street is the small church of *Ayios Dimitrios* which contains four fine paintings by *Panayiotis Doxaras* (1662–1729), father of Nicholas and founder of the Ionian School. The Italian-influenced style of his late work is best seen in the majestic *St John the Baptist*.

On the W outskirts of the town, the small *Archaeological Museum* has Bronze Age finds from Nidri.

A pleasant walk through the town, taking in most of the features of interest, starts at the 17th-c. church of *Ayios Spiridon* in the main square (reached from the end of the causeway) and follows Odos Ioannis Mela to the church of Ayios Minas. With the shore road taking most of the through traffic this street (once known as the 'Bazaar') belongs to the walker, who at a leisurely pace can enjoy the activity of the multitude of small shops along the way. Churches which either survived the earthquake or have since been reconstructed may be seen on the route, or by short diversions (see map). The walk can be made circular by going right at Ayios Minas, past the hospital and right again along Pefaneromeni and Marinou. Interesting relics of the British Protectorate on Pefaneromeni are two early 19th-c. stone buildings, formerly the *British Residence* and *Courthouse*.

Odos Ioannis Mela with the church of the Pantokrator, Levkas town

The Yiro and Ayios Nikitas
(5km and 24km return journeys)

Two separate routes can be taken from Levkas town to the most popular local beaches. The first, the *Yiro*, is the rectangular sandspit which encloses the lagoon to the N of the town (5km circular tour). The broad sand and pebble beach which runs along the N edge of the spit and then sweeps W to the tiny fishing village of Ayios Ioannis, is exposed to rough seas but is good for sunbathing. The flat shoreline of the lagoon, broken only by thickets of calamus and the towers of old windmills, provides a strange contrast to the mountain backdrop of the island's other beaches.

To reach Ayios Nikitas, leave Levkas town by Odos Faneromeni (see map). A poor road climbs via a hillside village (*Frini*), a pinewood and the modern *Faneromeni Monastery* (the original was destroyed in the 1948 earthquake) to the village of *Tsoukalades* (5.5km). Having negotiated the island's NW mountain spur the road then descends along its flank to the exposed but magnificent sands of *Pefkoulia* beach to the village of *Ayios Nikitas*, a further 6.5km.

The parking space is outside the village, which despite the number of taverns (the beach is popular with Greek visitors from the mainland) has kept much of its character. The beach itself is sheltered by a promontory with rocks and a sea-cave. The unmade road running S from Ayios Nikitas leads to two more good W coast beaches at *Kathisma* (1km) and *Kalamitsi* (5km).

Round-island tour from Levkas
(81km)

The island can be covered by car in a single day, but this does not allow time for excursions from points on the route. An ideal itinerary would include a night at Vasiliki.

Leave Levkas town by road s/p 'Vasiliki' (see map). In 1.5km, a church with a belfry close to the road and an adjoining rock face carved with niches for votive offerings indicate a sacred spot. This is the site of the spring which supplied the ancient town of *Leucas* (*Nerikos*) and today supplies the modern capital. On the bend 800km further on, running down the hillside, is a line of polygonal walling. This belongs to the ancient town founded by the Corinthians, a well-preserved perimeter wall that can be followed to the summit of the hill. Further up, a tower with superimposed square-cut Hellenistic blocks and rougher Byzantine masonry shows the

continuing improvement of the city's defences in later periods.
In 2km is the left turn for the Alikes Saltworks (a further 1km).

> *Diversion 1:* **Alikes** From the salt pans, which resemble a sunken village with the salt mounds covered by their tiled roofs, there is a view across the channel between Levkas and the mainland. In the middle of this channel is the small island of *Alexandros*, formed by the dredging of the canal, on which stands a Russian *fort*. Named after Tsar Alexander, this is a rare monument to the Russian protectorate of the Ionians during the Napoleonic Wars. Further S, on the promontory guarding the S entrance to the channel, is the medieval *Castle of Ayios Yeoryios*, at one time occupied by Ali Pasha, who coveted Levkas but never won it.

Returning to the main road, a pleasant coastal route leads to **Nidri** (13km) the island's most popular resort. Its setting is certainly unique: on the inlet to the tranquil Bay of Vlikho, and faced by a number of thickly-wooded islets. Its interest, however, is in more than just the surroundings, for it was here that Wilhelm Dörpfeld carried out excavations to prove his theory that Levkas was the ancient Ithaca and that Nidri was the site of Odysseus' city. He found Bronze Age remains here, but the topography argues against the site. In the time of Odysseus, Levkas was still attached to the mainland and there was no channel to the N. In addition, Levkas' proximity to the mainland made it ill-placed for the command of the Ionian Sea and the shipping routes to the W of the island on which Odysseus' pirate vessels preyed. However, Levkadians will argue to the contrary and Dörpfeld is an honoured name here. (His tomb lies on the point of the curving E arm of the bay and may be visited by following the road from Vlikho, s/p 'Desimi-Geni', and keeping left.) Nidri's long shingle beach, N of the harbour, is ideal for bathing, but the calm sea here, protected by the inlet, is particularly suitable for water sports.
In high season ferries run from Nidri to Ithaca and Cefalonia, and there is a continuous service to the nearby island of Meganisi.
Two of the islets facing Nidri were the homes of famous, if very different, men. On *Madouri*, the nearest, stands the Italianate villa of the poet A. Valaoritis (1824–79) whose work celebrated the Greek national struggle. *Skorpios*, the furthest, is the resting place of Aristotle Onassis (1906–75), who bought the island in the '60s and

married Jackie Kennedy here. Further S is the larger island of *Meganisi*, which can be reached by caique from Nidri. There are sea caves here, and good swimming and fishing. Rooms are available, and tranquillity ensured by the lack of development.

The *Bay of Vlikho*, which is almost landlocked, is a perfect haven for small boats. Its village, Vlikho, specialises in building them. For an overall view of the bay and islets and the fertile plain of Nidri, take the road up to *Neokhori* (5km SW of Nidri). At *Vlikho*, 3.5km S of Nidri, the left turn mentioned above ('Desimi-Geni') leads (turn right after 1km) to a shingle beach and camp-site.

8km S of Nidri is a left turn for *Poros* (3km).

> *Diversion 2:* **Poros** The village is built on a hillside overlooking Rouda Bay to the S. A fragment of a Hellenistic *tower*, surviving to a height of 5m in a nearby field is worth mentioning if only because of the lack of ancient sites in the island. To reach it, walk for 10 min beyond the church at the highest point of the village. Below the village on *Rouda Bay* – a 4km descent—is Poros' double beach (*Mikro Yialos* and *Aspro Yialos*) with a camp site and bungalows.

From the Poros junction, continue 2km to the next turn, s/p 'Sivros'.

> *Diversion 3:* **Ayios Ilias** This diversion offers a view of the S of the island from the highest accessible point and can be used as an alternative inland route to Vasiliki. (The coastal route is 11.5km; the inland route, excluding diversions, is 13.5km.)

After 4km on the Sivros Road there is a turning left to *Ayios Ioannis sto Rodaki*. A rough road leads in 3km to this monastery church, built on the foundations of a Doric temple. The dedication and original size of the temple are a mystery, but much of the ancient building may be discovered, incorporated in the interior and exterior of the church. The church has 17th and 18th c. frescoes.

At *Sivros*, in 1.5km, a turning by the school at the E end of the village leads in 6km to *Ayios Ilias*, the highest village in the island, which is overshadowed by the Stavrotas range (summit 1158m) to the N. Stop anywhere on the way up for the view across the Ionian Sea to Ithaca, Cefalonia and Zakinthos. The road from Sivros back to the main road (7km) is rough in places but quite driveable.

4km after the Sivros turn is another point of access to the S coast, s/p 'Sivota' (3km).

There is no beach here, but a clue to the charms of *Sivota*, tucked into its deeply indented bay, lies in the number of pleasure craft and fishing boats which vie for space in the harbour. The tavernas lining the bay offer a variety of excellent fish.

1.5km after the Sivota turn the s/p to Evgiros (2km) mentions 'The Cave of Odysseus'. The cave (real name *Khirospilia*) where Dörpfeld found late Neolithic relics to support his 'Ithacan' theory, is not however worth a diversion. 2km further on a rough road leads in 5km to *Cape Kastri* (camp site).

A descent of 5km, with fine inland views, terminates at **Vasiliki**. This seaside village is the most attractive in the island, set in the corner of a wide bay edging a beautiful fertile plain, with the barren grey backdrop of the Stavrotas. The colours of the fishing boats filling the harbour vie with those of the typically Levkadian houses with their brightly painted upper storeys. Though somewhat isolated, this is becoming a popular alternative resort to Nidri, with development along the bay to the W. The inter-island ferry to Cefalonia, which docks here, has also created some excursion traffic for the port. Like Nidri, the sheltered harbour is ideal for water sports, and there is a 3km stretch of sand and shingle beach at the head of the bay.

From Vasiliki the road turns up the E flank of the Levkatas peninsula, with marvellous views to the E of the Vasiliki plain. The road winds 12km to the turn for *Komilio* (1km) where commences the major excursion from the circular route.

> *Diversion 4:* **Cape Dukato** The return trip to the cape from Komilio is 40km (allow 4hrs), negotiating difficult terrain to the S tip of the island. After *Athani* (6km) the road is unmade, continuing to the cape past two beautiful beaches (*Egremni* and *Porto Katsiki*) accessible only by climbing down from the cliffs (for those who wish to 'cut a corner' there are boat excursions to these beaches from Vasiliki).
>
> Cape Dukato is the Venetian name for the White Rock (Levkas Petra) from which the island takes its name, and which Homer mentions in the *Odyssey*. The end of the cape is marked by a lighthouse and the dramatic cliff view known as 'Sappho's Leap'.
>
> It was from this point that a strange ritual was carried out by the ancient Levkadians, initiated, it is said, by Sappho to purge herself of an un-

Vlikho Bay

requited love. The ritual, performed annually in honour of the god Apollo, involved an enforced plunge from the cliff by a criminal. This was not an execution, more an involuntary exile; the victim having birds and wings attached to him to arrest his flight and boatmen waiting below to pick him up and row him to another shore. In this way the community was able to expiate its sins for another year.

Apart from the cliff there is little to see here, but it was thought that stones found in the vicinity of the lighthouse could belong to a temple of Apollo.

From the Komilio turn the route to the N continues 2km to *Khortata* and thence 3km on a barren mountainous route with superb coastal views to the junction for *Kalamitsi*.

Diversion 5: **Kalamitsi** The winding 5km descent to this village, tucked into the flank of Meganoros, is rewarded by a glimpse of the old Levkas, where women—many wearing traditional costume—weave blankets on their looms. A rough road drops down from the village and diverges to the series of rock-strewn, white sand beaches which are among the finest in the island. From Kalamitsi there is a rough road to Ayios Nikitas (see p. 107) which will eventually link the village to the coastal route N to Levkas town.

From the Kalamitsi turn, the main road follows a winding loop around the N spur of Meganoros to the junction at *Frias* (13km).

Diversion 6: **Karia and N peaks** Turn right for *Karia* (3km). This is Levkas' largest inland village, beautifully located on the slopes below the twin peaks of *Meganoros* and *Ayios Ilias*. The village is renowned for its needlework, which is sold throughout Greece and abroad: unfortunately the embroiderers are now elderly and the craft may soon die out.

At the entrance to the village a road s/p 'Levkas Air Station' goes right and climbs the vine-terraced mountainside 8km to the telecommunications station below the summit of the first peak: the second peak is reached in a further 1.5km where, beyond a second station, the surfaced road ends and becomes a rough road by which there is an alternative descent to Karia (11km). The views from the vantage points on this route are superb: taking in Levkas town, the lagoon, the protective arm of the Yiro, the flat coast of Akarnania and the distant mountain ranges.

From the Frias junction it is 12km back to Levkas town. After 9km, look out for the ruined monastery church of the *Panayia Odiyitria* below the road on the left. Founded in 1450, this is the only surviving Byzantine building in the island, an example of the High Paleologian architecture that prevailed in the area under Byzantine influence before the Turkish occupation. The cross-in-square is replaced by the long-naved basilican plan, similar to the churches in S Italy. The Renaissance influence is also seen in the apse frescoes (apply for entrance to the Archaeological Museum in Levkas).

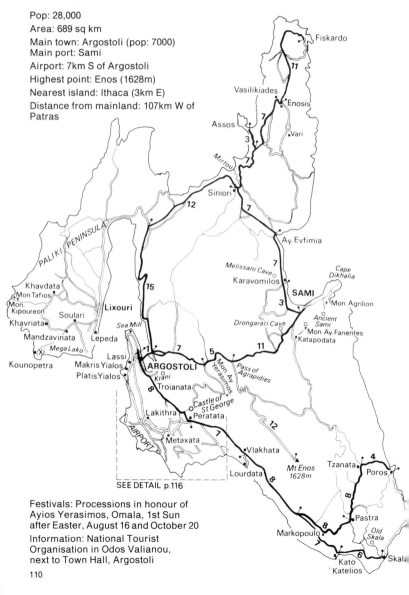

Cefalonia

(Kefallinia)

Pop: 28,000
Area: 689 sq km
Main town: Argostoli (pop: 7000)
Main port: Sami
Airport: 7km S of Argostoli
Highest point: Enos (1628m)
Nearest island: Ithaca (3km E)
Distance from mainland: 107km W of
Patras

Fiskardo

11

Vasilikiades

Enosis

7

Assos

3

Vari

7

Mirtou

12

Siniori

7

Ay. Evfimia

7

Melissani Cave

Cape
Dikhalia

Karavomilos

SAMI

PALIKI PENINSULA

3

Mon Agrilion

Khavdata

Mon.Tafios

15

Drongarati Cave

Ancient
Sami

Mon.
Kipoureon

Soulari

Lixouri

Mon. Ay. Fanentes

Katapodata

Khavriata

Sea Mill

Mandzavinata

Lepeda

Mega Lako

Lassi

1

7

5

11

Kounopetra

Makris Yialos

ARGOSTOLI

Platis Yialos

Krani

8

Mon. Ay.
Yerasimos

Pass of
Agrapidies

Troianata

Lakithra

Castle of
St George

Peratata

12

Metaxata

7

4

Vlakhata

Tzanata

Poros

Mt Enos
1628m

8

AIRPORT

Lourdata

8

SEE DETAIL p.116

Pastra

Markopoulo

8

Old
Skala

7

6

Kato
Katelios

Skala

Festivals: Processions in honour of
Ayios Yerasimos, Omala, 1st Sun
after Easter, August 16 and October 20

Information: National Tourist
Organisation in Odos Valianou,
next to Town Hall, Argostoli

110

Travel to Cefalonia

By air
Direct charter flights from London and
Manchester
Flights from Athens to Cefalonia by
Olympic Airways, Jun–Sep daily, twice
weekly rest of year

By sea
Car ferry

From Brindisi to Sami (*Ionis*)
Alternate days Jun–mid Sep, weekly
service in winter (14¾hrs)

From Patras to Sami
Daily (4hrs)
Also *Ionis* on the route Patras–
Cefalonia–Ithaca–Paxos–Corfu–Brindisi.
Alternate days Jun–mid Sep, weekly
winter service

**From Astakos (mainland) via Ithaca to
Ayia Evfimia**
Daily (3½hrs)

From Ithaca
See From Astakos, above (Ithaca to Ayia
Evfimia 1¾hrs)

From Levkas to Fiskardo and Sami
Daily from Nidri (Fiskardo only, 2 hrs) and
Vasiliki (Fiskardo 1½hrs)

From Killini (Peloponnese) to Poros
Twice daily (1¾hrs)

From Killini (Peloponnese) to Argostoli
Twice daily (3hrs)

Note: Inter-island routes are subject to
variation or curtailment out of season.

By land
By car from Athens via Corinth to Patras
(222km) then car ferry. By bus from
Athens (daily, 9hrs) via Corinth, Patras
and ferry link to Sami or via Corinth,
Patras, Killini and ferry link to Poros. By
train from Athens to Patras, several times
daily (5hrs) then car ferry.

Travel in Cefalonia Buses run from Sami
to Argostoli at least four times daily and
from Argostoli at least once daily to the
larger villages. In the summer there is a
service from Argostoli to the beaches of
Platis and Makris Yialos. A local car ferry
service runs from Argostoli-Lixouri and
return, up to 12 times daily. Taxis may
be hired at Sami and in the main square
of Argostoli, and car and scooter hire is
available in Argostoli, Skala and Poros.

Accommodation Hotels (see p. 28), villas
apartments and private rooms are
available in the towns and main resorts,
and camping at Sami and Argostoli
(Fanari).

Restaurants In Argostoli most restaurants
and tavernas are located around the
main square (Plat. Valianou) and on the

Mirtou

waterfront. There are also modest eating
places in Sami and Lixouri. Lassi, and
the resort area S of Argostoli, is well
provided with tavernas, and the seaside
places and resorts of Ayios Thomas,
Lourdata, Katelios, Skala, Poros, Assos
and Fiskardo have restaurants or
tavernas open in the summer.

Beaches What Cefalonia's beaches lack
in quantity they make up for in quality.
Near Argostoli are the attractive and
adjoining sand beaches of *Lassi, Platis
Yialos* and *Makris Yialos* (1–3km S). On
the NW coast the bay of *Mirtou* (28km N
of Argostoli) is particularly fine, also the
beaches on either side of the Assos
peninsula further N. Accessible beaches
on the S coast are at *Ayios Thomas,
Lourdata, Katelios* and *Skala* (12, 17.5,
30 and 36km from Argostoli). Beaches on
the E coast are at *Sami, Karavomilos*
(27km from Argostoli) and *Poros* (43km).
In the Paliki peninsula there are good
beaches at *Lepeda* and *Xi* (Kounopetra).

Museums and monuments

Argostoli

Archaeological Museum (p. 115)
Daily 08.00–14.00. Closed Thurs

Koryalenios Library & Museum (p. 115)
Daily 09.00–13.00, 17.30–20.30

S of Argostoli

Castle of St George (Ayios Yeoryios) (p.
116)
Daily 08.45–15.00, Sun 09.30–14.30.
Closed Tues

Lixouri

Iacovatos Museum (p. 121)
Daily 08.00–14.00

The largest and most sparsely populated of the Ionians is dominated by its spinal massif, whose peak is the highest point of the island group. In relation to its size it is also the least visited by tourists—a contradiction to the attractions of a number of fine beaches and pleasant excursions, and the remarkable lake-caves of Sami.

History In the Homeric Age the people of the Ionian islands which constituted Odysseus' kingdom were known as 'Cephallenians'. The place of Cefalonia itself in the *Odyssey* has been determined by the association of two city states with the island. First of these, *Same* or *Sami*, was the most important of the four ancient cities of the island, captured from the Greeks by the Romans in 189BC: traditionally, it was the name by which the whole island was once known. The second city, *Dulichium*, is more problematical. In Homer's *Iliad* Dulichium is credited with supplying 'forty black ships' to the Trojan expedition, in contrast to the 12 ships supplied jointly by Ithaca, Zakinthos and Sami. This would suggest that Dulichium was the largest and most resourceful of the states in Odysseus' kingdom: a strong argument for its identification with Cefalonia.

Archaeology has not as yet supplied any answers to the question of Dulichium's location, or of the association of the whole island with the *Odyssey*. Mesolithic finds have, however, established a tradition of settlement for Cefalonia that can be related to the fertility and great natural resources of the island, a tradition continued into the Bronze Age.

Evidence of Mycenaean occupation (rock-cut tombs at Mazarakata and elsewhere) is stronger here than in the other Ionians, and it is apparent that Cefalonia's position on the sea routes to southern Italy and Sicily

from the western Peloponnese encouraged trade with the Mycenaean world, and settlement by its refugees after the Dorian invasions. It has also been suggested that the Achaean immigration might have brought with it the ancestors of Odysseus— and another possible location for Homeric Ithaca.

Colonisation of the island after the Dark Ages remains a mystery, although the Corinthians who colonised Corfu and Ithaca are assumed also to have settled here, c. 9th–8th c. BC. Known in ancient times as 'Tetrapolis', the island had four major cities—*Sami*, *Krani*, *Pali* and *Proni* which were independent states, sometimes united and sometimes divided. Under threat from Philip V of Macedon in 218BC they joined forces to repel him: a similar occupation by the Romans in 189BC was resisted only by Sami, which submitted after a long siege.

Under the Romans the island was an imperial backwater, becoming at one time the private estate of a Roman senator and at another time the gift of the Emperor Hadrian to the city of Athens, which he greatly admired. Although accorded the status of a *theme* (major administrative district) of the Byzantine empire, the island fared no better in this period, exposed to the continuing ravages of pirates and sea-going adventurers.

In 1082 the island was seized by the Normans, whose leader, Robert Guiscard, died here in 1085. In 1194, after intermittent Norman rule, it was handed over to the Orsini family, vassals of the Sicilian king. Later Latin rulers were the Tocco family.

In 1479 the Turks occupied Cefalonia, but by 1500 had lost it to the Venetians, who captured the Castle of St George and slaughtered the Turkish garrison. Turkish revenge came in 1537 withen their forces raided the island and carried off 13,000 of its inhabitants into slavery. The Venetians ruled the

Argostoli

island until the French occupation (1797).

Under the subsequent British Protectorate (1809–64) Cefalonia was in the vanguard of the struggle for liberation and union with independent Greece. Two insurrections (1848–9) were put down by British troops, and in 1858 Gladstone came here on his abortive peace mission. A benevolent British Resident, Col Charles Napier (1822–30) carried out many important public works, including the construction of the quay at Argostoli. During his residency the island was visited by Lord Byron, who at his house in Metaxata received delegates from the Greek factions engaged in the independence struggle prior to his departure for the mainland.

In 1943, after Italy's armistice with the Allies, the Italian forces occupying Cefalonia refused to surrender to the Germans. The ensuing battle for the island resulted in the massacre of 5000 Italian soldiers. Much of the island was destroyed in the 1953 earthquake.

The island Straddling the entrance to the Gulf of Corinth between Zakinthos and Ithaca, Cefalonia is the dominant island of the Ionian group, with the greatest area and the highest mountain. It has, however, only three small population centres—Sami, Lixouri and the capital Argostoli, and a number of minor villages mostly located in the cultivated areas on the south coast, the Paliki peninsula, and in the valleys on the north-east and south-east coasts. Much of the rest of the island is wild and mountainous, rising to the peak of *Mt Enos* (1628m). The slopes of this mountain, the dominant feature of the south of the island, are forested with the native fur (*abies Cephalonensis*) a traditional source of timber for ship-building through the centuries from the Bronze Age to the Venetians. It was from these dense and dark pines, now reduced to a sparse coverage of the peak, that Enos earned its popular name, the 'Black Mountain'.

The fertility of the south of the island —the result of the precipitation of rainfall on Mt Enos—has produced the mainstay of the island's economy —market gardens, vineyards and currant growing. The most successful local wine, *Robolla*, is produced on the drier west slopes of Enos.

Since the war, and as a result of the earthquake, there has been a progressive decline in the island's population. This has only been partially arrested by tourist development, mainly concentrated on the south-west coast. The small number of beaches has made tourism a limited objective, but the island offers many other physical attractions which make it ideal for the holidaymaker with an explorer's instinct.

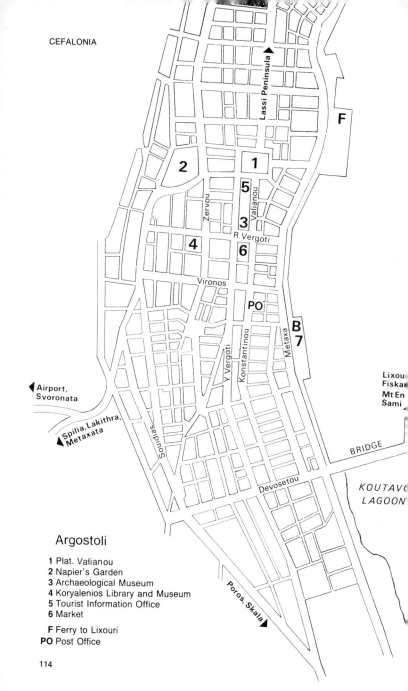

CEFALONIA

Lassi Peninsula

F

2

1

5

Zervou

Valianou

3

R. Vergoti

4

6

Vironos

PO

B

7

Y. Vergoti

Konstantinou

Metaxa

Airport,
Svoronata

Spilia, Lakithra,
Metaxata

Souidias

Lixou
Fiska
Mt En
Sami

BRIDGE

Devosetou

KOUTAVO
LAGOON

Poros, Skala

Argostoli

1 Plat. Valianou
2 Napier's Garden
3 Archaeological Museum
4 Koryalenios Library and Museum
5 Tourist Information Office
6 Market

F Ferry to Lixouri
PO Post Office

Argostoli

The capital of Cefalonia is situated on a small peg of land on the W side of the island, looking out over a shallow lagoon (Koutavas Lagoon). The 'peg'—the Lassi peninsula—juts into the Gulf of Argostoli, the inlet which lies between Argostoli and the opposite coastline of the Pali peninsula. As a result of this unusual location the small harbour has the oddity of facing inland, with its back to the sea.

The town was originally the port of the old Venetian capital of the island, San Giorgio (Ayios Yeoryios) and took over as capital when the hill fortress was abandoned in 1757. Seat of an archbishop, Argostoli was rebuilt after the 1953 earthquake, largely with one-storey buildings of reinforced concrete. Now that even the shades of Venice have departed there is probably insufficient 'ambience' here to compel a visit of more than a few days—but as the focus for the island's bus services, the town is the best base for excursions.

To the W of the Leoforos Yeoryiou Vergoti, which runs S from the central Plateia Valianou, a record of the pre-earthquake town can be found in the **Koryalenios Library and Museum**, a private bequest which combines a wide-ranging collection of books and manuscripts (including the papers of Col Napier) with an excellent 19th c. historical and folk collection. The museum also houses the archives of the Venetian occupation (1500–1797). Other features are a reconstructed elaborately carved iconostasis from a church destroyed in the earthquake, and an exhibition of photographs of the pre-earthquake town.

Nearby, on Vergoti, the **Archaeological Museum** contains prehistoric finds from numerous sites (Early Helladic, Late Helladic and Mycenaean). The latter period is represented by pottery, jewellery and weapons from the tombs at Mazarakata, Lakithra, Diakata and other sites. Finds from the Archaic to Roman periods include coins from the 'Four Cities', and a fine bronze *portrait head* (3rd c. AD) from Sami. There is also a selection of terracotta votive offerings from the Sanctuary of Pan in the Cave of Melissani, one of which is a circular tablet depicting nymphs dancing around a flute-playing Pan.

To the W of Plat. Valianou lies an attractive *public garden* dedicated to Colonel—later General Sir—Charles Napier (1782–1853), the British Resident of Cefalonia, who in later life achieved distinction in the Indian campaigns as the conqueror of Sind. Although he never returned to the island, Napier greatly cherished the memory of his years here.

Sea mill, Lassi peninsula

Lassi Peninsula A pleasant walk or drive may be made around Argostoli's small peninsula, following the coast road between the pinewoods and the sea. After 2.5km, at the point, is an old *sea mill*, erected by the British in the 19th c. above an underground flow of sea water which was sufficient to power the mill. The mystery as to where the sea water flowed was solved by Austrian scientists, who poured in a yellow dye and observed the tinted water emerge at the Cave of Melissani on the far side of the island—after flowing 16km under the central mountain range. In a further 500m is an attractive *lighthouse*, built in the form of a Doric rotunda c. 1820 and rebuilt after the earthquake. It is the only surviving building of the British period in the island. From the lighthouse the road continues 4km back to Argostoli.

Koutavas Lagoon and ancient Krani The lagoon to the S of Argostoli is separated from the sea by a causeway and a *bridge* 700m long, the latter built by the British in 1813 (commemorative obelisk at centre). The shore of the lagoon, shaded by pine and eucalyptus, offers a pleasant walk. Halfway round, an old spring house and a modern waterworks provide a marker for the site of *Krani*, one of the four ancient cities of the island. Founded (it is assumed by the Corinthians) in the 6th c. BC, Krani's walls extended 5km over the two hills and connecting ridge to the S and E of the lagoon (the ancient harbour). The spring would have supplied the city with its water, in the same way that it now supplies Argostoli. Access to the *city walls* is impracticable at this point, as the area is thickly overgrown. The more accessible NE section can be reached from the road to Sami (see p. 121).

Excursions from Argostoli

South: Short Excursion

Argostoli–Lakithra—Metaxata–Castle of St George–Kourkoumelata–Svoronata–Argostoli (30km)

This excursion is ideal for short-stay visitors to Argostoli and can include an afternoon on the beach at Platis or Makris Yialos.

Leave Argostoli by the route s/p 'Spilia' (see map). This is the central of the three roads which run S from Argostoli, a pleasant elevated route with striking views of the plain of Argostoli which in 6km reaches *Lakithra*. Here the entrance to the village is dominated by the sign 'Byron's Rocks', a reminder of the poet's sojourn in the island. A path ascends to a small white chapel, beside which some flat grey rocks offer a panoramic view over the sea and S coastline. This was a favourite retreat of Byron, whose debt to the landscape of Greece is recorded in an inscription here. (The present view of the runway of Cefalonia's airport might prove less inspirational.)

In 2km take the right turn at the crossroads s/p 'Kourkoumelata'. This is the entrance to the village of *Metaxata*, and shortly on the right (*plaque*) is the site of the house where Byron stayed from August to December 1823, awaiting news from Greece before his fateful departure for Missolonghi. The house itself was destroyed in the 1953 earthquake.

A 1km circuit is made to rejoin the main road (turn right). In 1km a rough road joins the main road opposite the junction (s/p 'Pesada'). Turn left up this for 300m. Within a fenced enclosure on the right are the rock-cut tombs of *Mazarakata*. These

chambers, approached by narrow *dromoi*, contain rows of rock-cut graves. They were dated from the pottery recovered from them as Late Mycenaean (12th c. BC).

Returning to the main road, turn left and continue 1km to the T-junction at *Travliata*. Turn left and then right at the s/p 'Kastro'. A 2km climb reaches the gate of the **Castle of St George**. This, the best-preserved castle in the Ionian Is., stands on a conical hill (322m) originally fortified in the Byzantine period but more substantially by the Orsini in the 13th c. At this time the castle, and its surrounding houses and churches, comprised the island's capital, Argostoli being only an insignificant port. The Venetians strengthened the castle after their capture of the island in 1500, and at its height the citadel had a population of 15,000. After an earthquake had destroyed the town (1636) it was eventually abandoned for Argostoli. The castle was maintained, however, until the time of the British Protectorate (Private Wheeler mentions a garrison here in 1824).

A caretaker will escort visitors round the castle. Within the walls, the buildings present a ruinous sight. The central keep, the site of the original Byzantine stronghold, is now an enclosure for a forest of trees; the Latin cathedral below it a shell. The *powder magazine* with its double chamber on the S range is, however, well preserved, and there is an impressive *cistern* nearby with two openings, 35m long. (Note the escutcheons of the Orsini, and Venetian commanders, in various places.)

It is the walls and bastions themselves which hold the castle's secrets. Within the bastion guarding the main gate are the *dungeons*, deep caverns of darkness whose lamp niches mark the only source of light. From the NW corner of the castle a *tunnel* (now blocked) ran an incredible 8km to the Koutavas Lagoon at Argostoli. A secret escape route since the Middle Ages, this was last used in 1943 when a group of Italian soldiers, trapped in the castle by German troops, were led out through the tunnel by local people. (The guide will show visitors the entrance.)

The exterior of the towers, with their elaborate corbelling, is particularly fine. The views from the castle walls embrace Mt Enos to the E, the island of Zakinthos to the S, Argostoli to the N and beyond the inland bay and Paliki peninsula.

Below the castle, in the village called simply *Kastro* which has replaced the old capital, stands an attractive *church* fronted by a quaintly-carved belfry arch. This Venetian-built church has survived both the 17th-c. earthquake and that of 1953 and contains icons by Karantinos (*c.* 1660–1740).

Entrance, Castle of St George

South: Long Excursion
Argostoli–Poros–Argostoli (86km, with diversion to Skala 112km)

Attractive route beneath the forested slopes of Mt Enos, through cultivated terrain, with diversion to the sea at Katelios, and to the pine trees and sandy shores of Skala, and on to the small resort of Poros through the Vale of Arakli.

Leaving Argostoli by the route s/p 'Poros, Skala' (see map) the road passes beneath the Castle of St George (see *Short Excursion*, above) and reaches the village of *Peratata* (8km). Here the *Convent of Áyios Andreas*, rebuilt after the earthquake, contains reclaimed 12th c. *wall paintings*. At *Vlakhata*, 7km from Peratata, a road on the right to *Lourdata* runs down to a sandy beach (2.5km) fringed by allotments (cafébar open in summer). The road continues 8km to the Skala junction.

Diversion: **Skala** A right fork takes the road through the plain of Katelios, a corn-growing area, and a shaded coastal route to *Katelios* (7km) with its beach and taverna. In the following 6km stretch to Skala the soil becomes sandier and the olive gives way to pine. **Skala** is a quiet 'end of the road' place, built since the earthquake (it is also known as Nea Skala), which is popular with the islanders as a cool picnic spot and a holiday retreat by the sea. It has a greater range of sandy beaches than elsewhere in the island and as a result is now on the tourist map, though its remoteness should inhibit any uncontrolled development.
In a shady hollow to the immediate S of the *Skala Hotel* (ask in reception for a guide with a key) is a modest heirloom of the Roman period: a *Villa* (late 2nd c. AD) with two **mosaic floors**. Between illusionistic mosaics in the central room is one of a man being attacked by a lion, a tiger, a puma and a leopard, with an inscription below, pointing out the fate of the envious, signed by the artist Krateros. In another room is a scene from the Odyssey where Teiresias tells Odysseus to make a sacrifice of a ram, a bull and a boar to Poseidon. (The subject of this mosaic has stimulated local speculation that the villa might have occupied the site of Odysseus' palace: yet another claim to the legendary association.)
Two short detours from Skala are worth mentioning:
1) An unmade road to the NW of Skala leads in 4km to the *old village*, built by the Venetians and destroyed by the

For those interested in the island's wine industry, a road runs down the N side of the hill and on by a right turn to *Troianata* (4km), one of the five villages with a winery (open to visitors on application). The local vineyards produce the famous *Robolla*, one of the best wines of Greece.

Returning from the Kastro down to Travliata, the junction of the short and long excursions is reached. For the short excursion, go back to the *Kourkoumelata* junction and turn left for the village. This modern development, looking like a lush Californian estate, was built by a Greek shipowner to replace the village destroyed in the earthquake.
Immediately below Kourkoumelata is *Kalligata*, where the Kalliga winery produces *Robolla* and the other Cefalonian labels. The village has a Baroque-style *church* (1804) with an unusual silver *throne*. This is one of a number of old churches in the SW corner of the island to have survived, at least partially, the 1953 earthquake and is now restored. Others are at Domata and Svoronata, which follow.
The church at *Domata* guards a revered relic of the War of Independence: the coffin of the Patriarch Gregorios, the Orthodox Church leader who was hanged by the Turks in Constantinople at the time of the Greek uprising (1821). The coffin carrying the Patriarch's remains (which were subsequently buried at Odessa) was found floating on the waters of the Bosphorus by a Cefalonian ship and brought back to the island. Over the entrance to the church is a carved marble slab depicting the ship, which was owned by the village. The church at *Svoronata* (late 18th c.) is dedicated to St Nicholas, protector of seamen, and has a fine iconostasis.
The road runs back to Argostoli via the attractive sand beaches of *Platis Yialos* (owned by the White Rocks Hotel) and *Makris Yialos*.

earthquake. In the midst of olive trees, the ruins present a compelling if desolate spectacle. Beyond the ruins the unmade road forks left 4km to Pastra on the Poros road, a useful short cut for sturdy vehicles to save the 13km journey from Skala back to the junction.

2) A track which leads along the coastline from Skala to Poros reaches in 2km the remains of a 6th c. BC Doric *temple* with a nearby Venetian *chapel* which incorporates some of its columns (an Archaic capital from one of these columns may be seen in the Archaeological Museum in Argostoli).

Continuing on the main road from the Skala junction the village of *Markopoulo* (4km) is reached. This village is famous for an unusual phenomenon. Each year during the Feast of the Assumption (Aug 15) the village church is invaded by dozens of small snakes whose heads are marked with black crosses. At this time of the year the snakes, which are in the middle of their mating and egg-laying, are probably drawn out of their nests by the noise of the festivities, but the villagers, who believe they have miraculous powers, put a more divine interpretation on their appearance. The snakes are quite harmless and are reverently handled and caressed by the villagers.

In a further 4km the village of *Pastra* is reached, with fine views over the plain of Katelios. 1.5km from Pastra, beyond *Ayios Yeoryios*, the road descends rapidly to the fertile *Vale of Arakli*, enclosed by mountains. The terracing of the slopes is a legacy of the intensive farming carried out here during Napier's time when a colony of Maltese farmers was established in this part of the island. From *Tzanata* 6.5km further on, an unmade road branches left at the start of a route of 22.5km to Sami.

Approaching **Poros** (4km) the road is filtered through a narrow gorge at the end of the valley, a dramatic entry to this small but growing resort. A good pebble beach lies to the N, across the river; to the S is the jetty for ferry services to Killini in the Peloponnese.

In the hills to the S towards Pastra (about an hour's walk) lies the double acropolis of ancient *Proni*: apart from some polygonal walls there is little to see.

A return to Argostoli by the same route is recommended.

North and Centre
Argostoli–Assos–Fiskardo–Sami–Argostoli (125km)

This excursion to the extreme N of the island, returning via the port of Sami, offers the full variety of the island's mountain scenery, including the dramatic coastal stretch leading up to Assos and the winding, humpback journey over the central massif back to Argostoli. To allow a more leisurely enjoyment of the beaches (Mirtou, Assos) and the charms of Fiskardo, a night is recommended there: this would also permit a more relaxed exploration of ancient Sami and the lake-caves the next day. With short stops, however, the whole journey can be done comfortably in a day.

Leave Argostoli by the bridge, and then turn left for Fiskardo. (Before the turn is the *British Cemetery*, with its headstones commemorating the soldiers who died—most often of fever—serving the Protectorate.) For 15km the Gulf of Argostoli is followed to its N limit, where the road to Lixouri (see p. 121) branches left. In a further 4km (*Agonas*) the neck of the Paliki peninsula is crossed and the road runs precipitously along the E cliffs of the Gulf of Mirtou.

At *Siniori*, 8km further on, the junction with the road to Sami, there is a rough road (2km) down to the crescent-shaped *Mirtou Beach*, of white pebble and sand. The view of this beach, from a height of 330m, is stupendous. The route to Assos maintains the spectacle, the road a sinuous ledge above the corrugated cliffs. The peninsula of **Assos** comes into view, a fortress-crowned rock connected to the island by a slim hook of land. The branch road to it, 7km from Siniori, descends 3km through a curtain of cypress, levelling at the crook of the causeway where the village lies, tucked into the cliffside.

A rough road climbs steeply 2.5km to the *fortress*, whose circuit wall extends around the summit of the peninsula. Built by the Venetians in 1593, it served to guard the W approaches to the island, also the two small harbours on either side of the peninsula. Its vaulted entrance, with the subtly curved passage, is an excellent example of Venetian stonework. The interior of the castle, once cultivated by an agricultural community whose derelict houses may be seen, is now wildly overgrown.

At *Enosis*, 7km N of the Assos turnoff, a diversion may be made via Playia to *Vari* (6km) where the island's only complete surviving building of the Byzantine period may be found. This is the chapel of the *Panayia Kouyanna*, with wall-paintings of the 15th c.

The road continues through rich farming country, on a high plateau, and then descends through forest to **Fiskardo**, a total of 53km from Argostoli. This little port on Cefalonia's N coast has an immediate appeal, largely because it escaped the worst of the earthquake and retains its attractive, 19th c. character. The old houses not only survive but are well-kept, their walls freshly whitewashed and their woodwork painted in bright colours. On the point to the N of the harbour, below the modern lighthouse, is an interesting survival: a round *beacon tower*, possibly one of the lighthouses built by Napier.

Fiskardo owes its name to Robert de Hauteville, nicknamed Guiscard or 'weasel', a member of the family of Norman adventurers whose campaigns against the Byzantine empire in the 11th c. brought them regularly into the Adriatic and Ionian Seas. It was on such a campaign that Guiscard contracted the plague and died here, in 1085.

This is a popular port of call for yachts, and the car ferry from Levkas puts in here. There are rooms to let and several fish tavernas: the speciality lobster.

Returning to the Siniori junction (25km), take the Sami road. A fast drive through a valley route 7km to the small port of *Ayia Evfimia* continues S down the W coast of the Gulf of Sami.

In 7km a sign indicates the 'lake-cave' of **Melissani**, 150m to the right. This is one of Cefalonia's great natural wonders: an underground pool supplied by sea water from the *other side* of the island. The water, which rushes underground at Argostoli, powering the sea mill at the top of the Lassi peninsula, emerges again here, its saltiness somewhat reduced. This phenomenon was revealed in the '60s by researchers from an Austrian university, who used a yellow dye, poured into the water at Argostoli, to demonstrate the remarkable underground flow.

Interest in the cave was enhanced by the discovery here of clay votive tablets and figurines of the Hellenistic period. Depicting nymphs and the god Pan, these votive objects (now in the Argostoli Museum) showed that the cave was in ancient times a Sanctuary of Pan. Now the cave is a popular tourist attraction, and a rock tunnel has been cut down to it (admission fee). The cavern is open to the sky and the luminosity and beauty of the water is stunning. For an additional fee a boatman will take visitors around the pool and into a stalactite cave—a haunting experience.

Immediately to the S, in the village of *Karavomilos*, is a seaside pool, fed by the cave of Melissani. The restaurant here is a popular summer venue for the Samiots.

Fiskardo

In 3km the bay is rounded to **Sami**, the island's principal port. This town was almost totally destroyed by the earthquake in 1953 and rebuilt in reinforced concrete to a uniform pattern, but although the architecture is impersonal the place is intermittently lively when the ferries for Patras or Brindisi dock here. (It must have been even livelier in 1571, when the Christian fleet of Don John of Austria assembled in the bay before the Battle of Lepanto.) There are a number of waterfront tavernas, modest hotels and rooms to let. For those who are spending a few hours here there are a number of short excursions. These are:

Melissani Cave (3km, see above)

Drongarati Cave (3.5km, see below)

Ancient Sami (see below)

Ancient Sami (climb, 2hrs) Behind Sami rises a double hill, the lower summit towards the town known as *Ayia Fanentes*, the upper as *Paleokastro*. These two hills were the site of the flourishing capital city of Cefalonia in the 5th c. BC: the acropolis on the higher (N) and a connected fortress on the lower (S). The only one of the island's four cities to resist the Romans, Sami paid the price with its destruction after a four-month siege. The city later revived under the Romans but fell into decline after the 3rd c. AD.

Two relics of the Roman period may be seen in the area. From the wide Plat. Kyprou, where the Argostoli road runs into the harbour, a side road leads uphill off Leof. Anglias to a Roman *bath* with walls to a height of 5m. 300m along the Argostoli road (to the left) is a Roman *chamber tomb*. The approach to the ancient city is either from the rough road out of Sami to the NE or by a steep but more direct climb on foot from the harbour to Ayia Fanentes.

From NE (Dikhalia) From the square at the N end of the town (Plat. Konstantou) a rough road s/p 'Moni Agrilion' runs along the headland to Cape Dikhalia, diverging right to the *Monastery of Agrilion* (3km). The interest of this ruined monastery, situated on a hill at the head of the point NE of Sami (Dikhalia) is its association with Lord Byron, who visited it in 1823 during his stay in Cefalonia. The only survival of the church is its earthquake-shattered belltower (the bells hang below an olive tree nearby). The guest room in which Byron is supposed to have stayed is preserved in the restored monastery.

A branch from the road to the monastery (s/p 'Kastro/Ayia Fanentes') leads to the salient features of the ancient Sami. From the summit of *Paleokastro* with its well-preserved walls, a line of the city wall runs down to the ruined *Monastery of Ayia Fanentes* (3km). This incorporates a tower (c. 4th c. BC) to a height of about 4m, part of a fortress whose walls run along the N facing slope below the monastery. The regular courses of masonry are particularly fine. There is a new chapel up here. The rough road continues down to the village of *Katapodata*, 4km S of Sami.

From the harbour 200m from the Plat. Kyprou on the Argostoli road, a left turn is made opposite a large new church (Lesvou). At the top turn right and in 100m there is a path to the left under an old olive tree. This leads past smallholdings and then up the hillside (always keep the lower summit in view). Towards the top the path ascends by steps through terraces and after 50min reaches *Ayia Fanentes* (see above.)

Route from Sami to Argostoli (24km) From Sami the return journey to Argostoli is made over the central mountain range, a slow road somewhat inferior to those on the rest of the route (but nevertheless a testament to the determination of the British Resident, Col Napier, and the team of engineers who built it in the 1820s). 3km from Sami a minor road goes right to the **Cave of Drongarati**, a huge illuminated stalactite cavern (admission fee).

In a further 8km after the steep climb out of Sami, the summit of the road is reached at the *Pass of Agrapidies*. To the left is the approach road for Mt Enos (see *Excursion to Mt Enos*, below). The road descends a further 5km to the lower *Pass of Kouloumi*, where a side road leads left in 3km to the *Convent of Ayios Yerasimos*. Yerasimos (d. 1579) is Cefalonia's patron saint, an ascetic who founded a nunnery here in 1554. Like St Spiridon in Corfu, the saint's mummified remains, normally kept in a silver casket in the church in Argostoli, are carried in processions at Easter and other special occasions. The modern convent and church are situated at the end of the broad and fertile Omala valley and are approached by a straight tree-lined avenue, originally laid by Napier to honour the patron saint of his adopted island.

The road continues its descent to Argostoli with beautiful views of the bay and the Paliki peninsula. After 4km a rough road (left) is marked 'Cyclopean Walls of Krani'. This leads in 2km to a glimpse of the ancient *city walls*, partially concealed by the hillside vegetation and the rough walls of sheep-folds. See *Krani*, p. 115.

In a further 3km the road reaches the lagoon bridge to Argostoli (1km).

Mt Enos

Argostoli–Pass of Agrapidies–Mt Enos–Argostoli (50 km)

The afternoon is the best time for this excursion to Cefalonia's highest mountain, for the views from the summit.

Leave Argostoli by the bridge and take the Sami road. In 4km is the turn for the walls of ancient *Krani* (see above) and in a further 4km is the turn for *Ayios Yerasimos* (see above). In a further 5km, at the *Pass of Agrapidies*, a right turn is made for Mt Enos. The road first negotiates the S flank of *Mt Roudi* (1125m) to the *Pass of Ayios Eleftherios* (4km).

From here, beginning the ascent of Mt Enos itself, a 'Prohibited Zone' is entered below a telecommunications station. The surface road goes up to the station: at this point, 8.5km from the Agrapidies turn, a left fork is taken on an unmade road. This is the beginning of the greatest area of forest on the island (there is only one other, on the summit of Roudi). Prior to the Venetian occupation these beautiful native firs covered much of Cefalonia before their reduction by fire and the demands of shipbuilders.

The unmade road ends, after 3.5km, at the old 'Touristikon Peripteron' ruined by the earthquake. From here a path leads in 1hr to the summit (1628m) and superb views: NE beyond Ithaca and Levkas to the mighty Pindus range on the mainland, E to the Gulf of Corinth and S to Zakinthos.

Paliki Peninsula (Pali)

With its poor roads, arid landscape and inaccessible coastline, Cefalonia's W peninsula is undeveloped and little visited. The site of the ancient city of *Pali* lies close to the modern town of Lixouri, but there are few remains. **Lixouri** itself, the second town of the island, is a marketing centre for currants, the main product of the area, and a small port. It is most easily reached by car ferry from Argostoli (up to 12 crossings daily), avoiding the slow 32km route around the Gulf of Argostoli. The town, like Argostoli totally destroyed in the 1953 earthquake, is laid out on a grid plan and intersected by a cement river bed. In the *Iacovatos Mansion* which survived the earthquake, there is a fine collection of books, manuscripts and church treasures, including post-Byzantine icons of the Ionian School.

From the pleasant willow-shaded square to the S of the harbour a coastal road leads in 2km to the town's nearest beach at *Lepeda*. Calamus reeds and oleanders line the avenue to a colourful beach of red sand protected by a breakwater of rust-coloured rocks. Other less accessible beaches lie on the S coast of the peninsula, reached from a 6km circular route from Lixouri (leave by N exit and turn left before river).

The road which winds into the southern interior of the peninsula reveals its extraordinary landscape—unlike any other part of the island. Its geological formations — pinnacled fortresses of eroded grey marl rising out of the farmland plateaux—are not seen elsewhere in the Ionians. The marl, which breaks down into the rich soil of this area, still cultivated today, once produced most of Cefalonia's currant crop.

Though damaged by the earthquake, many of the villages preserve older houses, and the reconstructed churches retain their original carved screens and—in some cases—excellent post-Byzantine icons. Midway between Khavdata and Khavriata there is a rough road to the *Monastery of Kipoureon* (7km). The monastery, situated on the cliffside below its ruined brother (*Tafios*), was founded in 1744 and survived the earthquake. The monks offer rooms to those who wish to stay overnight. The road to the monastery offers the only point of access to the W side of the peninsula.

Access to the S coast is by rough road from Mandzavinata (on the circular route) to *Kounopetra* (4km) with corrugated marl cliffs and a red sandy beach (*Xi*) and from *Soulari* to the sandy bay at *Mega Lako* (3km, reached from the main road outside the village).

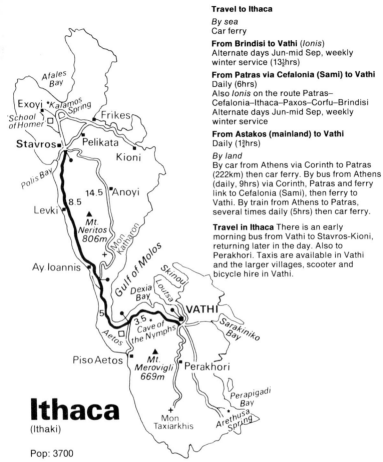

Ithaca
(Ithaki)

Map labels:

Afales Bay, Exoyi, *Kalamos Spring, 'School of Homer', Frikes, Stavros, Pelikata, Kioni, Polis Bay, 14.5, Anoyi, 8.5, Levki, ▲ Mt. Neritos 806m, Mon Katharon, Ay. Ioannis, Gulf of Molos, Skinou, Dexia Bay, Loutsa, VATHI, Sarakiniko Bay, 5, 3.5, *Cave of the Nymphs, Aetos, Piso Aetos, ▲ Mt. Merovigli 669m, Perakhori, Perapigadi Bay, Mon Taxiarkhis, Arethusa Spring

Pop: 3700

Area: 90 sq km

Capital/port: Vathi (pop: 2100)

Highest point: Mt Neritos (806m)

Nearest island: Cefalonia (3km W)

Distance from mainland: 139km NW of Patras

Festival: Assumption of the Virgin August 15. Service in the Monastery of Katharon and celebrations in Vathi

Information: From Town Hall (Dimarkion)

Travel to Ithaca

By sea
Car ferry

From Brindisi to Vathi (*Ionis*)
Alternate days Jun-mid Sep, weekly winter service (13½hrs)

From Patras via Cefalonia (Sami) to Vathi
Daily (6hrs)
Also *Ionis* on the route Patras–Cefalonia–Ithaca–Paxos–Corfu–Brindisi Alternate days Jun-mid Sep, weekly winter service

From Astakos (mainland) to Vathi
Daily (1¾hrs)

By land
By car from Athens via Corinth to Patras (222km) then car ferry. By bus from Athens (daily, 9hrs) via Corinth, Patras and ferry link to Cefalonia (Sami), then ferry to Vathi. By train from Athens to Patras, several times daily (5hrs) then car ferry.

Travel in Ithaca There is an early morning bus from Vathi to Stavros-Kioni, returning later in the day. Also to Perakhori. Taxis are available in Vathi and the larger villages, scooter and bicycle hire in Vathi.

Accommodation Hotels (see p. 29), villas, apartments and private rooms in Vathi. Also private rooms in Perakhori, Stavros, Frikes and Kioni.

Restaurants In Vathi, Dexia Bay, Perakhori, Stavros, Frikes and Kioni.

Beaches Near Vathi there are sand and shingle beaches at *Dexia*, *Loutsa*, *Skinou* and *Sarakiniko* (see p. 126) and on the W coast pebble beaches at *Piso Aetos* (5km SW of Vathi) and at *Polis Bay* (17km NW of Vathi). On the N coast there are pebble beaches between *Frikes* and *Kioni* (19 & 24km NW of Vathi).

The second smallest of the Ionian Islands, Ithaca lies to the north-east of Cefalonia, separated from the larger island by the 3km-wide Ithaca Strait. Although its attractiveness to the average tourist is limited by its barren and rocky character, Ithaca's appeal is in many ways equal to that of its sister islands, with its unusual contours and the village atmosphere of its delightful small port, Vathi. Above all, its Homeric associations as the home of the wandering hero Odysseus give it a special fascination to all travellers with an eye for the topography of legend.

History The importance of Homeric Ithaca, capital of a realm of neighbouring islands, passed with the legend. Although there is evidence of settlement by the 9th–8th c. BC, little is known about Ithaca's ancient past, and through the later centuries of conquest and piracy it shared the fate of the other Ionians.

In 1185 Byzantine rule was brought to an end by the Sicilian Normans, who ten years later handed over the island to their allies the Orsini, first of a series of feudal overlords who were finally ejected (the Tocchi were the last) in the struggles between the Turks and the Venetians. In this Turkish purge (1479) the island, along with neighbouring Cefalonia, Zakinthos and Levkas, lost much of its population, carried away into slavery.

Stability returned with the repopulation of the island from the mainland by the Venetians (1503) and their long period of rule (until 1797). Throughout this period the islanders developed their maritime skills, making use of the various safe harbours around their coastline.

The North African corsairs, originally a serious menace to the island, were eventually outmatched by the armed vessels of the Ithacan merchant fleet. Eluding both the Barbary pirates and the Venetian naval patrols the Ithacans were able to conduct a successful trade directly with the merchantmen of foreign countries. Their main exports—currants and olive oil—were to the British. Unable to exercise any control over this trade the Venetians had to resort to increased taxation, which contributed greatly to the final impoverishment of the island.

With the French and British occupations the island's history followed that of the other Ionians (see *Corfu*). In 1953 it suffered from the earthquake that devastated Cefalonia and Zakinthos.

The island Ithaca's striking double-humped outline represents its two mountainous masses, with the deep indentation of the Gulf of Molos between. In the north, rising to 806m, the *Neritos* range is topped by the plateau of *Anoyi*; in the south the *Stefani* range reaches its highest point at *Merovigli* (669m). The connecting ribbon of land has its own smaller peak, *Aetos* (380m).

After Paxos, Ithaca is the smallest of the Ionians, 23km in length and 6km at its widest point. It is largely barren, its cultivated areas confined to the hinterland of the port, and the fertile triangle north of Stavros, where olives, fruit trees and vines are grown. There is also some farming in the Anoyi plateau. The island produces an excellent dry red wine, thought by many to be the best in the Ionians.

Ithaca and the *Odyssey*

My home is under the clear skies of Ithaca. Our landmark is the wooded peak of windswept Neriton. For neighbours we have many peopled isles with no great space between them, Dulichium and Same and wooded Zakinthos.

Near the end of his great ten-year voyage, Odysseus describes his homeland to his host King Alkinoos, who has given him sanctuary on the island of Scheria (Corfu). His long years of absence, however, have weakened his memory of his island kingdom, which he is unable to recognise after he has been returned to its shores by the friendly Phaeacians. He is finally delivered from his quandary by Athena, who appears before him in the guise of a shepherd boy. The goddess, expressing surprise at his ignorance of his surroundings, asserts that the island's name 'is known to thousands'. She continues:

I grant that it is rugged and unfit for driving horses, yet narrow though it may be it is very far from poor. It grows abundant corn and wine in plenty. The rains and fresh dews are never lacking; and it has excellent pasturage for goats and cattle, timber of all kinds, and watering-places that never fail. And so, my friend, the name of Ithaca has travelled even as far as Troy . . .

This was enough to reassure the exultant Odysseus that he had, at last, found his native land. Modern visitors will require a little more information, but will heed the reference to the island's ruggedness and unsuitability for horses. This will at least eliminate another candidate for the title of Homer's Ithaca, the island of Levkas proposed by Dörpfeld. Here there are meadows aplenty, ideal for driving horses. More topographical details are necessary, and here Homer obliges us:

Now in that island is a cove named after Phorkys, the Old Man of the Sea, with two bold headlands squatting at its mouth so as to protect it from the heavy swell raised by rough weather in the open and allow large ships to ride inside without so much as tying up, once within mooring distance of the shore. At the head of the cove grows a long-leaved olive tree and nearby is a cavern that offers welcome shade and is sacred to the Nymphs . . . and there are springs whose water never fails . . .

All these features can be related to sites in Ithaca associated with the legendary homecoming. Not evidence in itself, but the island's strategic position, on Greece's western seaboard and at the entrance to the Gulf of Corinth, together with its excellent harbours, make it an obvious choice as the site of the maritime capital.

The search for relics of the Bronze Age, to establish the existence of the city and palace, has brought limited results. Numerous early 19th c. romantics, notably the enthusiastic Sir William Gell, saw an affinity between various topographical features and the Homeric descriptions. The scholars were followed by the archaeologists: in 1878 Heinrich Schliemann claimed that the ruins of ancient *Alalkomenai*, on the slopes of Aetos, marked the site of Odysseus' capital. In fact these are the remains of an Archaic foundation associated with the Corinthians (9th–8th c. BC).

British excavations from the '30s which have revealed late-Mycenaean artefacts, and some masonry, at *Pelikata* in northern Ithaca, suggest a more likely location for the palace, with a harbour at *Polis Bay*. Polis Bay has also been suggested as a site for Homer's *Phorkys*, where the Phaeacians deposited Odysseus after the journey from Scheria. Objects found in a cave at the north-west corner of the bay have identified it as a shrine devoted to the hero (see p. 129).

Rival claims for Homeric sites in the south of the island date back to the early 19th c (Gell). The *Bay of Dexia* is suggested as Odysseus' landing place, and inland from it the *Cave of the Nymphs* as an alternative cave for Odysseus' treasure. The *Arethusa Spring*, watering place for the swine of Eumaios, has been located near Perapigadi at the south-east corner of the island.

The only location not in dispute between north and south—but no less controversial—is the isle of *Asteris*, where the Suitors lay in wait for Odysseus' son Telemachus on his return from the Peloponnese:

Out in the open strait, midway between Ithaca and the rugged coast of Same, lies the rocky isle of Asteris, which small as it is can offer ships a harbour with two mouths.

This description would seem to fit the topography of the Ithaca Strait between Ithaca and Cefalonia, with the islet of Daskalio representing Homer's Asteris, visible today from the high road between Levki and Stavros. But whether this tiny refuge—little more than a sandbank—would be capable of concealing the Suitors' ships is unlikely.

Vathi

Vathi

The approach to Ithaca's port is one of the most tantalising in Greece. As the steamer enters the Gulf of Molos, there is only a desolate arc of mountains to be seen, with no sign of a suitable landfall. Turning into the pincer-shaped Bay of Vathi the port is finally glimpsed at its narrow head—a horseshoe-shaped cluster of red-tiled, whitewashed houses. The Greek word for 'deep' (*vathis*) aptly describes this port, where the huge liners tied up at the quay overshadow the rows of tiny waterfront houses.

The town only came into existence in the later Venetian period, the island's earlier medieval settlement being at Perakhori on the E slope of Merovigli. It is now the seat of a bishop. At the entrance to the harbour is an islet (formerly used as a *lazaretto*) with a chapel. During his visit in 1823 Lord Byron rowed out here for his morning swim. Main features of the town are the central quayside *Plateia* which is particularly lively at night; the *Metropolis* with its detached Italianate belltower and finely carved iconostasis; and the *Museum*, hous-

ing a collection of finds from the Corinthian settlement at Aetos. The museum is just around the corner from the Metropolis: between them is a little garden with *Byron's Stele*, commemorating the poet's stay in Ithaca. The stele is inscribed with a quotation by the poet: 'If this island belonged to me, I would bury all my books here and never go away.'

Accommodation in Vathi is limited, but the people are well-known for their hospitality and offer rooms to visitors. The arrival of the steamers is always a lively event, with the townsfolk thronging the quay.

There are shingle beaches at *Loutsa* on the E side of Vathi Bay (2.5km from Vathi) and at *Skinou* (3.5km from Vathi) in the small coves in the inlet to the N, the latter reached by track from the road to Loutsa. On the island's lower E coast is the bay of *Sarakiniko*, with shingle and sand coves. To reach the bay turn right off the promenade at the Hotel Mentor and left at the Metropolis (Karavia) and continue 3km. There is also a shingle beach at *Dexia Bay* (2km W of Vathi on the main road).

Excursions from Vathi
Three short local excursions and one long excursion (to the N of the island) can be made from Vathi.

Fontana Arethusa (Arethusa Spring)

The site (proposed by Gell) of the legendary watering place of the swineherd Eumaios is 6km S of Vathi. At least 3hrs should be allowed for this excursion, which is partly on foot (if wholly on foot, allow 2hrs more). Leaving Vathi by the promenade (s/p 'Fontana Arethusa Marathia') a rough road through olive groves and vineyards is followed 5km to a small bridge and a s/p 'Cave of Eumaios' (15min climb). 200m beyond the s/p a ridge offers commanding views of the SE coast, including the *Bay of Perapigadi* with its small island. A path, s/p 'Fountain of Arethusa', leads downhill to the left: a steep descent and then a horizontal track that girdles two headlands. After the second, a dramatic view opens of the chasm with a rock-filled floor, headed by a red-streaked bluff identified by Gell as Homer's *Korax* (the 'Raven Rock'). The spring lies beneath it: a hole in the rock at the top of a shale-covered slope. In the summer months it is invariably dry: in the time of Eumaios it was presumably a perennial spring. A track from the main path leads in a 10-min scramble to a small but inviting beach.

Perakhori

The interest of this village lies in its location (300m above Vathi) near the ruins of the 16th c. capital of the island (Paleokhora). By car or moped it is easily reached (4km) by the road which runs up from the W end of the promenade: on foot it is quicker to take the unmade track to the right 500m out of town. The views of Vathi on the way up are among the finest of the port. Just before reaching the highest point of the village a s/p right by a modern church shows the path to *Paleokhora*. Apart from a fragile belfry and a few walls, almost indistinguishable from the terracing on the steep hillside, little remains of the town established here by the Venetians after their 1503 occupation.

An extension of this walk along the E flank of Mt Merovigli may be made to the *Monastery of Taxiarkhis* (2.5km).

Cave of the Nymphs and Mt Aetos

Identification of these two 'Homeric sites' owes more to imagination than scientific evidence. Leaving by the town's W exit, ascend the road on the W side of Vathi Bay. After 1.5km, by the bend into the next bay, an unmade road leads left in 2.5km to a stalactite cavern in the hillside. This has been questionably identified as the *Cave of the Nymphs*, where Odysseus hid his treasure after landing in the island. The cave would seem too far from the bay to make this practicable, so its interest is confined to its geology. A small outer chamber opens into a larger inner chamber, into which a shaft of light plays from an opening. This is sufficient to reveal a large central stalactite, and a block of stone on the left which may have been the altar of a shrine. Just beyond the turning to the cave is the *Bay of Dexia* or *Forkinou*, the latter a revival of the Bay of Phorkys in which Odysseus came ashore on Ithaca (panorama from the *kastro* on its E headland).

Back on the main road, a turn in 1.5km (s/p 'Piso Aetos') leads to *Mt Aetos*, suggested as the site of Odysseus' palace. The theory was pursued by both Gell and Schliemann, the latter carrying out excavations here. Later archaeology, however, has shown that nothing existed here before the Dark Age, and that the stronghold was probably the *Alalkomenai* associated with the Corinthians and mentioned by Strabo.

At the summit of the road, in 1.5km, a sign on the right stands below the 'Archaeological Site of Aetos'. Beyond it another sign indicates 'The Palace of Ulysses'. Directly behind these signs, going uphill, are three flights of stone steps set into the

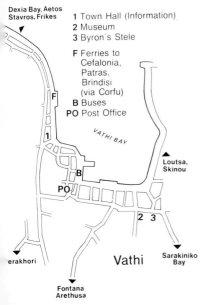

Dexia Bay, Aetos
Stavros, Frikes

1 Town Hall (Information)
2 Museum
3 Byron's Stele

F Ferries to
Cefalonia,
Patras,
Brindisi
(via Corfu)
B Buses
PO Post Office

VATHI BAY

Loutsa,
Skinou

erakhori   Vathi   Sarakiniko
Bay

Fontana
Arethusa

terraces. These lead to a path (turn right) by which there is a 20min ascent to the summit of *Mt Aetos*. The polygonal walling of the citadel (*c.* 700BC) has been ruined by earthquakes, but is intact in places.

Although a strategic site, on the narrow land route between the northern and southern halves of the island, and overlooking the Ithaca Strait on one side and the Gulf of Molos on the other, Aetos ('The Eagle') does not command Homer's 'three seas'. This, and the lack of archaeological evidence, should make it concede to Pelikata as the most obvious site of the city and palace of Odysseus.

The road continues 1.5km down to the small port of *Piso Aetos*.

Odysseus statue, Stavros

North
Vathi–Stavros–(Kioni–Stavros–Anoyi)– Vathi (34km, with extension 73km)

This route takes in the proposed Homeric sites in the N of the island, with an optional extension to the seaside villages of Frikes and Kioni and an optional return via Anoyi and the Monastery of Katharon.

Leaving Vathi by the W exit, the junction for Piso Aetos is reached in 3.5km. Circling the bay of the Gulf of Molos, the road then ascends the S slope of *Mt Neritos* (a steep climb not recommended for mopeds). After 4.5km, a rough road drops sharply to the village of *Ayios Ioannis*; in a further 500m at the summit of the climb, a surfaced road runs right to the Monastery of Katharon (4.5km, see below).

The run along the W flank of Neritos, looking out across the channel to the parallel coastline of northern Cefalonia, is most enjoyable (look out for the tiny isle of *Daskalio*, thought to be Homer's Asteris, off the E coast of Cefalonia: see also p. 125). There is a single village on this road (*Levki*) and then, after a further 8.5km (a total of 17km from Vathi) **Stavros** is reached.

This pleasant little village, dominated by its ungainly twin-towered church, is ideal for a pause or even an overnight stay (one of the cafés in the square has guest rooms). A tiny public garden has a bust of Odysseus to mark the general recognition of the nearby hill of Pelikata as the site of Odysseus' palace (with Stavros as a contender for the site of the city). Appropriately the bust looks out on the *Bay of Polis* (1km descent from here) where the most substantial evidence of an Odysseian connection was found by the British School in the '30s.

The site was a cave in the NW corner of the bay where a local farmer found the crushed remains of a bronze tripod. Although the cave had collapsed, the British team were able to investigate it by pumping out the contents. Their search revealed a further twelve tripods, which recalled those given by the Phaeacians to Odysseus as prizes at the games held in his honour by King Alkinoos in Scheria (Corfu). Dated to the 9th–8th c. BC, these could not have been the original tripods, but were representations in what was apparently a shrine devoted to the hero. Further evidence of the significance of the cave was supplied by a tiny clay sherd scratched with Odysseus' name: the date of this relic (2nd—1st c. BC) shows a continuing cult worship at the site.

An association of the cave with that in which Odysseus hid his treasure is natural, and it would seem a better candidate than the Cave of the Nymphs in the S of the island. This would make Odysseus' landing place the Bay of Polis rather than the Bay of Dexia: more problematical, however, as good seamanship would favour the more protected E side of the island.

The name of Polis ('city') is itself intriguing. It is said that a Byzantine 'city' slipped into the sea here during an earthquake in the 10th c. AD, and the sign in Stavros points suggestively to the 'Ancient City'. The thought that the name may relate to the Odysseian capital on the heights above is more tempting.

From the N end of Stavros a left fork (s/p 'Platithria, School of Homer, Exoyi') leads in 1km to the **Museum of Pelikata**. This lies near a site excavated by the British School which revealed evidence of settlement from 2200BC to Mycenaean times. With its commanding views the ridge here offers a topographical argument for this as the site of Odysseus' palace. A clear view, unimpeded by modern buildings, would encompass three bays: Afales to the N, Frikes to the E. and Polis to the SW (Homer's 'three seas'?). These would have provided alternative harbours for the vessels of the Ithacan fleet, depending on wind direction. The view would also embrace the inland sea to the E through which vessels bound for the Gulf of Corinth would pass, and the sheltered waters of the Ithaca Strait to the W.

Though small and unkempt, the museum (if closed enquire in house or village for custodian) has some interesting relics. Parts of the tripods found in the Bay of Polis can be seen, also the piece of terracotta inscribed with a dedication to Odysseus. Of the same period as the tripods (8th c. BC) is the painted and incised Corinthian *plate* with the rooster symbol of Odysseus. Other finds from the Polis cave —the proto-Geometric pottery—show its much earlier use as a shrine. Finds from the hill of Pelikata and other local sites offer similar evidence of the long occupation of the area. More recent are Hellenistic objects recovered from the chapel of Ayios Athanasios, the 'School of Homer'.

From the museum continue a further 1km to *Platithria*. At the entrance to the village, follow the path (left) by the s/p **'Homer's School'** and in 10min turn right at the cane brake and follow the path upwards. In a further 10min the ruins of the chapel of *Ayios Athanasios* will be glimpsed to the right through olive trees. This 19th c. building, destroyed in the 1953 earthquake, looks out over the Bay of Afales. It stands on a platform of ancient masonry, belonging to a watch-tower of the 5th–6th c. BC. Leading up to it is an ancient staircase cut in the rock. Apart from the ruins of Aetos,

*Odysseus sherd,
Museum of Pelikata*

this is the only ancient building still standing in the island. The name is fanciful, but enough to induce a visit from Lord Byron, travelling by boat from Vathi.

Returning to Platithria, take the fork left s/p 'Kalamos'. A rough road with two signposted turns leads in 3km to the *Spring of Kalamos*, a fountain with three spouts of refreshing water near an old hotel damaged by the earthquake. Inevitably the claim has been made for this as the 'Fountain of Arethusa'. (The fountain itself is interesting, being one of the island's few surviving monuments of the Venetian period.) The area is extremely fertile and rich in citrus fruits.

From Platithria the journey can be extended 2.5km to the small port of *Frikes* on the bay of the same name, and thence a further 4.5km to the attractive seaside village of *Kioni*, one of the most pleasant places to stay on the island (bus service to Vathi).

An alternative return route to Vathi from Stavros is by the unmade road which runs E from the square to *Anoyi* (6.5km), the highest village on the island. Located on an elevated plateau on the E side of Neritos, remarkable for its scattering of huge monolithic rocks, Anoyi has lost much of its population to the coastal Kioni. Its church has 17th c. frescoes. 3.5km further on is the *Monastery of Katharon*, rebuilt after the 1953 earthquake. In 4.5km, after completing the circuit of Mt Neritos, the main Vathi–Stavros road is rejoined. The views on this route are magnificent.

Zakinthos

(Zante)

Pop: 30,000

Area: 435 sq km

Capital/port: Zakinthos (pop: 10,000)

Airport: 6km S of Zakinthos

Highest point: Vrakhionas (756m)

Nearest island: Cefalonia (15km N)

Distance from mainland: 31km SW of Killini

Festival: Processions in honour of Ayios Dionisios, Easter Saturday, August 24 and December 17

Information: Tourist Police in Town Hall near harbour pier S of Plat. Solomou

Travel to Zakinthos

By air

Direct charter flights from London and Manchester

Flights from Athens to Zakinthos by Olympic Airways, Jun–Sep daily, twice weekly rest of year

By sea

Car Ferry

From Killini (Peloponnese)

Frequent services in summer, 4 times daily in winter (1¼hrs)

By land

By car from Athens via Corinth and Patras to Killini (293km) then car ferry. By bus from Athens (daily, 7½hrs) via Corinth, Patras and Killini and ferry link to Zakinthos. By train from Athens to Killini via Patras, several times daily (6½hrs) then car ferry.

Travel in Zakinthos Buses run from Zakinthos town (station at junction of Filita and Eleftheriou) to all the main villages. In the summer there is a regular service from Zakinthos town to Laganas and other beach resorts. Most taxis are based in Zakinthos town, with the main rank near the principal square (Plat. Solomou). Car and scooter hire is also available in Zakinthos town.

Accommodation Hotels (see p. 29), villas, apartments and private rooms are available in Zakinthos town and the main resorts, and camping at Laganas.

Restaurants In Zakinthos town most restaurants and tavernas are in the area of the Plat. Ayiou Markou (St Mark's Square) and in the side streets off the

waterfront. At Bokhali, on the way up to the castle, are convivial eating places where the local songs, the *kantades*, are performed. Resorts and seaside places with good restaurants and tavernas are Argasi, Vasiliko, Laganas, Alikes, Planos and Tsilivi; country tavernas at Lithakia, Mouzaki, Keri and Katastari.

Boat trips Agents on Lombardou (the Strada Marina in Zakinthos town) offer boat excursions to the Blue Cave on Cape Skinari in the N of the island.

Swimming There is a Lido at the N end of Zakinthos town, beyond the Xenia Hotel.

Beaches The nearest beaches to Zakinthos town are on the stretch of coastline before *Argasi* village (4km SE). These are sand and shingle: better sand beaches are further S along the Skopos peninsula at *Porto Roma* and *Yerakas* (both 16km SE of Zakinthos). The island's most popular beach is at *Laganas* (10km S of Zakinthos) in the great bay between the Keri and Skopos peninsulas—a wide strand of flat golden sand with perfect swimming conditions. To the N of the island there are good sand beaches at *Tsilivi* (Planos) 6km NW of Zakinthos and at *Alikes* (17km NW), the latter with shallow, safe swimming.

Museums

Zakinthos Museum (p. 136)
Daily

Solomos Museum and Mausoleum (p. 136)
Daily

The third largest of the Ionian Islands and the most southerly of the main group, Zakinthos (a revival of the ancient name, replaced in the Venetian period by Zante) has a gentler landscape than its sisters and some of the finest beaches. Its popularity with tourists has greatly increased in recent years and it is now the most visited of the Ionians after Corfu. The attractive capital which shares its name is a broad reconstruction of the original, destroyed by the 1953 earthquake.

History Although 'wooded Zakinthos' receives only a passing mention in Homer's *Odyssey*, as a neighbour of Odysseus' Ithaca and subject of his kingdom (and the source of no less than 20 of the unfortunate Penelope's suitors) there is a significant reference to the island by Herodotus. The historian's description of one feature of the island—the pitch lakes—offers a compelling association with the legend.

First settled in the Mesolithic period, and in legend by Zakinthos from Arcadia, the historical occupation of Zakinthos began with an Achaean colonisation (8th c. BC) recorded by Thucydides. Forced into an alliance with the Athenians (455BC) Zakinthos remained on their side during the Peloponnesian War, but the island was subsequently taken by Sparta. Occupations by the Macedonians and Romans followed, then Zakinthos became a part of the Byzantine empire for nearly nine centuries until the island was conquered by the Norman King William II of Sicily (1182).

Following the fall of Constantinople (1204) the island was held by the Venetians and then by various dynasties, subject initially to the Latin emperor and later to the Angevins. Most powerful of these dynasties, vassals of the Angevins, were the Tocchi, who controlled the island from 1404 until their brief expulsion by the Turks (1479) and then by the Venetians (1482).

From 1482–1797 Zakinthos (Zante) was a Venetian colony, ruled efficiently but oppressively by a *Provveditore Generale* in Corfu. The Venetians encouraged the cultivation of olives and the production of currants, which brought great wealth to the island in the 16th and 17th c. (the population of 30,000 was the same as today). The Zakinthiots were great seamen and provided many of the ships which fought alongside the Venetians and their allies at the Battle of Lepanto (1571).

To strengthen their position the Zakinthiot merchants formed exclusive trading guilds, becoming a powerful group which in 1628 rose against the old feudal aristocracy and became the island's new ruling class. Each guild endowed their own church, which they embellished with paintings and other treasures.

The Turkish conquest of Venetian possessions in the Morea (Peloponnese) and the Aegean brought a great influx of Greek refugees to the island, many of them artists working in the Byzantine tradition whose skills were employed by the Zakinthiot guilds.

With its indulgence of the aristocracy, Venetian rule became increasingly unpopular in the island. When the Ionians fell to Napoleon (1797) the social reforms of the French Republic were welcomed. French rule, however, with its strong anti-clericalism, was otherwise unpopular.

After the departure of the French and the imposition of the Russo-Turkish protectorate (1800) Zakinthos became part of the independent Septinsular Republic. The constitution drawn up for the islands continued to favour the aristocracy, however, and the Zakinthiots rebelled, demonstrating their objections by raising the British flag. Links had already developed between Zakinthos and Britain through the currant trade, with Britain as the island's major customer. (At the peak of production in the early 18th c. currant vines covered two-thirds of the island's cultivated land.)

As the protecting power, however, the Russians were responsible for restoring order to the island, and it was they—after the Treaty of Tilsit—who conceded a second period of occupation to the French. This lasted two years until the British finally ejected the French and commenced their own rule of Zakinthos and the neighbouring Ionians (1809), five years before their occupation of Corfu.

In 1814 Zakinthiot support for Greek nationalism was symbolised by the meeting here of the *Philike Etairia*, the 'Friendly Society' pledged to fight for an independent Greece. Although its status as a British protectorate denied Zakinthos' participation in the war, the island became a harbour for refugees.

Later on, when the British became committed to the Greek cause, the island served as the Allied naval base, and it was from here that the British, French and Russian fleets sailed for their decisive engagement with the Turco-Egyptian fleet at Navarino (October 20, 1827).

Two Englishmen who fought for Greek freedom have particular—and in both cases sad—associations with Zakinthos. In April 1824 the body of Lord Byron arrived here from Missolonghi en route to England: tragically, the first instalment of the money raised by the London Greek Committee for Byron's use only reached the island after his body had been delivered to the lazaretto. Another sad association is that of Frank Abney Hastings, captain of the steam gunboat *Karteria*, which took a heavy toll of the Turkish fleet in the Gulf of Corinth. Wounded off Anatoliko in 1828 Hastings was brought to Zakinthos for treatment but died from tetanus shortly after his arrival.

A Zakinthiot who championed the patriotic cause and is recognised as Greece's greatest modern poet was Dionysios Solomos (1798–1857). His *Hymn of Liberty*—the Greek 'Marseillaise'—expressed the hopes and ideals of his countrymen in their struggle to throw off the Turkish yoke. Other famous poets born in Zakinthos were the Italian Romantic poet Ugo Foscolo (1778–1827) and Andreas Kalvos (1792–1869).

Wartime occupation, first by the Italians and then the Germans, left the island unmarked, but in 1953 Zakinthos shared in the devastation of the earthquake which also struck the neighbouring islands of Cefalonia and Ithaca.

The island The Venetians called Zakinthos 'Zante, fior di Levante', an apt description for one of the Serene Republic's most prized possessions which excelled not only in flora and fine architecture but was a flourishing commercial centre for the export of currants and olive oil. Today the description is just as fitting. Although two thirds of the island is mountainous (*Vrakhionas Mts* to the west, *Skopos* to the east) the remaining third, the central plain, is the most fertile area in the Ionian islands, producing an abundance of wheat, grape vines, currants, olives and citrus fruits. A well-known local wine, with a sherry-like flavour, is the amber-coloured *Verdea*.

Zakinthos is refreshingly unspoiled, with tourist development confined to *Laganas*, with its long sandy beach; *Argasi*, east of Zakinthos town, and *Alikes* on the central north coast also with a fine beach. There are no beaches on the mountainous west side of the island, but a special attraction is the series of sea grottoes on the extreme north coast, collectively known as the *Blue Cave*.

An excursion to one of the remoter parts of the island offers a chance to visit some of the charming villages of the interior which were spared at least in part by the earthquake: here the way of life has hardly changed since the becalmed days of the Venetian Zante.

Artistic heritage Many of the island's artistic treasures, the inheritance of the diaspora of artists from the Turkish conquests of the 15th c. onwards, were unfortunately lost in the disastrous earthquake of 1953, but there has been some splendid work in reconstruction and preservation.

The surviving churches are mostly 17th c., built in the simple basilica style of the Roman tradition. The belltowers, similar to the Italian campanili, are usually detached from the church, to protect the church itself in the event of their collapse in an earthquake. Inside the churches the most dominant feature is always the altar screen (iconostasis) which is high and elaborately carved. All the churches of the period in Zakinthos town, reduced to rubble in 1953, are reconstructions.

The churches were decorated by artists whose roots were in the Byzantine tradition but who were increasingly influenced by the West. Notable among the artists working in the island in the 16th–17th c. were the Cretans *Michael Damaskinos* and *Emmanuel Tzanes*, whose paintings may be seen in the Zakinthos Museum. Founder of the island's 18th c. school of painting which also flourished in Corfu was *Panayiotis Doxaras* (1662–1729) who studied in Italy and exemplified Renaissance ideas and techniques in an important textbook of religious painting.

Founder of the first Ionian Academy of Arts, Doxaras did little painting himself. None of his work survives in Zakinthos and he is best known for the ceiling of St Spiridon in Corfu: his influence however extended through his school, which included his son *Nicholas* and the priest-painters *Kandounis* and *Koutouzis*. Examples of these artists' work and of the many treasures rescued from the damaged churches may also be seen in the Zakinthos Museum (p. 136).

In addition to its poetry (see above) the island has a strong musical tradition. In pre-war days the pride of Zakinthos was its opera house (Corfu and Cefalonia also had them) which was visited annually by touring companies from Italy. Victim of the earthquake, the splendid building is now reduced to a fading memory—and a model in the museum. The operatic spirit, however, continues in the island's own unique and colourful folk songs, the *kantades*, performed in restaurants by local groups.

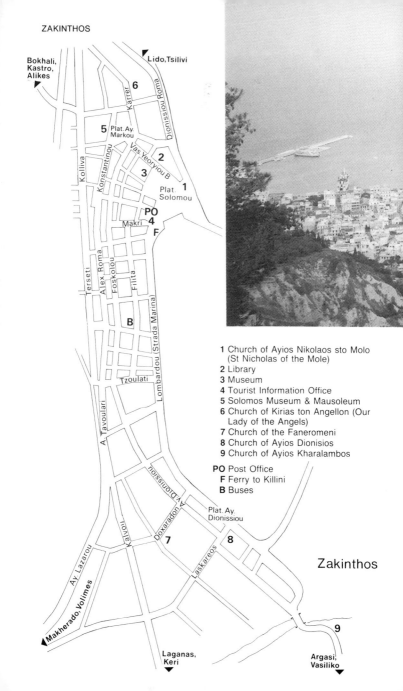

ZAKINTHOS

Bokhali,
Kastro,
Alikes

Lido, Tsilivi

Karrer

Dionissiou Roma

6

5 Plat. Ay.
    Markou

Kolliva

Konstantinou

Vas Yeoryiou B

2

3

Plat.
Solomou

1

PO

Makri

4

F

Terseti

Alex Roma

Foskolou

Filita

Lombardou (Strada Marina)

B

Tzoulati

A. Tavoulari

Ay. Lazarou

Makherado, Volimes

Kalou

Doxaradon

Ay. Dionissiou

Plat. Ay.
Dionissiou

7

Laskareos

8

Zakinthos

Laganas,
Keri

Argasi,
Vasiliko

9

1 Church of Ayios Nikolaos sto Molo
  (St Nicholas of the Mole)
2 Library
3 Museum
4 Tourist Information Office
5 Solomos Museum & Mausoleum
6 Church of Kirias ton Angellon (Our
  Lady of the Angels)
7 Church of the Faneromeni
8 Church of Ayios Dionisios
9 Church of Ayios Kharalambos

PO Post Office
F Ferry to Killini
B Buses

Zakinthos town

Despite the destruction of most of its buildings in the 1953 earthquake, Zakinthos is still undoubtedly the most charming town in the Ionians after Corfu. Stretching along its 3km bay, guarded to the N by Castle Hill and Cape Krioneri, the town retains a semblance of the old Venetian port. Although the post-earthquake buildings are of concrete they imitate many of the features of the Venetian *palazzi*, notably the arcades at street level. The church towers are replicas of the typical Venetian *campanile*.

Rebuilt on its former street plan, the town has a simple layout which hinges on two main thoroughfares: the waterfront (Strada Marina) and the principal shopping street (Alex. Roma) which is the third parallel street. At the N end of the waterfront by the mole is the broad white expanse of *Solomos Square* (Plat. Solomou), named after Greece's great national poet Dionysios Solomos (1798–1857) who was born in Zakinthos.

Part of the space occupied by the square was originally a small harbour guarded by a fort (Castello San Nicolo). This fort was demolished by the Venetians for the construction of the mole which now closes the N side of the modern harbour. The mole was enlarged by the French (1797–98) and further by the British when they took over the island in 1809. Zakinthos became an important base for the British navy during their campaigns against the French in the Mediterranean and served them in their final capture of Corfu (1814).

In the NE corner of the square is the small 16th c. church of **Ayios Nikolaos sto Molo** (St Nicholas of the Mole) which originally existed as a fishermen's chapel on a small island flanking the old harbour. Rebuilt as a church on the Venetian mole, it was later brought firmly into dry land with the filling in of the square.

Restored after the earthquake, this is now the town's oldest surviving building and maintains its dedication to the patron saint of seamen. The sandstone of its exterior walls—a warm contrast to the cool concrete of the post-earthquake buildings—was used in many of the Venetian buildings of the old town. The Byzantine method of construction used in the earlier chapel—stones interlaid with courses of tiles—was imitated in the Venetian rebuilding, as can still be seen on the N side.

The Venetian-style public buildings of Solomos Square include the *Library* (N side) which has a collection of photographs of the pre-earthquake town, and the Museum (W side).

Solomos Square

Zakinthos Museum contains a fine collection of icons from various churches in the island from the 12th–19th c, painted not only by Zakinthiots but by artists in exile from many parts of the Byzantine empire occupied by the Turks. In the entrance hall is the splendid frieze of the *Procession of the Relics of St Kharalambos* by Ioannis Korais (1756) which shows the dignitaries of the period—the aristocracy, the presidents of the guilds, the ecclesiastics—escorting the holy relics. Other works on the ground floor include paintings of the 18th c. Ionian School by *N. Doxaras*, *Kandounis* and *Koutouzis* and beautifully carved altar screens from churches destroyed by the earthquake. Upstairs is an interesting reassemblage of the 17th-c. frescoes of a church in Volimes, also destroyed, and part of a 12th-c. wall painting from the ruined Catholic cathedral in the Kastro.

Three blocks to the W (reached by Vassileos Yeoryiou B) is the smaller square of *Ayiou Markou*, with its pavement cafés and restaurants and diminutive flanking 'neo-Venetian' buildings resembling a stage-set. The central of these is the *Solomos Museum and Mausoleum* which commemorates the life and work of Dionysios Solomos and his two fellow poets Andreas Kalvos and Ugo Foscolo, all natives of Zakinthos (see above). The mausoleum contains the tombs of Solomos and Kalvos: the museum is upstairs.

At the other end of the town, its campanile a prominent landmark on the waterfront, is the town's major church of **Ayios Dionisios**, which houses the relics of the saint. Built of concrete before the war, the church survived the earthquake. The neo-Byzantine style, harsh on the exterior, is vivid and pleasing in the interior, and there is some fine decorative work, notably the embossed silver reliquary of the saint (early 19th c.) by Baffas. St Dionysius, born in Zakinthos in 1547, was for a period Archbishop of Aegina and then came back to the Ionians as Archbishop of Cefalonia and Zante. He spent his last years as abbot of Anafonitria Monastery and died

in 1622. The saint's relics, like those of St Spiridon in Corfu, are highly revered and carried in procession during the most important religious festivals. Like St Nicholas, St Dionysius is specially regarded by the island fishermen, whose needs are so diligently attended by the saint that he is presented with a new pair of sandals each year to assist his perambulations.

Other churches of interest in Zakinthos town

Church of the Faneromeni At the S end of the town, two blocks NW of the Church of Ayios Dionisios, this reconstructed church (1659) has the island's most decorative exterior. Considered before its destruction the finest Greek church in the Ionians, the Faneromeni possessed a beautiful painted ceiling by N. Doxaras of the Ionian School—the most precious of the many lost treasures of Zakinthos.

Church of Our Lady of the Angels In Odos L. Karrer, leading N off Vassileos Yeoryiou B, this reconstructed sandstone church (1687) has fine carving on its W front.

Church of Ayios Kharalambos Shortly after the bridge, at the start of the Argasi road, is this typical example of an Ionian church in the Venetian Baroque style (1728). As with so many similar churches in the island, the decorative stonework of the exterior has been reset in the concrete reconstruction.

British Cemetery At the N end of the town, a turning left after the Lido (Botsari) leads up to this relic of the Protectorate, which lies behind the ruined church of *Ayios Ioannis*. The earthquake which shattered the church also had its impact on the tombs here, the last resting places of the British consuls and merchants who were in the island in the Venetian period, and the officers and soldiers of the garrison and their families who served the Protectorate. The many children's graves recall the high incidence of disease (malaria, dysentery etc.) in the islands at the time.

Excursions from Zakinthos town

Bokhali and Kastro

The most popular short excursion from the town is a visit to the Venetian castle whose massive ruined walls straddle the hill above it. The route is via the small village of Bokhali, with its aerial view of the town.

Leaving by Plat. Ayiou Markou (s/p 'Bokhali') the hill is ascended to the cross-roads (1.5km). To the right a diversion may be made to *Akrotiri*, a wooded headland where the Lord High Commissioner of the Ionian Islands, Sir Frederick Adam (1824–32) built a summer residence (now a private villa). A short distance further on to the right, a paved walk 'Lofos Strani' leads to the point where the poet Solomos composed his 'Hymn to Liberty' in 1823.

To the left the road climbs in 500m to **Bokhali** where it enters a terraced square offering a panorama of Zakinthos town. The small church on the E side of the terrace (*Panayia Chrissopiyi*) has historic associations. An earlier church on the site was a secret meeting place for the *Philike Etairia* (Friendly Society) formed in 1814 to promote the cause of Greek independence. One of the restaurants here, facing the square, is well known for its *kantades*, songs of the island performed by a popular local trio. Further up is another restaurant with a belvedere: continuing uphill the N entrance of the castle is reached.

Kastro Built on the site of Byzantine and Frankish fortifications, the castle is now largely 17th c., although some features such as the round NE bastion are earlier. Restored by the British in 1810, it was subsequently damaged by earthquakes.

In the Middle Ages the castle contained the whole of the city of Zakinthos, with a population of several thousand; now it contains only a pine wood, and the derelict remains of a few buildings. At the N end are *barracks* and *stables* used by the British during the Protectorate, in the centre the ruinous apse of the medieval *cathedral*, at the S end the *arsenal*. The wellheads of a number of *cisterns* may also be seen. From the W wall there are fine views of the central plain, Alikes Bay and the Vrakhionas Mts.

In addition to visiting the castle a pleasant walk may be made along the E wall. Instead of going to the entrance on the N side, take the path to the left, skirting the round bastion: this follows a beautiful avenue of pines flanking the E wall (note the *triple entrance*, with inscriptions, towards the end). The path ultimately ends at the point of the fortress rock, with an exceptional view to the S and W.

South-west: Plain of Zakinthos and Keri

(42km return)

Leave the town by Plat. Ayiou Dionissiou (left at s/p 'Laganas'). The route runs through the fertile and productive central plain. Passing the turn for the airport a diversion may be made for **Laganas** (second s/p) at 8km. The village, now the island's principal resort, is at the centre of the *Bay of Laganas* (2km) with its 8km of brown sandy beach—a flat, firm strand used as a road by local drivers. Fish tavernas and restaurants abound.

Continuing W, a three-storey mansion, *Sarakina*, can be seen on the left in a setting of wooded hills. This 18th c. building, the country villa of the Lunzi family, was shattered by the earthquake but survives as a record of the splendours of the architecture of the Venetian period. 7km beyond the Laganas turn, passing the road junction for Lithakia, the road runs S to Keri. 2.5km beyond the junction (s/p 'Limni Keriou') a diversion is made left to *Keri Lake* (1km).

> The 'lake' is in fact a swamp, fringed by cane and enclosed to the E by a causeway at the little port. This is the source of the island's pitch wells, an unusual feature mentioned by Herodotus and Pliny. In recent times, as today, the pitch was used for caulking ships, and Homer's reference to Odysseus' 'black ship' would refer to the covering of black tar needed to protect the vessel from sea and weather.

3km from the turn to Keri Lake a charming country inn, the *Alepati* (rooms) is worth a pause. In a further 1.5km the road ends at the cliff-top village of **Keri**, which retains many fine old pre-earthquake buildings. Most interesting, down in the valley below the village, is the 17th c. church of *Panayia Keriotissa*, incorporating a baroque portal and window mouldings on the S. Inside is an elaborate gold baroque iconostasis: note also the women's gallery at the W end, with a painted frieze of a religious procession beneath.

Beyond Keri, *Cape Marathia* with its lighthouse forms the S tip of the island.

East: Mt Skopos and Yerakas Peninsula

(32km return)

Leave Zakinthos by S exit (over bridge, s/p 'Argasi'). A diversion can be made shortly to *Kalamaki* (4.5km) at the E end of Laganas Bay, which is becoming an extension of the Laganas resort. On the seashore, beyond the Kalamaki turn, is a curious relic of the Venetian period: a three-arched *bridge* originally spanning an inlet and now—as a result of earthquake movements—isolated by the encroaching sea.

At 6km is **Argasi**, the most popular resort after Laganas. Although the beach is shingle, Argasi has the virtue of being near the town and modest in scale—a 'village' of small hotels and villas. Once out of Argasi, the road starts to climb the lower slopes of Mt Skopos. After 1.5km a diversion may be made up the quarry road (100m after the bridge over the ravine) for the ascent of **Mt Skopos**. The road is driveable for 2km, but at the quarry the climb must be continued on foot (45min) to the summit. At 492m this is the highest point in the island and affords splendid views, especially of the E peninsula (Cape Yerakas) and the N, with the hazy bulk of Cefalonia's Mt Enos in the distance. At the summit stand the earthquake-shattered ruins of the *Monastery of Panayia Skopiotissa*, built in the 15th c. on the site of an ancient Temple of Artemis. (The church rises again in concrete, guarding a precious icon of the Virgin.)

The peninsula road continues its route above the coastline, with a diversion 4.5km from the Mt Skopos turn for *Porto Zoro*, an attractive sandy bay with a beach taverna reached by a 1km track. The road subsequently passes through pine woods and lush slopes, watered by springs from Mt Skopos. In a further 3km the road is at sea level with a diversion to the beach of *Vasiliko* (1km) and then, 1km further on, the village. From Vasiliko two further beaches may be visited. *Porto Roma* to the left (2km) has sand and rocky coves, *Yerakas* to the right (1km) has a broad swathe of brown sand. This beach, at the E extremity of the island, is better known as Turtle Bay, and is a nesting ground for the loggerhead turtle, a protected species. The turtles come ashore on summer nights to lay their eggs and there are notices asking visitors to respect the area and leave the beach by sunset. The bay is enclosed, to the E, by the serrated arm of Cape Yerakas.

North

Zakinthos–Makherado–Ayios Nikolaos–Maries–Volimes (Blue Cave)–Katastari–Alikes–Ayios Dimitrios–Zakinthos (91km)

This trip, which covers much of the island's attractive interior, can be done by car in a comfortable 4hrs. To make a day of it, a lunch break is recommended at Volimes with an excursion to the Blue Cave.

Leave Zakinthos by Plat. Dionissiou (straight ahead at s/p 'Makherado').

Following the signs to Makherado the route passes through the island's major wine-producing area. Most notable is the Comouto estate (*Agria Comouto*, founded in 1638) which also produces much of the island's olive oil. 10km from Zakinthos the large village of **Makherado** is dominated by the Venetian-style campanile of the church of *Ayia Mavra*. The church, which houses the 500-year-old icon of the saint (paraded in the village on the first Sunday in July on one of the island's major saint's day celebrations) was rebuilt after an earthquake in 1872; the campanile after 1953. Just outside Makherado on the way to Melinado is a particularly graceful example of the island's Venetian Baroque architecture in the 17th c. church of *Ipapanti* (Presentation at the Temple). Earthquake damage was also suffered by this church, but the arched detached belfry survives.

At the crossroads in the centre of Makherado the left turn (s/p 'Ayios Nikolaos') begins the ascent to the island's N range (Vrakhionas Mts). In 7km *Ayios Nikolaos* has an imposing 19th c. *church* whose campanile has unusually elaborate stone carving. The route continues, over the Vrakhionas plateau, through a number of attractive hill villages to *Maries*, 13.5km from Ayios Nikolaos. In a further 6km a left turn is made at the T-junction (s/p 'Anafonitria') for a short diversion to the *Monastery of Anafonitria*.

The turning for the monastery is in 500m on the left: a track is then followed for 1km. Founded in the early 15th c., the monastery was the home of the ascetic St Dionysius, who became the island's patron saint. The main surviving feature is the ruined three-storey belltower, entered by a flight of steps inside the courtyard: its function would seem to relate more to a fortress than a church. To see inside the little church, which contains some 17th c. wall paintings, visitors may ring one of the bells in the tower: this will summon the man with the key in the nearby *cafenion*.

Returning to the T-junction the route continues to *Volimes* (7km), a hill village scattered in three parts. From the upper part a road branches right for the *Blue Cave* (Spileo Kyanoun). The attractive route to the headland (Skinari) divides half-way, both routes going to the Blue Cave: keep to the left, surfaced route and after 6km descend to the harbour at Skinari. Here are two or three taverns providing not only refreshments but a boat trip to the

Above: Makherado
Below: Blue Cave

Blue Cave (1hr). The swimming in the clear water of the harbour is delightful.

Returning to Volimes, a pause should be made in the main village (*Meso Volimes*) to note a charming ornamental detail on the church of *Ayia Paraskevi* in the main street: the carved shells over the windows, seen in other churches throughout the island. Those who can pause for longer to look at another survival of the Venetian period should ask for directions to the *Monastery of Ayios Yeoryios Kremna*, reached by a 3km path to its location in pine woods overlooking the sea.

> Like its brother at Katastari, described below, the monastery retains a defensive *round tower* complete with the machicolation from which missiles could be dropped on attackers. The *church* has fine interior detail.

Returning to the main road, a corniche road crosses the scrub-covered mountain range to begin the descent to Alikes Bay. 13km from Volimes (3km before Katastari) a group of white, tile-roofed buildings will be seen above the road: this is the *Monastery of Ayios Ioannis o Prodromos* which can be reached by a track at the point where the road remounts the spur after the bend. Though now derelict, this is the most intact monastery to survive the earthquake and is well worth the short climb. To reach the main entrance on the E side it is necessary to walk around the exterior wall. The 17th c. *entrance gate* itself is most attractive with a belfry above ornamented with a stone flagstaff holder in the form of a clenched fist. The defensive *round tower* at the NE corner survives to the level of the string course. Within the gate, note the Byzantine twin-headed eagle on the keystone: the monastery was founded at about the time of the fall of Constantinople. Steps on the left of the courtyard lead up to the refectory over an arcaded loggia: a less attractive detail, in the walled courtyard at the SW corner, is a niche with the skulls of monks who served here. The *church* contains some venerable icons, including one by the Cretan Poulakis (17th c.).

From *Katastari*, reached in 3km, a short diversion (1.5km) may be made to **Alikes**, where salt pans are fed by a network of canals connecting them to the sea. The salt pans (*alikes*) were originally Venetian and are still in production—a dazzling sight in high summer when the sea water has dried out and the salt lies in gleaming white hills. Alikes' long sandy beach is a good alternative to Laganas, although the hotels and facilities are more modest.

The return from Katastari to Zakinthos (17km) is made via *Ayios Dimitrios*.

Kithira

Pop: 3500

Area: 227 sq km

Capital: Kithira/Khora (pop: 300)
Main port: Ayia Pelayia

Airport: 21km N of Kithira town

Highest point: Mermingaris (507m)

Distance from mainland: 14km SW
of Cape Maleas (Peloponnese)

Nearest mainland port: Neapolis
(20km)

Festival: Assumption of the Virgin
(August 15) at Mirtidia Monastery
and Potamos

Information: Travel office at Ayia
Pelayia, Police at Potamos and
Kithira town

Platia Ammos

Ay. Pelayia

Ay. Nikolaos

4.5

Potamos

Paleokhora

AIRPORT

Diakofti

8

Cave of
Ay. Sofia

3

Paleopolis

Avlemonas

Kato
Khora

Milopotamos

Kastri

Fratsia

Mt.
Mermingaris
507m

Karvounades

Mon.
Mirtidia+

Kontolianika

Kalokernes

11.5

Livadi

KITHIRA
(Khora)

Kapsali

Travel to Kithira

By air
Daily flights from Athens to Kithira by Olympic Airways

By sea
Car ferry

From Piraeus to Ayia Pelayia via Monemvasia
Weekly (11hrs)

From Neapolis to Ayia Pelayia
Daily in summer, three times weekly in winter (1½hrs)

Hydrofoil ('Flying Dolphins', no cars) From Pireaus (Zea Port) via Argo-Saronic Is. and E Peloponnese. Four times weekly in summer (5hrs)

The small port of Kapsali, in the S of the island, is included in some sailings from Piraeus, Githio (Peloponnese) and Crete. In bad weather the small port of Platia Ammos in the N of the island is sometimes used as an alternative to Ayia Pelayia

Travel in Kithira Buses from Kithira town to Kapsali, Potamos and Ayia Pelayia, with extra services in the summer. Taxis available in Kithira town, Potamos and Ayia Pelayia.

Accommodation Apart from small hotels in the area of Kithira town and at Ayia Pelayia (p. 29), accomodation in Kithira is limited to holiday villas and private rooms. The villas are concentrated in Ayia Pelayia, Kapsali and the inland village of Livadi (details of the latter from the Pefkaki Inn on the main road into the village). In addition, private rooms are available in Ayia Pelayia, Avlemonas, Kithira town, Kapsali, Livadi, Potamos and Milopotamos.

Restaurants All accommodation locations mentioned above have simple eating places, but most only open in summer.

Beaches Accessible beaches are by Kithira's ports: *Ayia Pelayia* on the NE coast and *Kapsali* on the S coast. Less accessible but worth the drive over rough roads are *Avlemonas* and *Kastri* on the E coast.

Administered from Piraeus, Kithira's title as an Ionian island is now purely historical, the result of its position on maritime routes linking it to the other islands. Geographically it is quite separate, lying off the SE coast of the Peloponnese. Though its remoteness has preserved its anonymity, the arrival of a domestic airport and hydrofoil service from Piraeus has brought a recent increase in visitors, attracted to the island by its rural charm and tranquillity.

History Excavations on the island's E coast have shown that between *c*. 1900–1400BC Kithira, which lies north-west of Crete, was a Minoan colony. According to Herodotus, the Phoenicians later had a commercial interest in the island, which was the source of the murex used for their purple dye, and founded a temple to Aphrodite here. In the mid-6th c. BC the Spartans won the island from the kings of Argos: in the later conflict with Athens they had to defend it, finally losing it to the Athenian general Nikias in 424BC. The Byzantine period was marked by Slav and Arab raids, and the period after the Fourth Crusade and up to the end of the 18th c. was dominated by the Venetians, notably the Venieri vamily. Their protection did not, however, save the island from a devastating attack by the Ottoman admiral Barbarossa, who sold the inhabitants into slavery. After the occupation of Kithira by the French Republic in 1797 the island's history followed that of the other Ionians.

The island has two low mountain ranges, rising to a maximum height of 507m, with a central plain where olives, grapes, almonds and some cereals are grown. Otherwise there is little cultivation and fresh fruit has to be brought in from the mainland. Emigration has greatly depopulated

Kastro, Kithira, looking down on Kapsali

the island and the Kithirans are now largely dependent on the earnings of their relatives abroad, notably in Australia. The mountainous west side of the island drops sharply into the sea and there are no beaches. The east side has a gentler aspect and there are beaches at *Platia Ammos*, *Ayia Pelayia*, *Ayios Nikolaos*, *Diakofti*, *Avlemonas* and *Kastri*.

The two main centres of population are *Potamos* in the north of the island and *Kithira* or *Khora*, the capital, in the south. The island's principal port is *Ayia Pelayia* (car ferry, hydrofoil and steamer) but there is also a steamer service to *Kapsali* and the car ferry occasionally puts in at *Platia Ammos* instead of Ayia Pelayia. The island has few hotels, but there are numerous villas and guest houses (enquire in the restaurants in the larger villages).

Kithira town (Khora) is one of the most attractive small towns in the Ionians: its whitewashed box-shaped houses, banked against a mountain spur at the S tip of the island, could happily blend into an Aegean landscape. On the highest point of the rock stands the Venetian *Kastro*, commanding the passage into the Aegean. The castle, reached by the main street of the town, is a rebuilding (1503) of the fortress started by the Venieri in the early 14th c. Within the enceinte are many of the ruined buildings of the original fortified town, including a surprising number of churches (also perched on the E slope below). Many of these churches, of the 17th and 18th c., were the private chapels of some of the noble Venetian families. From the castle walls there are splendid views of the crescent bay of Kapsali to the E and the Trakhilos peninsula to the S.

Kithira's *Museum*, at the entrance on the left, has a mixed collection, which includes finds from the Minoan site at Kastri. The port, *Kapsali*, lies 2.5km below the town at the foot of a winding road, its horseshoe bay and curving terrace of port buildings, fishermen's houses and cafés forming a

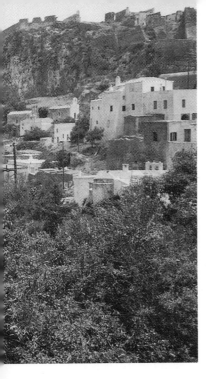

8km S of Potamos (11.5km N of Kithira) a turning W leads in 3km to the attractive village of **Milopotamos**. This is a well-watered place (the name means 'river mill') located over a spring which feeds a fountain below the shady plateia. The houses and churches of the village are well-kept and it is hard to believe that it supports only a few elderly inhabitants, many of the younger generation having emigrated. An even smaller population lives in the lower village of *Kato Khora* (1km W). This semi-derelict village, built shortly after the destruction of Paleokhora, is an architectural curiosity. Overlooking the square is a yellow-walled building with Gothic windows resembling a chapel: this is a *School*, built by the British Resident Macphail in 1825. Immediately behind it is the entrance to the 16th-c. *fortified village*, with a gateway crowned by the Lion of St Mark. Inside is a maze of cobbled streets, crumbling houses, and small stone-tiled churches, some restored.

A popular excursion from Milopotamos is the *Cave of Ayia Sofia* to the W of the village. The cave has a rock chapel with well-preserved Byzantine frescoes and consists of several chambers with stalactite and stalagmite formations. It is reached by a tortuous descent to the rocky W coastline and the crossing of a gorge: a guide is essential. (Ask in the square).

10km S of Potamos (9.5km N of Kithira) a road leads E 1.5km to *Fratsia*. From here an unmade road (a slow and rough drive) leads in 9.5km to the coast. The route passes through the area which was the focus of Kithira's population in prehistoric and ancient times: the valley which opens the interior of the island to its eastern approach, the sheltered bay of Avlemonas. 5km from Fratsia the road passes the site of ancient Kithira (*Paleopolis*) located on a hill marked by a chapel and remains of polygonal walling. From here it descends in 4.5km to *Kastri*, at the outlet of the Paleopolis River.

The ridge E of the stony river bed is the location of two ancient sites of which there are scant traces: the Minoan colony and the classical port of *Skandia*. Two splendid beaches, separated by a headland with tunnels eroded by the sea offer the best bathing in the island. 2km to the E is the fishing port of **Avlemonas** with a small Venetian fort.

15.5km S of Potamos (4km N of Kithira) is *Livadi*, a village with a friendly inn which offers accommodation both on the premises and in local hamlets. To the S of the village there is a view to the E of the 12-arched *Katouni Bridge*, built by Macphail to carry a road to Avlemonas: the bridge, and the project, were never completed.

perfect composition. The bay offers safe swimming and this is the island's most popular holiday place: it is not, however, a resort, and accommodation is limited both here and in Kithira town.

Routes

The main access to all parts of the island is by the central N–S road, from Potamos to Kithira (19.5km). The majority of the other roads are unmade, and should only be attempted with a strong vehicle.

An asphalt road connects Potamos with **Ayia Pelayia** (4.5km), a much used route. Although its existence is largely dependent on its port, Ayia Pelayia has the added virtue of two fine beaches on either side of the jetty. From *Potamos*, the island's largest village and market centre, the main road runs S. At 3.5km (16km N of Kithira) an unmade road leads 4km E to *Paleokhora* (the 'old place'). This was the medieval capital of the island, sacked by Barbarossa in 1537: its lofty inland site was no protection. Since its destruction and the removal of its population it has not been reinhabited and remains a shattered relic of the Byzantine age.

Writers and Rulers

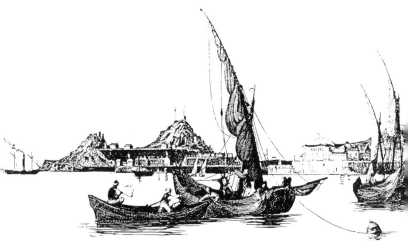

Ionian travellers

> Corfù.—Arrival. Boat to or from the steamer 1 dr.,
> with heavy luggage 1½–2 dr. The boatmen are insolent,
> there is no tariff, and great confusion prevails . . .
> Passengers intending to continue their voyage by the
> same steamer may bargain with a boatman to be taken
> on shore and brought back to the ship for 1 dr.

THE strictures and cautions of Baedeker's 1909 *Handbook to Greece* strike a curious note in the current age of well-organised, mass-market travel when service, if at times strained, is usually obliging, when most of the transport is prepaid, and when confusion—even in the departure lounge—is generally contained. Modern travellers to Corfu will feel little identity with the travails of their predecessors—but should know that they are following in a great tradition.

Homer probably never visited the Ionians, but this did not prevent him from providing us with the first description of the islands in the *Odyssey*, drawing on the observations of the bards who preceded him. The setting for the greatest work of Greek literature became the starting point for the travellers and writers who followed him.

The accounts of the great chroniclers of the classical age—Herodotus, Thucydides, Xenophon—are mainly historical (though Herodotus describes the pitch springs of Zakinthos) and for the earliest topographical descriptions of the islands from personal observation we rely mainly on the works of two writers who travelled widely in the eastern Mediterranean during the early years of the Roman empire: the *Geography* of Strabo and the *Natural History* of Pliny.

The pioneering travellers of the 17th century, on the pilgrimage route to the Middle East, must have felt they were abandoning civilisation as they set sail from Italian ports into the pirate-infested waters of the Adriatic and Ionian seas. An appreciation of topography was far from the mind of William Lithgow of Lanark, whose *Rare Adventures and Painfull Peregrinations* (pub. 1632) include an account of an attack on his ship by a Turkish galley off Levkas.

Piracy was not the only peril for the early travellers. Edward Dodwell, author of *A Classical and Topographical Tour Through Greece* (pub. 1819) had special memories of a night in Corfu. Following the hallowed tradition of the Grand Tourists he had embarked with a Roman artist, Signor Pomardi, on a voyage of some uncertainty:

Every thing being arranged to our mutual satisfaction, we provided ourselves each with a small bed, some trinkets, to serve as presents in Turkey, and a fortnight's provisions for our voyage to Corfu; which we expected to perform in ten days, although, on account of calms and contrary winds, it took us near a month. The distance is only 500 geographical miles.

Corfu, at that time part of the Russo-Turkish Septinsular Republic, had yet to enjoy the civilising influence of the British:

We presented our passport and letters to Mr Foresti (British consul-general, and since minister), who received us with all possible civility. We took up our abode at a miserable inn, the only one in the town, where every thing was so filthy, that during the nights, we were quite infested with insects; and the first morning after our arrival, as soon as I awoke, I saw a scorpion on my pillow. The sting of the scorpion is not mortal in Greece, and is easily cured by the application of the Oleum Scorpionum, or oil in which scorpions have been infused; the animal itself, mashed and put immediately on the wound, is said to effect a rapid cure.

Col. W. M. Leake, who visited the Ionians at the same time as Dodwell, has left us a particularly detailed record of the antiquities of Cefalonia, Levkas, Ithaca and Kithira in his *Travels in Northern Greece* (pub. 1835). After the islands had fallen to the British he was followed by other travellers from his country, curious to explore the new Mediterranean possessions. Two of the most observant were medical men: Dr Henry Holland, later physician to Queen Victoria, who explored the minor islands from 1812–13 and Dr John Davy, Inspector-General of Army Hospitals, who though preoccupied with the 'fevers' prevalent in the region and the important subject of quarantine—in those days the only effective preventive of plague—was also enlightened on many other aspects of life in the Ionians.

Although Corfu had its own native historians (Baron Theotoki, who wrote in French, is remembered for his *Details sur Corfu*, published in 1826), English readers have a natural curiosity about the experiences of their countrymen, despite the unedifying prejudices of the majority of these self-appointed chroniclers. When it came to a discussion of the fate of Britain's Greek colonies—soon to be re-united with the motherland—the establishment view was well represented. Captain Henry Jervis-White-Jervis MP, author of *The Ionian Islands During the Present Century* (pub. 1863) felt obliged to speak on behalf of a continent:

Europe is naturally surprised to find that the Ionians, after forty years of British protection, after having had every political boon granted to them which the most democratic government could desire, are not only still dissatisfied, but almost in a state of revolution . . .

For his part Prof D. T. Ansted, author of *The Ionian Islands in the Year 1863* could not understand how their people could contemplate exchanging 'the mild protectorate of the Queen of England' for the 'miserable mismanagement and real tyranny of an Otho.'

An intemperate remark, in a book which is otherwise a fascinating account of the islands in the last year of British rule. Jingoism apart, Ansted had some perceptive comments to make about the effect of tourism on the most visited island, Corfu, with a reflection on its enduring impact which has resonances today:

The beautiful ridge near Peleka is greatly visited from Corfu, being among the places resorted to for celebrating that singularly British institution the picnic. Large deposits of oyster shells and broken champagne bottles will clearly indicate to future generations the important uses and sacred character of the place, and long after Great Britain has ceased to act as the Protecting Power of the Ionian Islands, long after even our roads—the most durable mark of England's Empire—have become obliterated, future travellers will discover in their search after the remains of a former people, these unmistakable proofs of the taste and habits of the western rulers of the world.

Of all the travellers and writers who visited the Ionians in the 19th century there are two outstanding figures: Lord Byron and Edward Lear.

George Gordon, 6th Lord Byron (1788–1824)

Undoubtedly the most celebrated of all visitors to the Ionians was Lord Byron, who made them his headquarters in 1823 at the commencement of his mission to gather support for the Greek revolution. His choice of Cefalonia as a base was encouraged by the presence of the British Resident, Col. Charles Napier, a known sympathiser with the Greek cause. Despite the neutral status of the British Ionian Islands, Byron was able to receive emissaries from the various military and political leaders serving the cause and devised a strategy for his final commitment, which would involve his passage to Missolonghi on the mainland and his eventual death there from fever (April 1824).

His time in Cefalonia (four months) was mostly a waiting game; in expectation of money from the London Greek Committee to supplement his own diminishing funds. The demands on his purse from rival revolutionary groups and his own retinue of Suliot bodyguards was exhausting, but Byron was able on occasion to put aside the cares of his heroic undertaking to enjoy the tranquil pleasures of the only part of his beloved Greece that was, at least, safe from the conflict. From his villa at Metaxata and from the belvedere of the nearby village of Lakithra ('Byron's Rocks') he was able to admire the landscape which had, he claimed, made him a poet: that first glimpse of the realm of Odysseus, admired from his brig-of-war on the earlier, pre-revolutionary voyage (1809) was recalled by views of the Black Mountain and of the olive and vineyard-covered slopes descending to the sea.

An excursion to Ithaca fulfilled some romantic yearnings, with visits to the Homeric sites. Less romantic was the journey to the island from Cefalonia, which involved a nine-hour mule trek across the mountains between Argostoli and the eastern port of St Euphemia (Ayia Evfimia), followed by a lengthy crossing of the Ithaca strait in a rowing boat.

This exacting trip did little to diminish Byron's ardour, however. A particular excitement was the discovery of the cave where, it was said, Odysseus had hidden his treasure. Reclining in its entrance the poet slipped into a trance-like slumber and had what was later described as a 'beatific dream or vision.'

The dreams and musings, which were a refuge from the

reality—and impossibility—of Byron's situation, were eventually dispelled by the march of events on the mainland. A newly-found fabric of unity among the Greeks needed the cement of leadership: Byron, the charismatic figurehead and natural choice, was ready to respond and move on to his tragic destiny.

Edward Lear (1812–1888)

The traveller who has left us the greatest visual record of the Ionian Islands in the 19th century is the artist and writer Edward Lear, who came here many times between 1848 and 1864. Originally sent abroad by his doctors for his health (he suffered from bronchitis, asthma and epilepsy) Lear became entranced by the landscapes of southern Italy, Greece and the eastern Mediterranean, which he sketched tirelessly on his travels. Corfu, the nodal point of these wanderings, had a special attraction for him, and the island was his home and the main base for his expeditions between 1855–58 and 1861–64, the end of the British Protectorate.

Better known as the writer of Nonsense Verse, Lear's fame should properly rest on his achievements as a landscape artist: it was, after all, in this field that he sought to earn his living. Although he travelled widely with his sketchbook in many other parts of Europe, the Near East and India, Lear's Ionian scenes form a major part of the topographical work which was his main output.

Corfu, with its exceptional physical charms, was to Lear's eyes a 'Paradise'. Of all his descriptions of the island in letters and journals, the best is probably that written to Chichester Fortescue, a friend in England, in December 1857:

Anything like the splendour of olive-grove & orange garden, the blue of sky and ivory of church & chapel, the violet of mountain, rising from peacockwing-hued sea, and tipped with lines of silver snow, can hardly be imagined. I wish to goodness gracious grasshoppers you were here.

Seeking a consummate view that would convey his essential image of the island, and provide a subject for the 'great work' that he would submit to the Royal Academy Summer Exhibition (1857), Lear chose the heights of the Kanoni peninsula above the village of Analipsis, looking north towards the citadel of Corfu on its rocky peninsula with the sea and snow-capped mountains of Albania in the background. The resulting oil painting, though lacking the appeal of his watercolour sketches, is probably one of the best known of Lear's Greek landscapes.

Despite the quality and accomplishment of his work Lear had difficulty for some time in finding patrons among the English community of Corfu, who in their fervent pursuit of social pleasures had little appreciation of the finer things of life. To Lear the activities of the 'court'—the entourage of the Lord High Commissioner and his wife—were a mindless distraction:

... at the Palace they are active—dancing & rushing about pauselessly and continually. I suspect Lady Young would not be happy in Heaven if she did not get up an immense ball & land and water picnics, among the angels. It is sadly frivolous work—this life for 'amusement' ...

The scarcity of what Lear called 'reddy tin' was an even greater distraction, and when the artist finally achieved a degree of acceptance, both for his work (sketches and paintings sold) and for himself (invitations to dinners and balls at the palace) he was quite happy to be a slightly larger fish 'in this very little fish pond of a place'.

The ultimate fulfillment of Lear's Ionian period was a project which demanded his greatest energy and endurance—a two-month tour of the islands in 1863 to carry out preliminary sketches for a book of lithographic plates, published by Lear in the same year (*Views in the Seven Ionian Islands*). It was the last full year of the British Protectorate, and Lear's valediction. He paid one more visit to Corfu in 1866, to find the island still exercising its charms:

The beauty of this place would strike a savage: how much more me ... So bright and glorious is all I now see & feel, it seems to overpay any outlay of pain—time—money! Can I give *no* idea of this Paradise island to others?

Lear's painting of the citadel, Corfu, from Analipsis (Private Collection)   149

The British in the Ionians

View of Vathi harbour, Ithaca, by Joseph Cartwright

On June 21 1814, General Donzelot, French Governor-General of the Ionian Islands, surrendered the fortress of Corfu to British troops under the command of General Sir James Campbell. The other islands had already succumbed to British blockade and occupation, and the British were now the sole masters of the islands which Napoleon had earlier described as 'of more importance to us than all Italy.'

Like the French (and the Venetians before them) the British could appreciate the strategic benefits of the Ionians. Their virtues were expressed in slightly different terms, however, by the British Foreign Secretary, Lord Castlereagh. Negotiator at the Treaty of Paris (November 1815) which confirmed the British protectorate, Castlereagh was happy to describe 'the principal utility of the islands being the convenience of their harbours for the purposes of refreshment and commerce . . .'

The British attitude to the Ionians, as elsewhere in their colonies, combined earnestness and indifference. The constitution which they drew up for the islands diligently ignored the clause in the treaty concerning their independence, and established a benevolent dictatorship which was joyfully administered by 'King Tom' (Sir Thomas Maitland, the first Lord High Commissioner). Although an Ionian Parliament was created, consisting of a Senate and a Lower House (Constituent Assembly), its most influential members were nominated by the Lord High Commissioner, and the rest elected on a limited franchise. The peasantry had no say in the running of affairs, but neither, ultimately, did the nobility, whom Maitland distrusted equally. A number of the old ruling families who had been powerful in the islands in Venetian times were represented in the Assembly and had some legislative power, but the Lord High Commissioner held the right of veto.

To set against this autocratic rule there were positive results for the Ionians, reflected in a prosperity unknown since their Venetian hey-day. While mainland Greece suffered ruination at the hands of the Turks and from the costly War of Independence, the islands were able to maintain their livelihood, guarded by redcoat garrisons and the cruisers of the British navy.

Trade with Britain was healthy, based on the export of the two staple products of the islands: olive oil and currants for 'John Bull's plum puddings'. In return the Ionians imported British manufactures.

For the British residents life was good. Corfu came in for particular praise from a colonial official, Viscount Kirkwall, who declared that:

the excellent shooting in Greece and Albania, with the delightful yachting excursions, and the paper hunts of the ladies and gentlemen, rendered Corfu in their eyes a kind of earthly paradise.

Paper hunts were, perhaps, one of the more eccentric sporting activities, ideal for young subalterns and their country-bred wives. A group of riders would take off across hills and meadows in pursuit of a leader whose trail would be marked by pieces of paper scattered behind him. Like so many of the British field sports it emulated, the otherwise harmless pastime showed the traditional disregard of local feelings. According to Ansted, the Corfiot farmers suffered a special anguish:

As the whole country is unenclosed, and there are plenty of small difficulties, the sport is often very exciting; but, not unnaturally, the cultivators complain that their crops are injured and their land cut up, by this wild romp . . .

Ansted's own sense of superiority suggests that he would have been quite happy to join in the romp. The assumption that he should be accorded special privileges by the subject race is apparent from his description of a visit to the Monastery of Katharon in Ithaca, where his reception was equally a testament to the generosity of his hosts:

As a visitor of distinction, whose coming had been announced, I was received by the superior at the gate with the greatest courtesy . . . Immediately on entering the walls of the convent, I and the gentleman who had been kind enough to accompany and take charge of me from Bathi, were served with delicious quince jelly, coffee and biscuits, with lemonade . . .

Edward Lear, who visited the islands several times towards the end of the Protectorate, had his own idiosyncratic view of English society in Corfu:

Everybody was overwhelmingly hospitable, from the Palace downwards: but as the balls, and small monotonous whist or tea parties are wholly out of my line in this very very very small tittletattle place, and as moreover night walks from this side of the city to the other don't suit me ... I decline all visiting on the plea of health and antiquity or what not ...

As the seat of government for the island it was inevitable that Corfu should be at the centre of affairs—and just as inevitable that the other islands should resent it. Although Cefalonia, Zante and the rest sent representatives to the Assembly in Corfu their needs were often subordinated to those of the political capital. A particular offender in this respect was Maitland's successor, Sir Frederick Adam, whose extravagant expenditure on schemes for Corfu and for his personal aggrandisement provoked the wrath of the Resident of Cefalonia, Col. Charles Napier (see p. 155).

The history of dissent in the islands, however, antedated the British, and had been shown most recently in the foundation of a branch of the Friendly Society (*Philike Etairea*) in Zante (see p. 132). Although there were disturbances over financial issues—taxes, export duties etc.—the root of opposition lay in the cause of Greek freedom espoused by the Society, and it was inevitable that after Greece achieved its independence in the 1830s there should be increased agitation for the union of the Ionians with the motherland. In 1834, following riots in Cefalonia, some palliative measures were introduced, relating mainly to the extended official use of the Greek language, but there were no serious constitutional changes until 1849, when reforms proposed by the Lord High Commissioner of the time, Lord Seaton, were adopted. These encompassed freedom of the press and an extension of the franchise—concessions which served only to fuel the flames of Greek nationalism.

The British, who had hoped their liberal gestures might encourage support for the protectorate, were disappointed. They might also have felt a lack of appreciation of the practical achievements of their administration: the roads, hospitals and secondary schools and—most importantly—the foundation of Greece's first university, the Ionian Academy. Inaugurated in 1824, the Academy was the inspiration of the Philhellene Lord Guilford, who in the dark days of Turkish rule had dedicated himself to the revival of the spirit of ancient Greece.

The Maitland Rotunda, Corfu town

The paternalistic British attitude to the Ionians was still being demonstrated thirty years later when another great Philhellene, William Ewart Gladstone, visited the islands. His appointment as Lord High Commissioner Extraordinary to execute reforms to the constitution, though reflecting his own liberal idealism, was seen by the islanders as another attempt by the British to prolong their rule. Predictably, his reception in the islands was turbulent and his ideas coolly received by the Assembly. After a few weeks of unsuccessful negotiation the great man was obliged to return home, his mission unaccomplished.

Six years later the Ionians were granted their wishes for *Enosis* and the British departed, taking the precaution first of selectively dismantling Corfu's fortifications.

A valedictory comment by the reactionary Lord Kirkwall, who had served on the Lord High Commissioner's staff in the twilight years of British rule, sums up the attitude of the colonial official of the day who had lost a perfect refuge:

It is of course mortifying to the pride of Englishmen that the Ionians should prefer to be united to poor, weak and distracted Greece, to remaining under the protection of strong, wealthy and well-governed England.

A more telling comment, from a representative of the majority of his compatriots back home, is also recorded in Kirkwall's memoirs:

I have been asked where the Ionians were? And what England could have to do with the people of Persia?

Sir Thomas Maitland Lord High
Commissioner of the Ionian
Islands, 1815–24

Something of a maverick in the
great tradition of British colonial
governors, the Ionians' first Lord
High Commissioner was aptly
named 'King Tom'. The guardian
and executor of a constitution
which ensured control of the
Assembly, and which could enact
legislation without the authority of
a British Parliament, Maitland was
effectively an independent sovereign
with complete power over his
subjects. His view of their political
rights was best summed up by his
confident assertion that: 'colonial
assemblies are injurious to the
people and disadvantageous to good
government'.

As the complete autocrat
Maitland was able to indulge
himself in a satisfying range of
antisocial behaviour, which
combined rudeness and
drunkenness with an unkempt
appearance. His disregard of
protocol and the sensitivities of his
subordinates was best illustrated by
his attendance at a meeting of the
Senate in the saloon of the palace
attired in nothing but a nightshirt
('in longitude . . . sorely scanty') a
red night cap and a pair of slippers,
in which garb he promptly
dismissed the Senate, telling them
all to go to hell.

Col Napier of Cefalonia, who
included this story in his memoirs,
also provided an insight into the
more calculating side of Maitland's
character:

'Maitland . . . knew that the leading
features in the characters of men are
the desire of *distinction* and the desire
of *money*. To gratify the first, he created
an order of knighthood called 'The
Order of St Michael and St George'
. . . he opened, ostentatiously, the 'Halls

of St Michael and St George' and saw
the Corfu 'galaxy' glittering in the
brilliant decorations of chivalry . . . he
also established another, and a lesser
distinction, a blue and yellow 'Ionian
uniform' . . . by these expedients he
established his government and thinned
the ranks of the Capo d'Istria
faction . . .

By appealing to their innate
snobbery with titles, and their
cupidity with generous salaries,
Maitland was able to keep the
Ionian elite in his pocket. Their
co-operation ensured the continuity
of his system, which though
undemocratic achieved a degree of
order, local justice and material
advancement for the islands
unknown in their history. The
constitutional changes which took
place 25 years after his departure
would be the beginning of the
eventual demise of British rule in
the islands.

Sir Frederick Adam statue, Corfu town

Sir Frederick Adam Lord High Commissioner of the Ionian Islands 1824–32 and **Col** (later **Gen Sir**) **Charles Napier** Resident of Cefalonia 1822–30

A celebrated diversion of the period of the British Protectorate was the quarrel between two of its most distinguished servants: on the one hand Sir Frederick Adam, successor of Sir Thomas Maitland, an old-style autocrat whose vanity was as legendary as his predecessor's rudeness, and on the other Col Charles Napier, Resident of Cefalonia, a soldier-hero whose imperialist ideals were tempered by a liberal conscience. Napier's sense of justice and loyalty to the people of Cefalonia provoked a resentment of the extravagance of his superior, who diverted funds intended for the common welfare of the islands to his—the Lord High Commissioner's—personal aggrandisement. In his memoirs Napier reserved particular contempt for Adam's equipage:

... men smiled when they saw Sir Frederick Adam, who has not a shilling in the world, broiling in his fine coat, with his two lancers before, two soldier-servants in liveries behind, and himself, in isolated splendour, like a gold fish in a glass globe! When we see this, and hear the old beggar women crying 'Jesu Maria!' as they cross themselves, while dogs and boys run barking, and shouting after: really the scene excites compassion for such pitiable weakness ...

At the heart of Napier's vexation was the fact that Cefalonia, though larger than Corfu in both size and (at that time) population, received a lesser share of the revenue, and that much of the money that might have been spent on public works and fortifications in the lesser islands was being used for Adam's own pet projects: a road to his favourite picnic place at Paleokastritsa, a second palace at Mon Repos ('Sir Frederick's Folly') and a country residence on Zakinthos (still standing at Akrotiri).

Sir Frederick, for his part, was greatly piqued by the criticisms of his subordinate. Here was the proconsul (the statue of Adam outside the Governor's Palace shows him appropriately toga-clad) being questioned by a petty official: a particular outrage for a man who had done so much to commend himself to his subjects through the benevolence of his civil projects— most notably the roads and water supply system for Corfu town (the latter was, in fairness, a remarkable achievement, enabling fresh water to be carried, by aqueduct and pipe, the eight-mile distance from the springs above Benitses). In the matter of public works, however, Adam knew that he was no match for the dedicated Napier, who made himself indispensable by his efficient administration of Cefalonia. The only riposte available to the Lord High Commissioner was a personal one, directed at Napier's beard (grown in contravention of army regulations), which he ordered the Resident to shave off. 'The order was obeyed to a hair', Napier dispatching the whiskers in an envelope to Adam in Corfu.

What Napier achieved in Cefalonia, though partly lost in the 1953 earthquake, survives as a testament to the more enlightened face of British colonialism. The 134 miles of road that he built, mainly over mountains, still form the island's basic road network: other major works were the draining of marshes and the building of the quay at Argostoli. By these works,

Col Charles Napier (Greville Napier)

Private Wheeler 51st Battalion King's Own Yorkshire Light Infantry, Ionian Islands 1823–28.

The experiences of a British soldier on garrison duty in the Ionians are recorded in the letters of Private Wheeler (see p. 41), which offer a unique glimpse of life in the islands in the early days of the British Protectorate. Wheeler, a veteran of the Peninsular War and Waterloo, was based initially in Corfu and subsequently in Cefalonia and Zante (Zakinthos). This was the time of the autocratic 'King Tom' (Sir Thomas Maitland, first Lord High Commissioner), his successor Sir Frederick Adam, and the latter's arch antagonist Col Napier, Resident of Cefalonia. The artless but wry observations of an enlisted man poke a rude finger through the drapery of pomp and self-esteem that typified the British colonial establishment:

Sir Frederick Adam is appointed Lord High Commissioner, nothing could have pleased the Greeks better. Sir F- is a great favourite, his lady is a Corfuot, her husband and brother are both living in Corfu. The story is that Sir F- was caught in such a situation with the lady that left no doubt on the mind of her Greek lord that Sir F- had just been measuring him for an enormous pair of horns which everyone knows is a disagreeable appendage to one's brows, particularly in a warm climate. Whether there was any foundation for the husband's fears I cannot say. Be that as it may he soon applied and obtained a divorce. This lady is now Queen of the Ionian Isles, and the Ladies, British as well as Greek, consider it an honour to receive a smile from 'Her Majesty'. Like most of the Greek women there is something interesting about her yet she must be content to be placed in the second class, her complexion is dark, features regular, eyes black as slows so is her hair, but the beard on her upper lip would ornament an huzzar.

and his firm stand against corruption, Napier earned the loyalty and affection of the Cefalonians, most strongly expressed when they asked him to lead an expedition against the Turks on the mainland. Napier, who had forged a friendship with Byron during the poet's stay in the island in 1823 *en route* to Missolonghi, was a natural champion of Greek independence, and after Byron's death went so far as to offer his services in such a command to the London Committee. The offer was refused, and Napier's military skills had to await the Indian campaigns of the 1840s, where he earned renown as the conqueror of Sind.

The devotion of the Cefalonians found its response in Napier's own sentiments. (His love for his Cefalonian mistress, Anastasia, bore fruit in their two daughters, one of them named Emily Cefalonia.) Though he never returned to Cefalonia after his departure in 1830 he retained warm feelings for the island, best expressed in a letter written from India 15 years later:

Here in Sind I am a King, it is true, but they say first love is truest and Cefalonia is mine.

On a more mundane level, Wheeler describes the privations of army life in a posting where the hazards were more of the animal than the human variety:

Our Barracks are any thing but comfortable, by day they are tolerable, but at night there's no rest, the walls, floors and beds are alive with bugs, fleas and mosquitos, then there is a little animal of the lizard kind fond of perambulating about at night. I do not know its propper name, the soldiers call it wood slave. This little creature that I believe to be perfectly harmless is looked upon with abhorance, it is said, if one of them should run over your leg or arm you instantly lose the use of the member, nay, it is farther affermed they are fond of p––g on people, and so poisonous is their water that the part becomes an incurable ulser. I have often taken them in my hand and found them harmless. They are persecuted the same as the poor inoffensive toad is in England, such is the prejudice of man . . .
Scorpions and centepees are very numerous and we often find them on the walls and in the rooms. We have a remedy against the bite or sting of these reptiles, it is simple and every company is provided with it. A bottle of rum is kept, into this every venemous reptile that can be caught alive is put. If any one should get stung you have only to wash the part with the liquor, the relief is instantaneous and a cure certain.

Wheeler, has much, also, to say about the Corfiot way of life, his comments ranging from the dedication of the Orthodox community's feasting and fasting to their unique method of bread-making:

The other day on going to see Manley, I passed a baker's shop. Hearing an old fiddle going I had the curiosity to peep in, how I was astonished to see five straping fellows as naked as they came into the world, their nasty greacy pelts as yellow as saffron, the sweat running down their bodies, as if they had been basted with oil or melted butter. These dirty Devils were dancing in a long kneading trough, they held on to something over their heads while the master was scraping a jig out of a miserable old fiddle. I had often been told this is the way they knead their dough, but never saw them at it before. It is seldom I ever put any bread to my mouth since, but that I have the picture before me.

Lending a narrative thread to Wheeler's final letters (1826–7) are the dramatic events of the Greek War of Independence, which with his posting to the southern islands of Cefalonia and Zakinthos was being fought just across the water in the Peloponnese. Their finely balanced relations with Turkey forbade British participation in the war on the side of the Greeks, and similarly obliged them to suppress any attempt by Ionian nationalists to join the struggle. International support for the Greek cause was, however, growing, and with it the frustration of sympathisers such as Wheeler, who having observed some German officers embarking at Zakinthos for the port of Navplion in the Peloponnese (a centre of Greek resistance) expressed the wish that if 'we could lend them a hand, we would soon turn the scales in their favour'.

His hopes were fulfilled a year later (October 1827), when having witnessed first the spectacle of the Turkish fleet in passage between Zakinthos and the Peloponnese, on the way to Navarino, and then the successive arrival of the Russian, French and British fleets bound for the same destination, he ultimately received the news of the Allied victory in the ensuing sea battle, which had the Greeks 'running mad with joy', and promised the eventual success of their cause.

Famous Ionians

John Capodistrias (Ioannis Kapodistrias) First President of Greece (1776–1831)

One of Greece's most eminent statesmen and patriots, Count John Capodistrias was born in Corfu, the offspring of a noble family who had come to the island from Istria in Dalmatia in the 14th century. The family's status ensured its involvement in the island's affairs and the tradition was continued by John, who though opposing the French occupation of 1797–9 was an ardent supporter of the Septinsular Republic (1800–1807) which he served as Secretary of State.

His work for the constitution through which the Russian guarantors administered the islands won him favour at St Petersburg, and after the French reoccupation he left Corfu, at the invitaton of Tsar Alexander I, to join the Russian foreign service.

Capodistrias' desire for the restoration of the Septinsular Republic, which would ensure a degree of independence for the islands, was thwarted by the British occupation and later protectorate, which he bitterly opposed. His nationalist sympathies, advanced during the siege of Levkas (see p. 103), which had brought him into contact with revolutionary leaders, committed him to the independence struggle on the mainland, and to the cause of *Enosis* (Union with Greece) for the Ionian Islands. In 1822, disappointed by the failure of the Tsar to support the Greek cause, Capodistrias resigned from his position as Russia's foreign minister and retired to Switzerland, where he devoted himself exclusively to raising material support for the independence struggle. In 1827 he was elected by the Greek National Assembly as the country's first President.

Although she had committed troops on the Greek side in the last stages of the war, and joined in the destruction of the Turkish fleet at Navarino, Britain displayed her traditional ambivalence when the leader of the new nation, anchoring off Corfu on his way to Greece, was refused permission to land. Well aware of Capodistrias' intentions towards his precious Ionians, Sir Frederick Adam had been unable to make the gesture.

In 1831 Capodistrias was assassinated by one of the Peloponnesian factions on the steps of the church of St Spiridon in Navplion. By his death Greece lost one of her greatest patriots.

Dionysios Solomos (1795–1857) poet, and **Nicholas Mantzaros** (1795–1874) composer

Born in Zakinthos, the poet Dionysios Solomos is best known for his 'Hymn of Liberty', written in 1823, which expressed the patriotic feelings of his fellow Greeks during their struggle for independence. He also made a significant contribution to the modern literature of Greece by writing in the everyday language of the people, a movement that achieved formal recognition in the Corfu Literary School. His house in Corfu, where he lived from 1828, was reconstructed as a museum after its destruction in World War 2 (see p. 73).

Solomos' 'Hymn to Liberty' was set to music by the Corfiot composer Nicholas Mantzaros, who founded Greece's first modern school of music in his native island. The song later became the national anthem of Greece.

Index

PLACES
Illustrations in italic; main entries for islands and main towns in bold; names of ancient cities and legendary sites in italic

C Corfu
Cef Cefalonia
I Ithaca
K Kithira
L Levkas
P Paxos
Z Zakinthos

Aetós (Mt, I) 123, 125–127, 128
Afiónas (C) 11
Agrapidiés Pass (Cef) 121
Agrílion (Mon, Cef) 120
Akharávi (C) 28, 60, 86
Akhílleion (C) 82, 82
Akrotiri (Z) 137, 155
Alalkomenaí (I) 12, 125, 127
Alikés (C) 28, 59, 89
Alikés (L) 107
Alikés (Z) 29, 131, 139
Amaxikhi (L) 15
Anafonítria (Mon, Z) 136, 138
Análipsis (C) 53, 78, 80, 149
Anemómilos (C) 28, 78
Angelókastro (C) 13, 19, 48, 83, 83
Anoyí (I) 123, 129
Antinióti Lagoon (C) 60
Antipaxos 96, 98, 99
Arákli (Mt, C) 53
Arákli, Vale of (Cef) 118
Argási (Z) 29, 131, 138
Argostóli (Cef) 15, 25, 28, 43, 110, 111, 113, 113, 115, 116–121
Arílas (C) 28, 60
Arkondíllas (Mon, C) 89
Artemis, Temple of, see Paleopolis (C)
Aryirádes (C) 28, 88
Ássos (Cef) 15, 19, 111, 118, 119
Asterís (I) 125, 128
Astrakerí (C) 28, 60, 87
Avlémonas (K) 141–3
Ay. Déka (Mt, C) 53, 59, 89
Ay. Evfimía (Cef) 29, 111, 119
Ay. Fanéntes (Mon, Cef) 120

Ay. Ilías (L) 108; Mt, 103, 109
Ay. Ioánnis (C) 28
Ay. Ioánnis (L) 101, 107
Ay. Ioánnis o Pródromos (Z) 139
Ay. Ioánnis sto Rodaki (L) 12, 108
Ay. Márkos (C) 85
Ay. Matthéos (C) 89
Ay. Mávra (L) 13, 15, 102, 102, 103–5
Ay. Nikítas (L) 101, 107, 109
Ay. Nikólaos (K) 142
Ay. Nikólaos (Z) 138
Ay. Pelayía (K) 29, 140–3
Ay. Sofía (Cave, K) 143
Ay. Spíridon (C) 60, 86
Ay. Stéfanos (C) 28, 60
Ay. Thomás (Cef) 111
Ay. Yeóryios, Castle of (Cef) 14, 15, 111, 112, 116, 117
Ay. Yeóryios (C) 28, 61, 89
Ay. Yeóryios Bay (C) 59, 60, 87
Ay. Yeóryios (Mt, C) 87
Ay. Yórdis (C) 28, 61, 88
Ay. Yeóryios Kremna (Mon, Z) 139

Barbáti (C) 28, 60, 86
Benítses (C) 28, 29, 52, 54, 59, 61, 88, 96, 155
Blue Cave (Z) 131, 138, 139
Bókhali (Z) 29, 131, 137
Boúkari (C) 28, 88
Cave of the Nymphs (I) 125, 129
Cefalonia 7 ff., 110–121
Corcyra (C) 12, 13, 46, 47, 57, 78, 80, 102
Corfu 7 ff., 44–95
Corfu town (C) 9, 14, 19, 22, 28, 29, 35, 39, 44, 48, 48, 53, 56, 58, 59, 61, 62, 63–73, 67, 90, 155
Main sights
Archaeological Museum 63, 71
Ayios Ioánnis o Pródromos, Church of 69
British Cemetery 63, 73
Byzantine Museum 63, 71
Campiello quarter 41, 57, 63, 70

Cathedral 70
Esplanade 22, 43, 64, 66, 66, 68, 90
Ionian Parliament Building 69
'Ioniki' 68, 69
Kremasti, Panayia, Church of 70
Liston 19, 43, 50, 51, 61, 63, 66
Market 63
Menekrates, Tomb of 63, 71, 79
New Fort 49, 50, 63, 70
Old Fort 47, 48, 56, 63, 66, 67
Old Port 70, 70
Palace of St Michael & St George 7, 19, 45, 63, 64, 64
Panayía ton Xénon, Church of 20, 69
Platitéra Convent 20, 63, 73
Porta Spiliá 70
St Nicholas Gate 65
St Spiridon, Church of (Ayios Spiridonos) 42, 63, 70
Solomos Museum 63, 73
Town Hall 18, 63, 68, 69

Dafnilá (C) 28
Danilia Village (C) 61, 83
Daskalió (I) 125, 128
Dassiá (C) 28, 59, 61
Desimi Bay (L) 101, 108
Dexiá Bay (I) 122, 125–7, 129
Diakófti (K) 142
Domáta (Cef) 117
Drongaráti Cave (Cef) 120
Dulichium 17, 112
Dukáto, Cape (L) 108

Egrémni (L) 101, 108
Eláti (Mt, L) 103
Enos (Mt, Cef) 8, 22, 110, 113
Episkopi (L) 101
Erimitis Cliffs (P) 98, 99
Érmones (C) 11, 28, 60, 61, 74, 88
Fiskárdo (Cef) 11, 15, 20, 29, 111, 119, 120
Frikes (I) 29, 122, 129
Fontana Arethusa (I) 125
Gáios (P) 13, 27, 28, 96, 97, 98, 98
Gardíki (C) 11, 13, 46, 89
Garitsa (C) 46, 49, 50, 71, 75, 78

Gastoúri (C) 28
Glifáda (C) 28, 61, 87
Gouviá (C) 28, 48, 49, 59, 85, 85
Halikiópoulos Lagoon (C) 46, 75, 78, 81
Homer's School (I) 12, 129
Ipsos (C) 28, 59, 60, 61, 85
Ithaca (Itháki) 8 ff., 122–9
Ithaca Strait 16, 125, 128, 129, 131, 147
Kalamáki (Z) 29, 60, 137
Kalámi (C) 28, 60, 86
Kalamitsi (L) 101, 107, 109
Kalligáta (Cef) 117
Kambi (Z) 11
Kanóni (C) 28, 58, 59, 75, 81, 88
Kapsáli (K) 141, 142, 142
Karavómilos (Cef) 111, 119
Kardáki Spring (C) 63, 80
Kardáki, Temple of (C) 71, 80
Kariá (L) 101, 109
Kariótes (L) 101
Karoussádes (C) 59, 87
Kassiópi (C) 12–14, 28, 60, 86
Kastro (Cef) 116
Kastro (Z) 136, 137
Kastri (K) 11, 141–3
Kastrí, Cape (L) 108
Kateliós (Cef) 111, 117
Katharón (Mon, I) 122, 129, 151
Kathisma (L) 101, 109
Káto Khóra (K) 15, 143
Kavadádes (C) 59
Kávos (C) 28, 54, 59, 61, 89, 96
Kerásia (C) 60
Keri (Z) 11, 131, 137
Kérkira 57 and see Corfu
Kióni (I) 122, 129
Kinopiástes (C) 59, 88, 89
Kithira town/Khóra (K) 14, 15, 29, 140, 141, 142–3, 142
Kithira 8 ff., 140–3
Koméno (C) 28
Kontókali (C) 28, 59, 85
Korifo 13, 47, 57
Korission Lagoon (C) 61, 89
Kouloúra (C) 60, 86
Kounópetra (Cef) 29

Koútavas lagoon (Cef) 115, 116
Krani (Cef) 12, 112, 115, 121
Laganás (Z) 29, 130, 131, 137
Lakithra (Cef) 115, 116, 147
Lákka (P) 96–99
Lákones (C) 83
Lássi (Cef) 29, 111
Lássi peninsula (Cef) 115, 115
Lefkátas peninsula (L) 101, 108
Lefkími, Ano (C) 54, 89
Leucas (L) 12, 102, 107
Levkás 8 ff., 100–9
Levkás town (L) 20, 26, 28, 43, 100, 101, 101, 103, 104, 104, 105–6, 106, 109
Liapádes (C) 28, 60, 83
Ligiá (L) 28, 101
Livádi (K) 141, 143
Lixoúri (Cef) 10, 15, 29, 111, 113, 121
Longós (P) 96, 98
Lourdáta (Cef) 111, 117
Loútsa (I) 122, 126
Madourí (I, L) 107
Magaziá (P) 99
Makherádo (Z) 18, 138, 139
Makris Yialós (Cef) 111, 119
Mandoúki (C) 49, 51, 58
Manitokhóri (K) 29
Markópoulo (Cef) 118
Mazarakáta (Cef) 11, 112, 116
Meganísi (I, L) 101, 103, 107, 108
Meganóros (Mt, L) 103, 109
Melinádo (Z) 139
Melissáni, Cave of (Cef) 119
Mermingáris (Mt, K) 140
Meroviglí (Mt, I) 123, 126, 127
Messongi (C) 28, 59, 88
Metaxáta (Cef) 113, 116, 117
Milopótamos (K) 141, 143
Mirtídia (Mon, K) 140
Mirtiótissa (C) 60, 87, 88
Mirtou Bay (Cef) 111, 111, 119
Mólos, Gulf of (I) 123, 128
Mongonisi (P) 96, 98, 99
Mon Repos (C) 51, 59, 71, 78, 80, 155

159

Moraïtika (C) 28, 59, 88

Neokhóri (L) 108
Néritos (Mt, I) 122, 123, 128, 129
Nidri (L) 11, 28, 101, 102, 103, 107, 108
Nikiána (L) 28
Nissáki (C) 28, 60, 60, 86

Odiyítria(Mon, L) 109
Omalá (Cef) 121

Paleokastrítsa (C) 19, 28, 54, 59, 60, 61, 75, 83–4, 84, 155
Paleókhora (I) 14, 127
Paleókhora (K) 14, 143
Paleópolis (C) 46, 63, 71, 75, 78–81; church 64, 80; Temple of Artemis 47, 71, 80; Church of Sts Jason & Sosipater 18, 56, 63, 79
Paleópolis (K) 13, 143
Páli (Cef) 12, 111–3, 121
Paliki peninsula (Cef) 113, 119, 121
Pantokrátor (Mt, C), 19, 44, 53, 65, 74, 82–83, 85
Pástra (Cef) 118
Paxos 8 ff., 96–9, 21, 39
Pefkoúlia (L) 101, 107
Pélekas (C) 87, 146
Pelikáta (I) 11, 125, 128, 129
Perakhóri (I) 126, 127
Pérama (C) 28, 59, 81, 88
Peratáta (Cef) 117
Perithia (C) 86
Petretí (C) 88
Piryí (C) 28, 59, 60, 85
Piso Aetós (I) 122, 128
Plános (Z) 29, 131
Platiá Ammos (K) 141, 142
Platis Yialós (Cef) 29, 111, 117
Plátonas (C) 29
Plitíri Point (C) 88
Pólis Bay (I) 11, 12, 122, 128, 129
Pontikonísi (I, C) 75, 80, 81
Póros (Cef) 29, 111, 118
Póros (L) 12, 101, 103, 108
Pórto Katsíki (L) 101, 108
Pórto Róma (Z) 131, 138

Pórto Zóro (Z) 138
Potámi (C) 89, 89
Potamós (C) 28, 51; river 75, 85
Potamós (K) 140–3
Proni (Cef) 12, 112, 118

Róda (C) 28, 59, 60, 71, 86
Rópa, Plain of (C) 53, 54; river 54, 88
Roúda Bay (L) 108

St George, Castle of (Cef), see Ay. Yeoryios
Same or Sami (ancient city, Cef) 12, 17, 112, 120
Sámi (Cef) 8, 15, 25, 29, 110–3, 119, 120
Santa Maura (L), see Ay. Mavra
Sarakina (Z) 137
Sarakiniko Bay (I) 122, 124, 126
Scheria 17, 46, 57, 74, 75, 78, 124, 125, 128
Sidári (C) 8, 11, 28, 46, 60, 86, 87
Sinarádes (C) 28, 88
Sívota (L) 101, 103, 108
Sivros (L) 108
Skála (Cef) 12, 29, 111, 117
Skandía (K) 143
Skínou (I) 122, 126
Skopós (Mt, Z) 138
Skorpiós (I, L) 107
Spartílas (C) 82
Stavrós (I) 122, 123, 125, 128, 128
Stavrotás (Mt, L) 100, 103, 108
Svoronáta (Cef) 29, 117

Tragáki (Z) 29
Troiannáta (Cef) 117
Troumpéta Pass (C) 84, 87
Tsiliví (Z) 131

Varí (Cef) 13, 119
Vasilikí (L) 26, 28, 101, 102, 103, 111
Vasilikó (Z) 11, 29, 131
Vathí (I) 15, 20, 29, 122, 123, 126, 126, 127–9, 150
Vátos (C) 59
Vído (I, C) 48, 51, 67
Vlakhérna (I, C), 80, 81
Vlikhó (L) 101, 103, 107, 108, 109
Volímes (Z) 29, 136, 138
Vrakhiónas (Mt, Z) 130, 138

Yíro (L) 101, 104, 107
Yérakas (Z) 131, 138

Zákinthos (Zante) 7 ff., 130–139
Zákinthos town (Z) 14, 15, 20, 29, 43, 130, 134, 135–6, 136

PEOPLE

Adam, Sir Frederick 64, 80, 83, 137, 152, 154, 155, 156, 158
Agathokles 46
Agrippa 47
Ali Pasha 103
Ansted, Prof. D. T. 146, 151
Apollodorus 47
Augustus 47, 102

Baffas, George 136
Barbarossa 48, 141, 143
Byron, Lord 113, 120, 126, 147, 156

Campbell, Gen Sir James 150
Capodistrias see Kapodistrias
Castlereagh, Lord 150
Charles of Anjou 48
Church, Maj Richard 103, 104

Damaskinos, Michael 20, 56
Davy, Dr John 10, 21, 146
de Hauteville family 47
Demetrius Poliorketes 46
Dionysius, St (Ayios Dionisios) 39, 130
Dodwell, Edward 145
Don Juan of Austria 49
Donzelot, Gen 52, 150
Dörpfeld, Wilhelm 17, 80, 103, 107, 125
Doxaras, Nicholas 20, 105, 136; Panayiotis 20, 70, 105
Durrell, Gerald 23, 24

Elizabeth of Austria, Empress 82

Frederick II, Emperor 48
Foscolo, Ugo 136

Gell, Sir William 125, 127
Gerasimus, St (Ayios Yerasimos) 39, 110, 121
Gladstone, W. E. 52, 97, 98, 113, 153
George I of Greece, 52
George II of Greece, 85

Gregorius, Patriarch 117
Guilford, Lord 52, 66, 68, 152
Guiscard, Robert 47, 112, 119
Hadrian, Emperor 112
Herodotus 131, 141, 145
Homer 16, 17, 57, 74, 103, 112, 125, 127, 128, 137, 144
Holland, Henry 146

Ibrahim Pasha 52

Jervis, Henry J-W. 146

Kalvos, Andreas 136
Kandounis, Nicholas 20, 73, 136
Kapodistrias, Ioannis 52, 65, 68, 73, 103, 158
Kassander 46
Khronis, Ioannis 136
Klotsas, George 73
Kirkwall, Viscount 151, 153
Kolokotronis, Theodore 97
Korais, Ioannis 136
Koutouzis, Nicholas 20, 73, 136

Leake, Col 145
Lear, Edward 7, 19, 83, 148, 149, 152
Lithgow, William 44, 145

Maitland, Sir Thomas 52, 68, 150, 153, 154, 156
Manfred 48
Mantzaros, Nicholas 158
Margaritone, Adml 14
Mark Antony 47, 102
Michael I Angelos 48
Michael II Angelos 48
Morosini, Francesco 49, 69, 103
Mussolini 52

Napier, Col Charles 113, 118–120, 147, 152, 154–6, 156
Napoleon 7, 50, 52, 103, 150
Nero, Emperor 47

Octavian 47
Odysseus/ Odyssey 16, 17, 74, 75, 83, 88, 107, 108, 112, 117, 123–5, 128, 129, 128, 129, 131, 137, 144, 147
Onassis, Aristotle 107
Orsini family 14, 112, 116, 123, 127

Paleologos, Catherine 79
Philip II of Macedon 46
Philip V of Macedon 102, 113
Pliny 145
Pompey 47
Poulakis, Theodore 73, 86, 139
Pyrrhus 46

Sappho 108
Schliemann, Heinrich 125, 127
Schulenberg, Count von der 49, 66
Seaton, Lord 152
Solomos, Dionysios 135–7, 158
Spiridon, St (Ayios Spiridonos) 39, 45, 47, 49, 55, 91, 121, 126
Strabo 145
Suleiman the Magnificent 48, 49

Theotoki, Nikiforos 69
Thucydides 46, 131, 145
Tocco family 14, 102, 112, 123, 131
Tzanes, Emmanuel 20, 73, 79
Tzenos, Michael 69

Valaoritis, Aristoteles 105, 107
Venieri family 141, 142

Wheeler, Private 156, 157
Wilhelm II, Kaiser 80, 82, 87, 88

Yerasimos, Ayios see Gerasimus, St

Xenophon 145